Fantastic Four
HOUSE OF M
IRON MAN

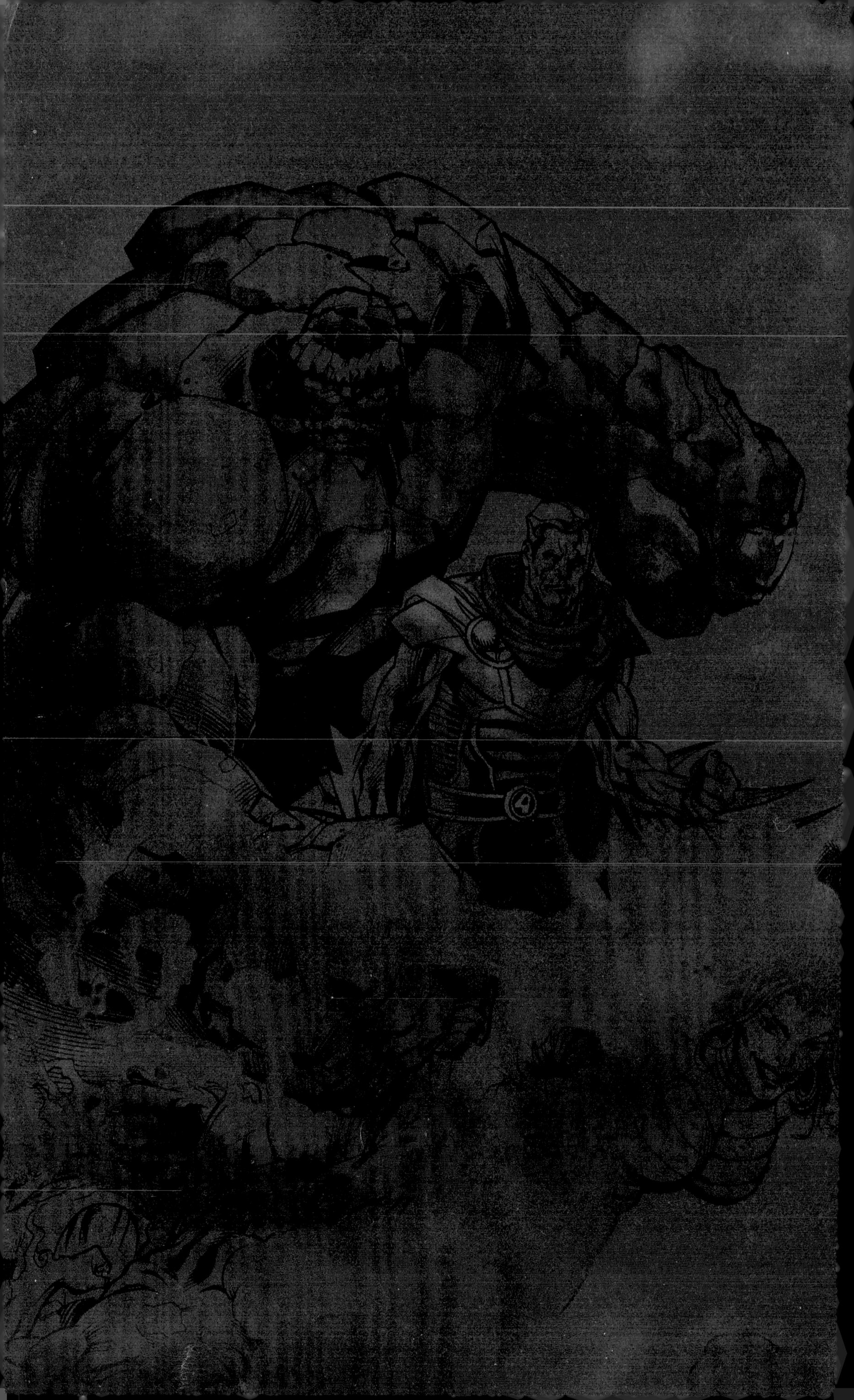

HOUSE OF M

Fantastic Four

Writer: JOHN LAYMEN
Pencils: SCOT EATON
Inks: DON HILLSMAN II
WITH RICK MAGYAR
Colors: DEAN WHITE
WITH AVALON'S ROB RO
Letters: VIRTUAL CALLIGRAPHY'S
CORY PETIT

IRON MAN

Writer: GREG PAK
Pencils: PAT LEE
Inks & Colors: DREAM ENGINE
Letters: VIRTUAL CALLIGRAPHY'S
RUS WOOTON

Collection Editor: JENNIFER GRÜNWALD
Assistant Editor: MICHAEL SHORT
Senior Editor, Special Projects: JEFF YOUNGQUIST
Director of Sales: DAVID GABRIEL
Production: LORETTA KROL
Book Designer: MEGHAN KERNS
Creative Director: TOM MARVELLI

Editor in Chief: JOE QUESADA
Publisher: DAN BUCKLEY

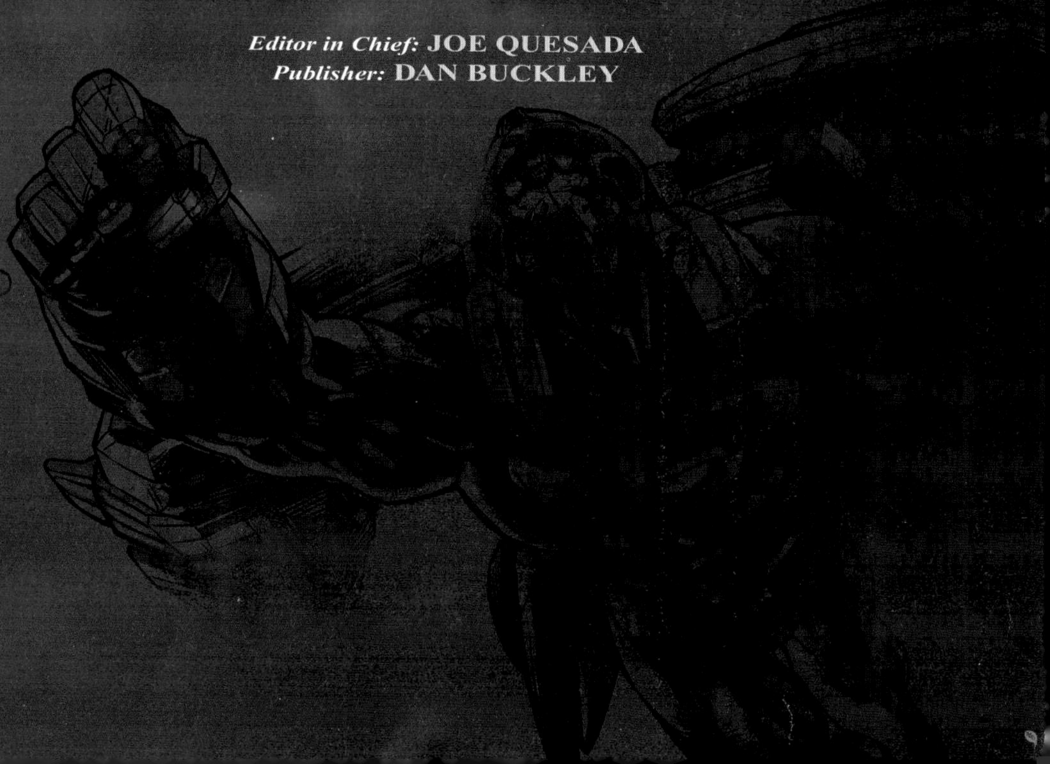

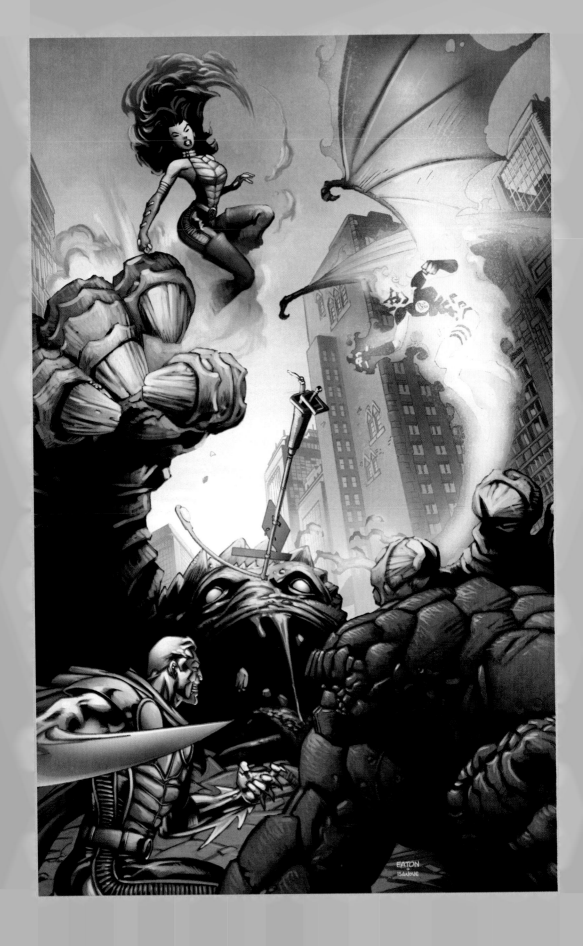

EATON
ISANOVE

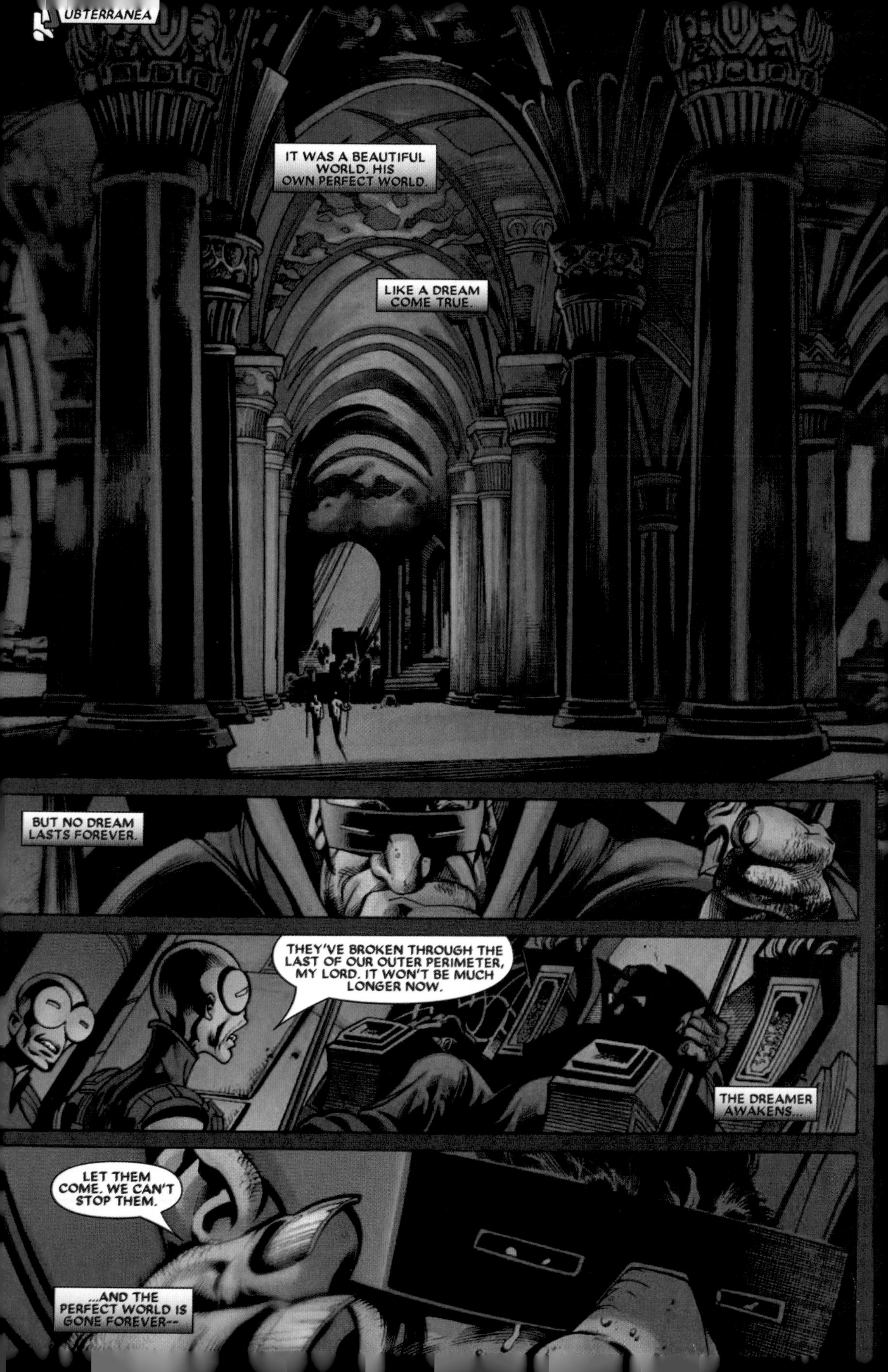

UBTERRANEA
IT WAS A BEAUTIFUL WORLD. HIS OWN PERFECT WORLD.
LIKE A DREAM COME TRUE.
BUT NO DREAM LASTS FOREVER.
THEY'VE BROKEN THROUGH THE LAST OF OUR OUTER PERIMETER, MY LORD. IT WON'T BE MUCH LONGER NOW.
THE DREAMER AWAKENS...
LET THEM COME. WE CAN'T STOP THEM.
...AND THE PERFECT WORLD IS GONE FOREVER--

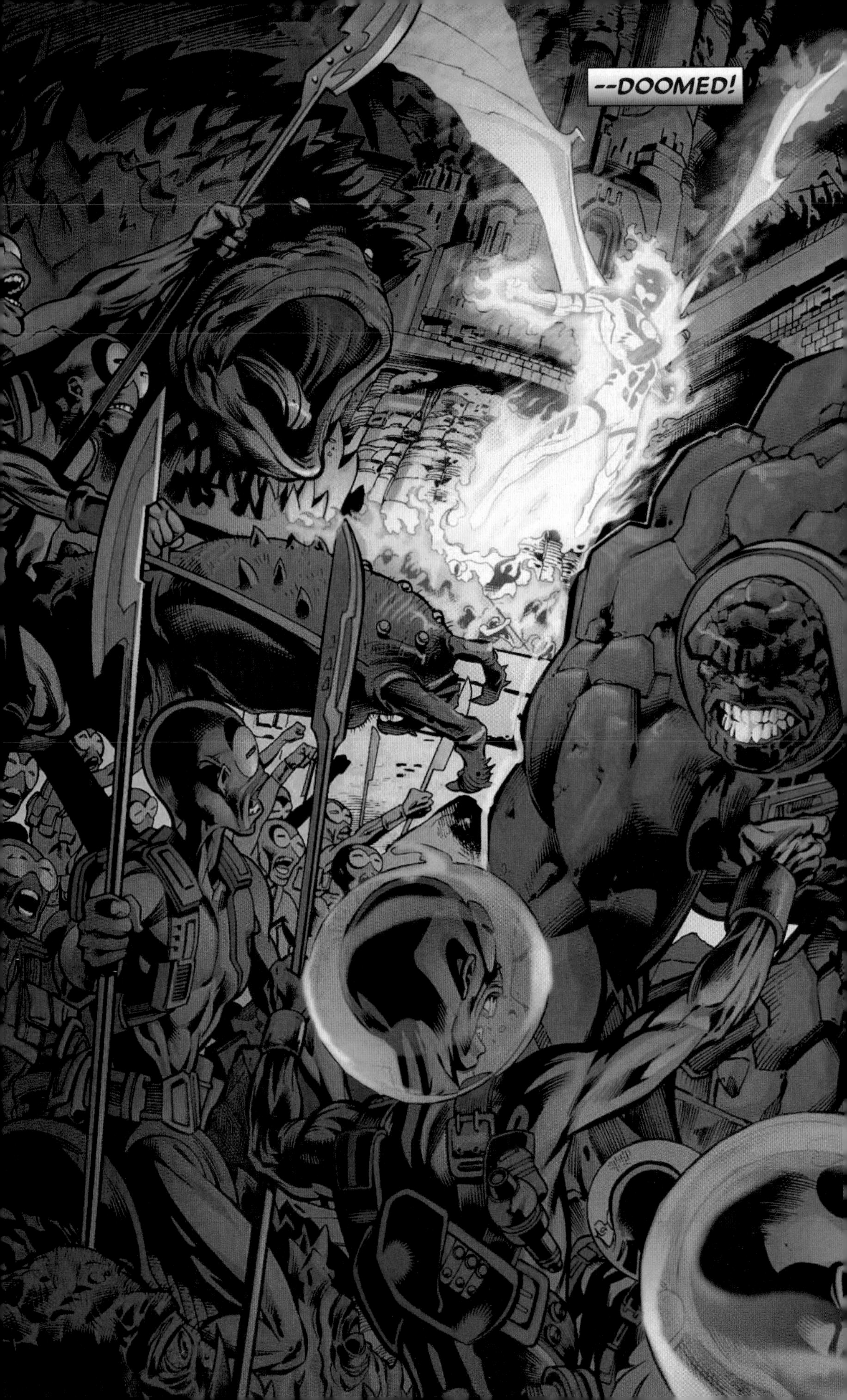
--DOOMED!

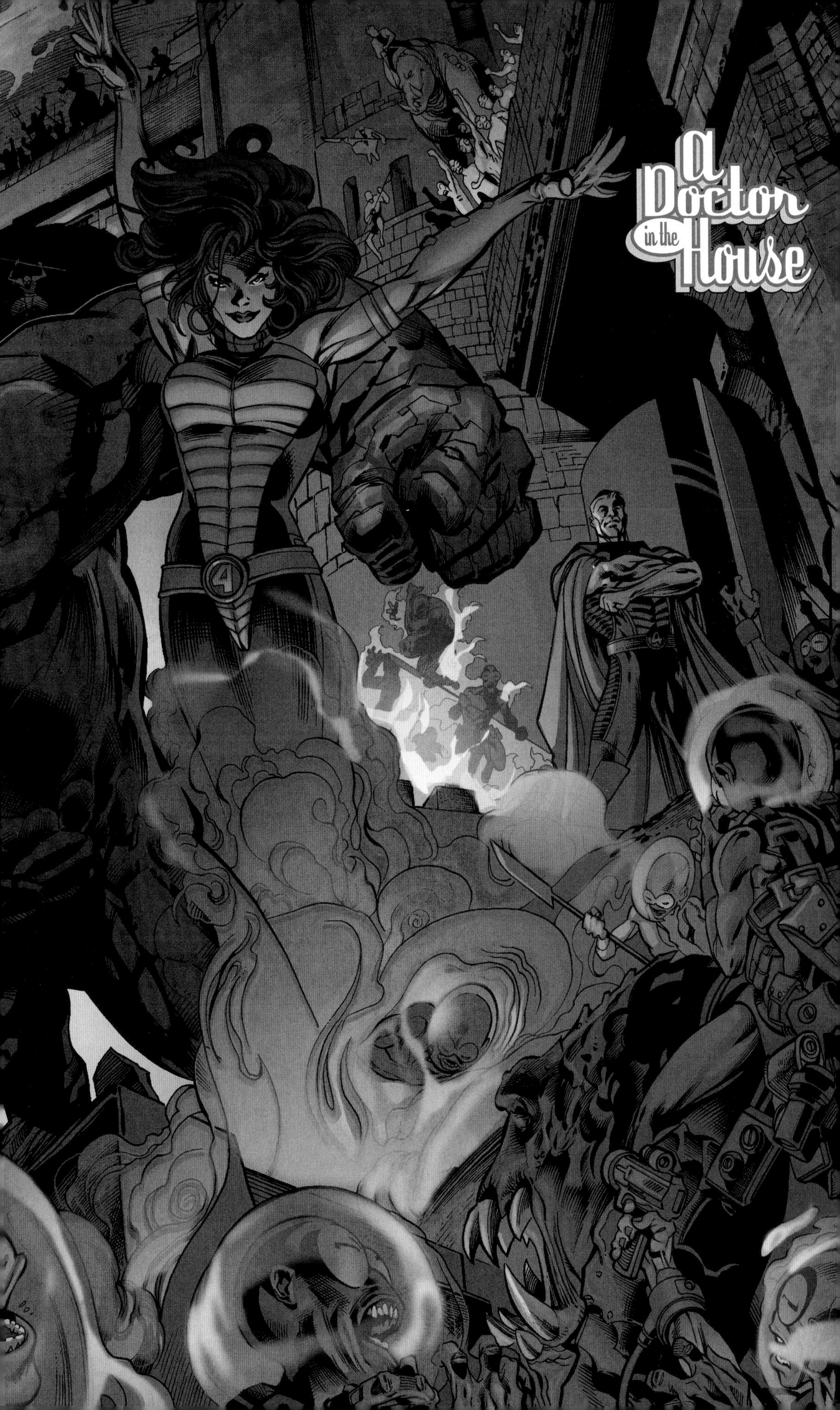
A Doctor in the House

The New Avengers and the Astonishing X-Men met to discuss the fate of Wanda Maximoff, the Scarlet Witch--the daughter of the powerful mutant terrorist Magneto. After losing control of her reality-altering powers and suffering a total nervous breakdown, Wanda unleashed chaos upon the Avengers, killing and injuring many of their number. Magneto intervened and took his daughter to the devastated island-nation of Genosha, where Charles Xavier--Professor X, the founder of the X-Men--was to help her recover. Xavier failed, and now it is up to Wanda's friends and teammates to decide whether she will live or die. But Magneto, Wanda, and her brother Pietro disappear...

Then the world burns to white. Reality as we knew it is gone...

...to be replaced by a society in which humans are the oppressed minority and mutants run the culture, ruling over all existing countries, religions, and politics. A kingdom united under the House of M.

HOUSE OF M

Mutants rule the world. Homo sapiens, few in number, cling to the margins, warming themselves on the last faint flickers of life before extinction.

The new masters won by changing the past. Those who would fight to restore the human order have been given impossible new lives, impossible new histories to keep them occupied.

Reed Richards is dead, and there is no Fantastic Four. Instead, Victor Von Doom leads a team called the Fearsome Four, which is frequently called upon to do the House of M's dirty work. But Doom is human, not a mutant--and despite having given himself and his family super-powers, he still feels mutantkind's continuing dominion over the globe is an insult he cannot abide...

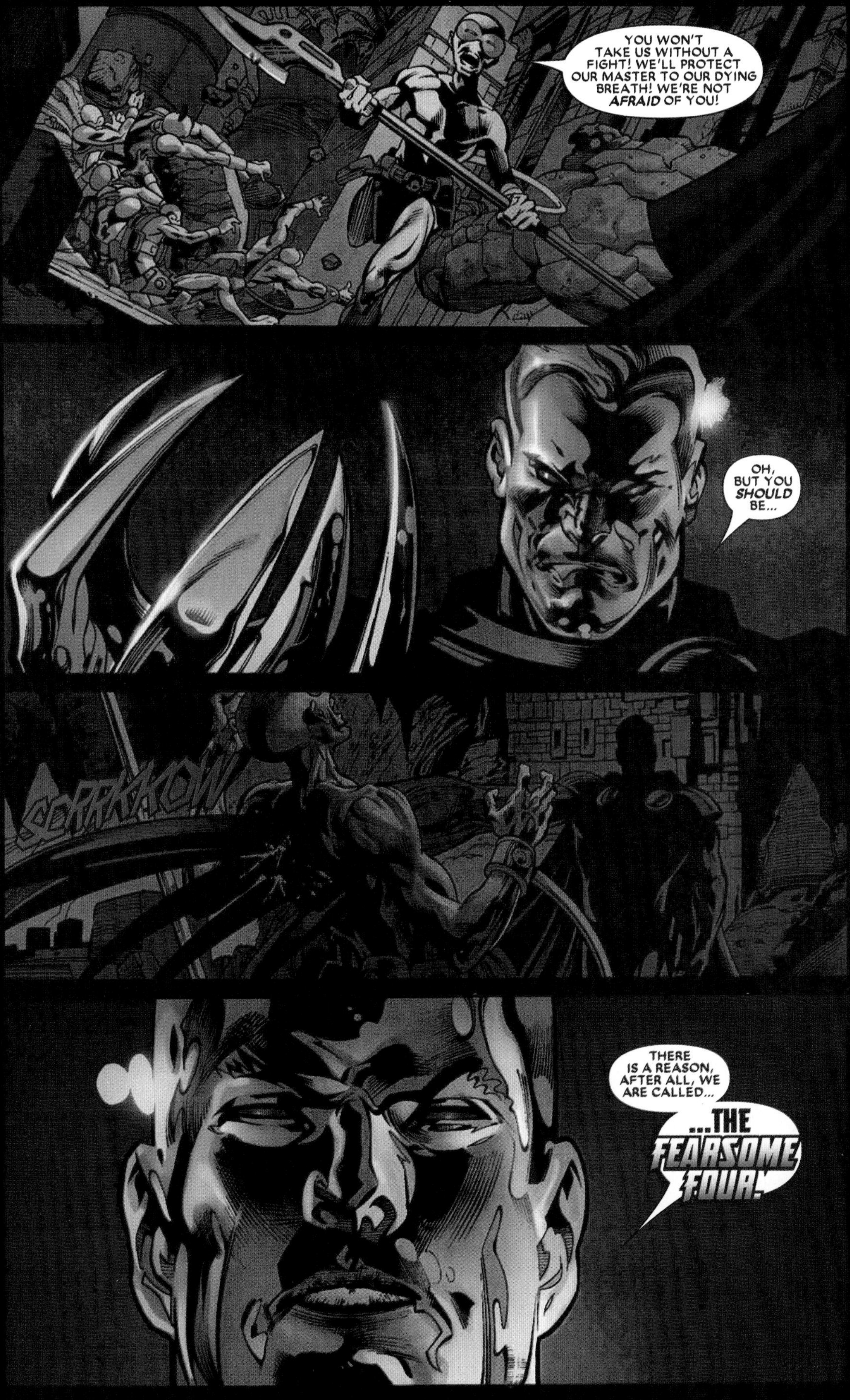
YOU WON'T TAKE US WITHOUT A FIGHT! WE'LL PROTECT OUR MASTER TO OUR DYING BREATH! WE'RE NOT *AFRAID* OF YOU!
OH, BUT YOU *SHOULD* BE...
THERE IS A REASON, AFTER ALL, WE ARE CALLED...
...THE FEARSOME FOUR!

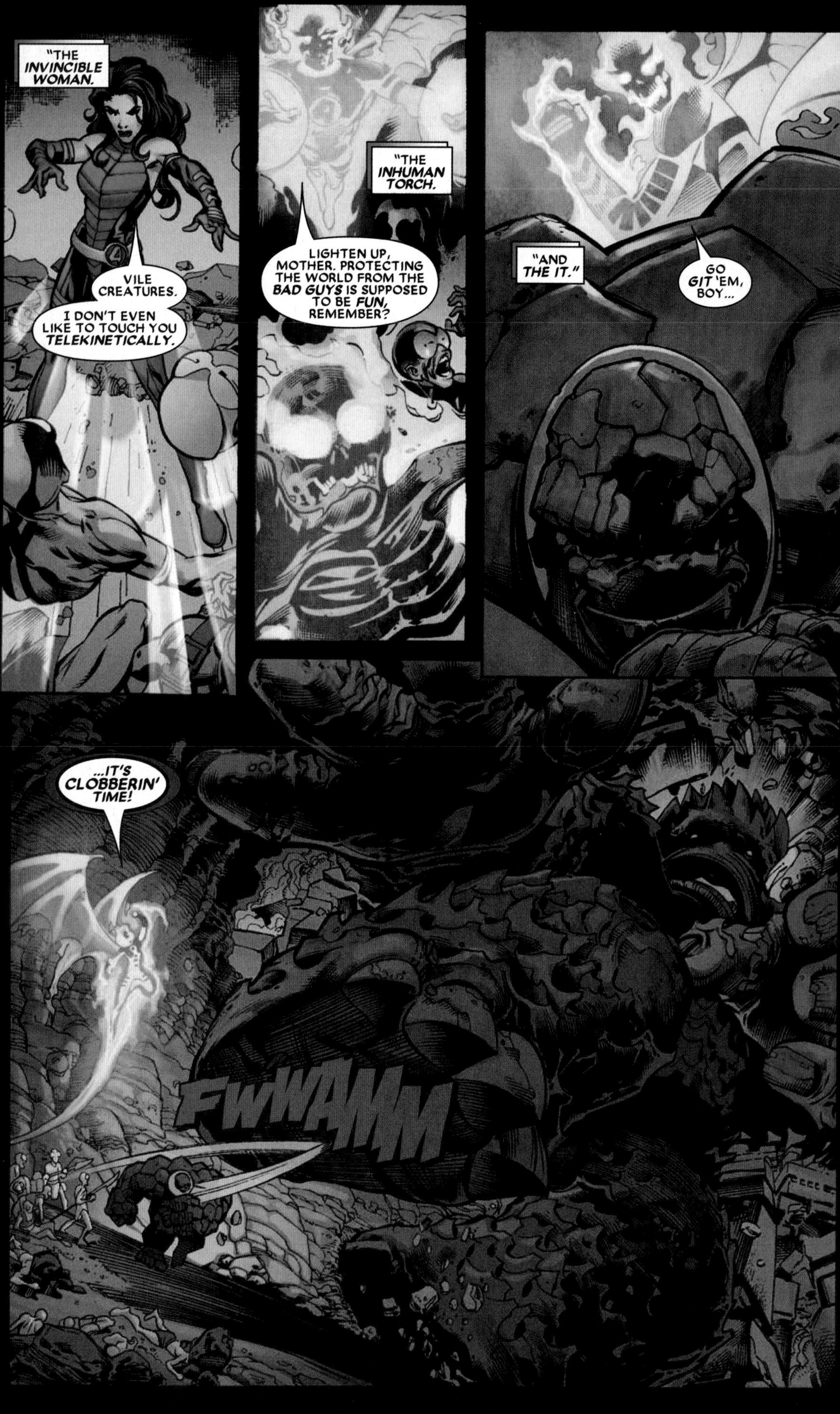
"THE INVINCIBLE WOMAN.
VILE CREATURES.
I DON'T EVEN LIKE TO TOUCH YOU TELEKINETICALLY.
"THE INHUMAN TORCH.
LIGHTEN UP, MOTHER. PROTECTING THE WORLD FROM THE BAD GUYS IS SUPPOSED TO BE FUN, REMEMBER?
"AND THE IT."
GO GIT 'EM, BOY...
...IT'S CLOBBERIN' TIME!
FWWAMM

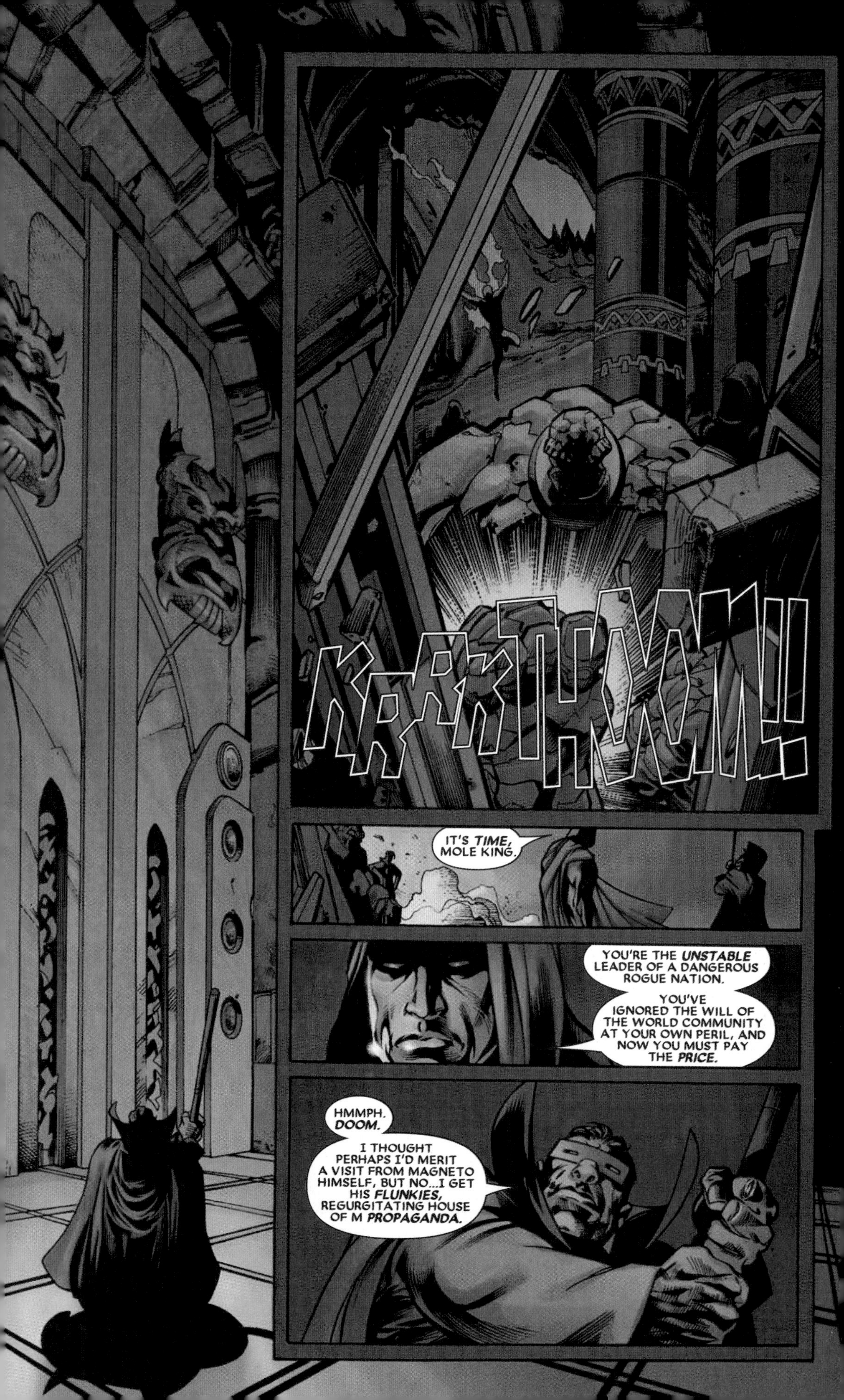

KRAKTHOOM!!
IT'S TIME, MOLE KING.
YOU'RE THE UNSTABLE LEADER OF A DANGEROUS ROGUE NATION.
YOU'VE IGNORED THE WILL OF THE WORLD COMMUNITY AT YOUR OWN PERIL, AND NOW YOU MUST PAY THE PRICE.
HMMPH. DOOM.
I THOUGHT PERHAPS I'D MERIT A VISIT FROM MAGNETO HIMSELF, BUT NO...I GET HIS FLUNKIES, REGURGITATING HOUSE OF M PROPAGANDA.

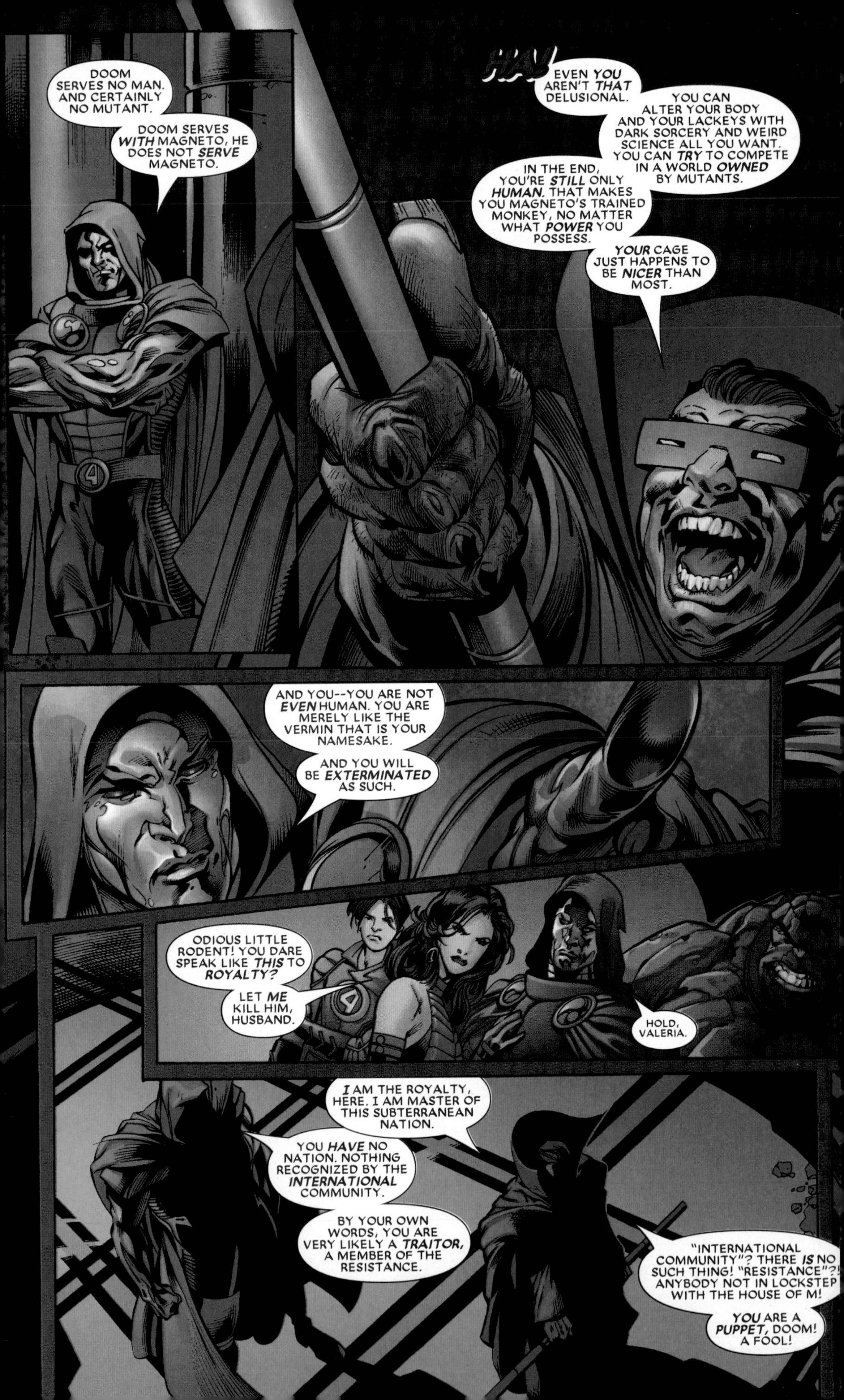
DOOM SERVES NO MAN. AND CERTAINLY NO MUTANT.
DOOM SERVES WITH MAGNETO, HE DOES NOT SERVE MAGNETO.
HA!
EVEN YOU AREN'T THAT DELUSIONAL.
YOU CAN ALTER YOUR BODY AND YOUR LACKEYS WITH DARK SORCERY AND WEIRD SCIENCE ALL YOU WANT. YOU CAN TRY TO COMPETE IN A WORLD OWNED BY MUTANTS.
IN THE END, YOU'RE STILL ONLY HUMAN. THAT MAKES YOU MAGNETO'S TRAINED MONKEY, NO MATTER WHAT POWER YOU POSSESS.
YOUR CAGE JUST HAPPENS TO BE NICER THAN MOST.
AND YOU--YOU ARE NOT EVEN HUMAN. YOU ARE MERELY LIKE THE VERMIN THAT IS YOUR NAMESAKE.
AND YOU WILL BE EXTERMINATED AS SUCH.
ODIOUS LITTLE RODENT! YOU DARE SPEAK LIKE THIS TO ROYALTY?
LET ME KILL HIM, HUSBAND.
HOLD, VALERIA.
I AM THE ROYALTY, HERE. I AM MASTER OF THIS SUBTERRANEAN NATION.
YOU HAVE NO NATION. NOTHING RECOGNIZED BY THE INTERNATIONAL COMMUNITY.
BY YOUR OWN WORDS, YOU ARE VERY LIKELY A TRAITOR, A MEMBER OF THE RESISTANCE.
"INTERNATIONAL COMMUNITY"? THERE IS NO SUCH THING! "RESISTANCE"?! ANYBODY NOT IN LOCKSTEP WITH THE HOUSE OF M!
YOU ARE A PUPPET, DOOM! A FOOL!

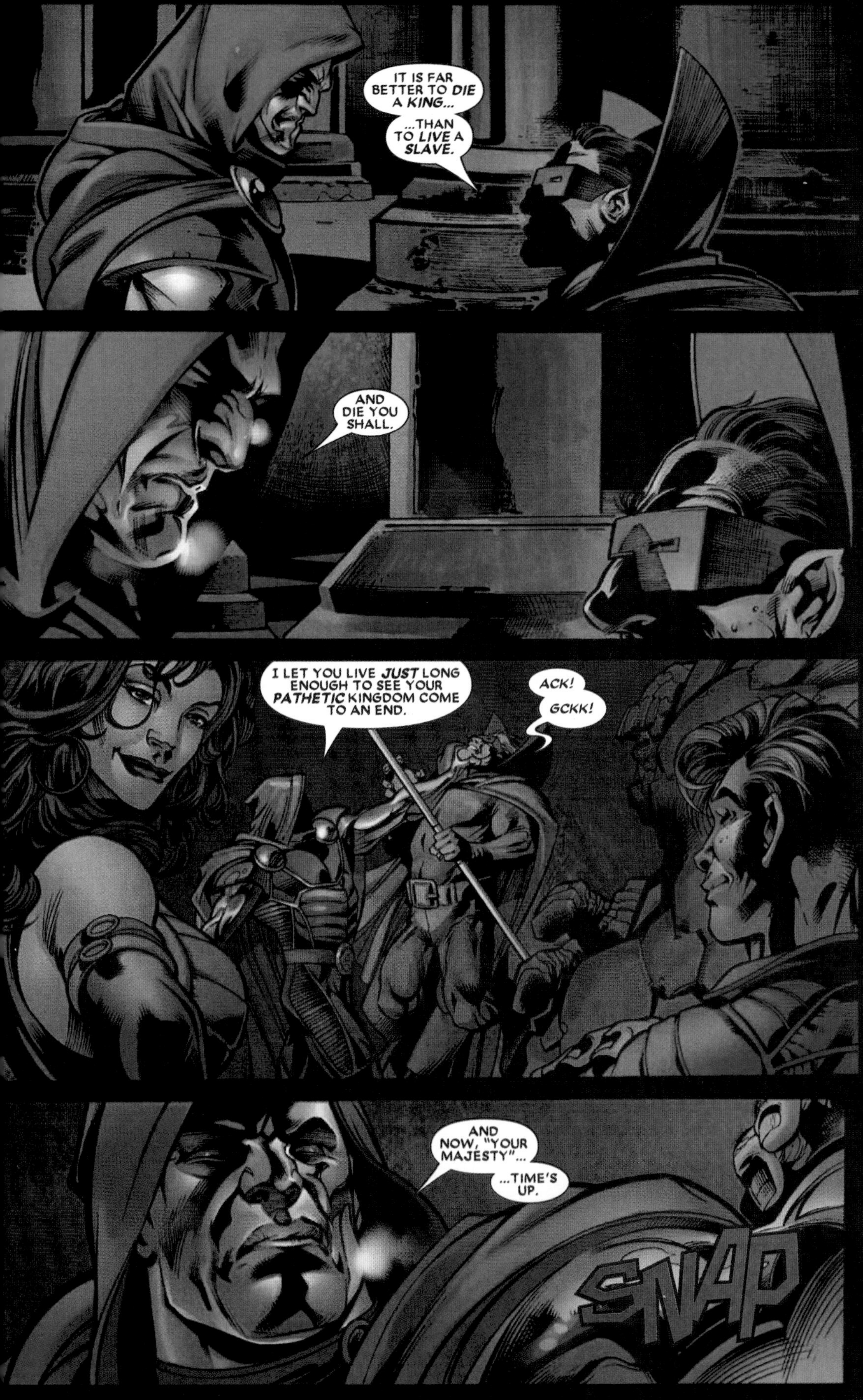
IT IS FAR BETTER TO DIE A KING...
...THAN TO LIVE A SLAVE.
AND DIE YOU SHALL.
I LET YOU LIVE JUST LONG ENOUGH TO SEE YOUR PATHETIC KINGDOM COME TO AN END.
ACK!
GCKK!
AND NOW, "YOUR MAJESTY"...
...TIME'S UP.
SNAP

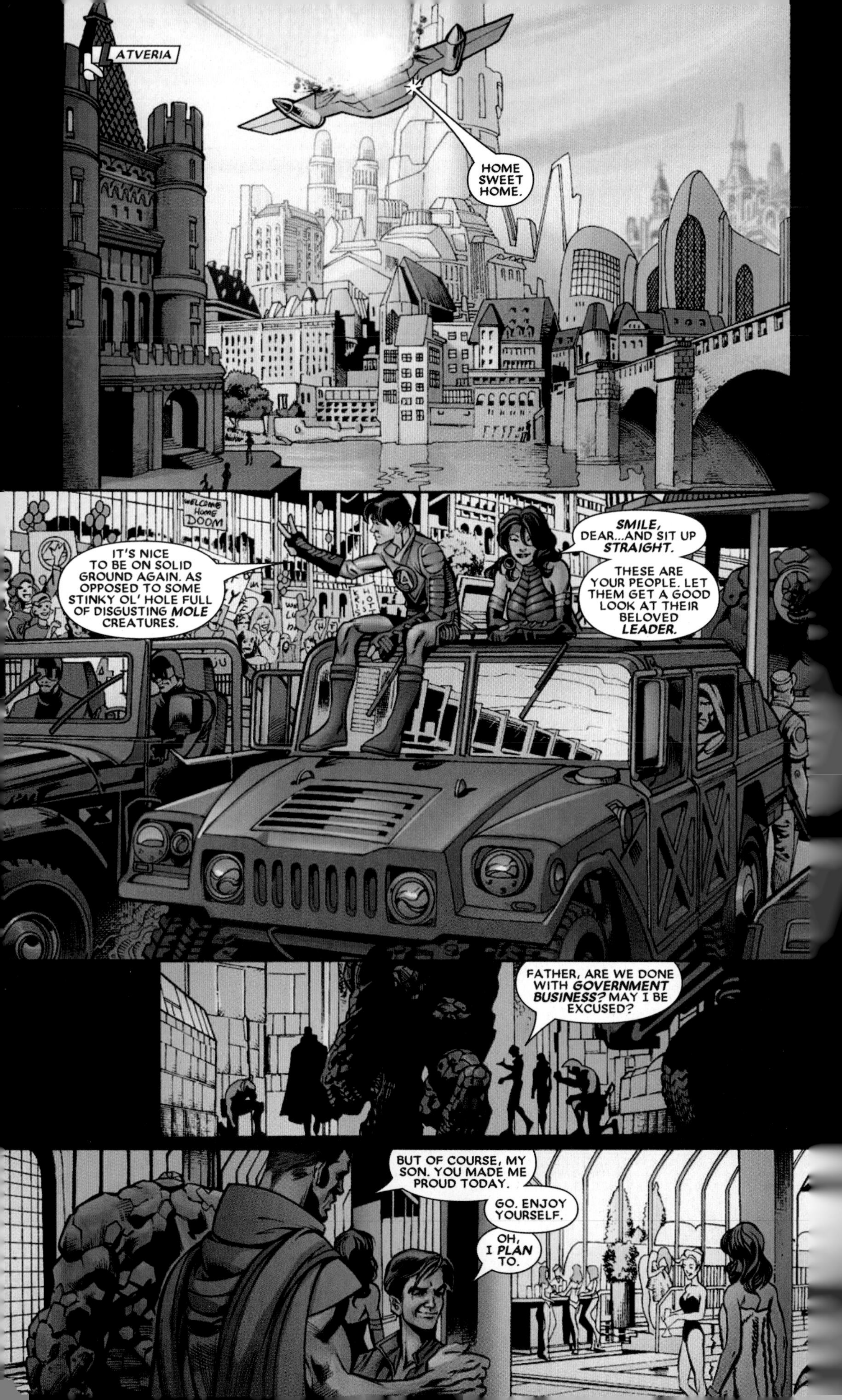
LATVERIA
HOME SWEET HOME.
WELCOME Home DOOM
IT'S NICE TO BE ON SOLID GROUND AGAIN. AS OPPOSED TO SOME STINKY OL' HOLE FULL OF DISGUSTING MOLE CREATURES.
SMILE, DEAR...AND SIT UP STRAIGHT.
THESE ARE YOUR PEOPLE. LET THEM GET A GOOD LOOK AT THEIR BELOVED LEADER.
FATHER, ARE WE DONE WITH GOVERNMENT BUSINESS? MAY I BE EXCUSED?
BUT OF COURSE, MY SON. YOU MADE ME PROUD TODAY.
GO. ENJOY YOURSELF.
OH, I PLAN TO.

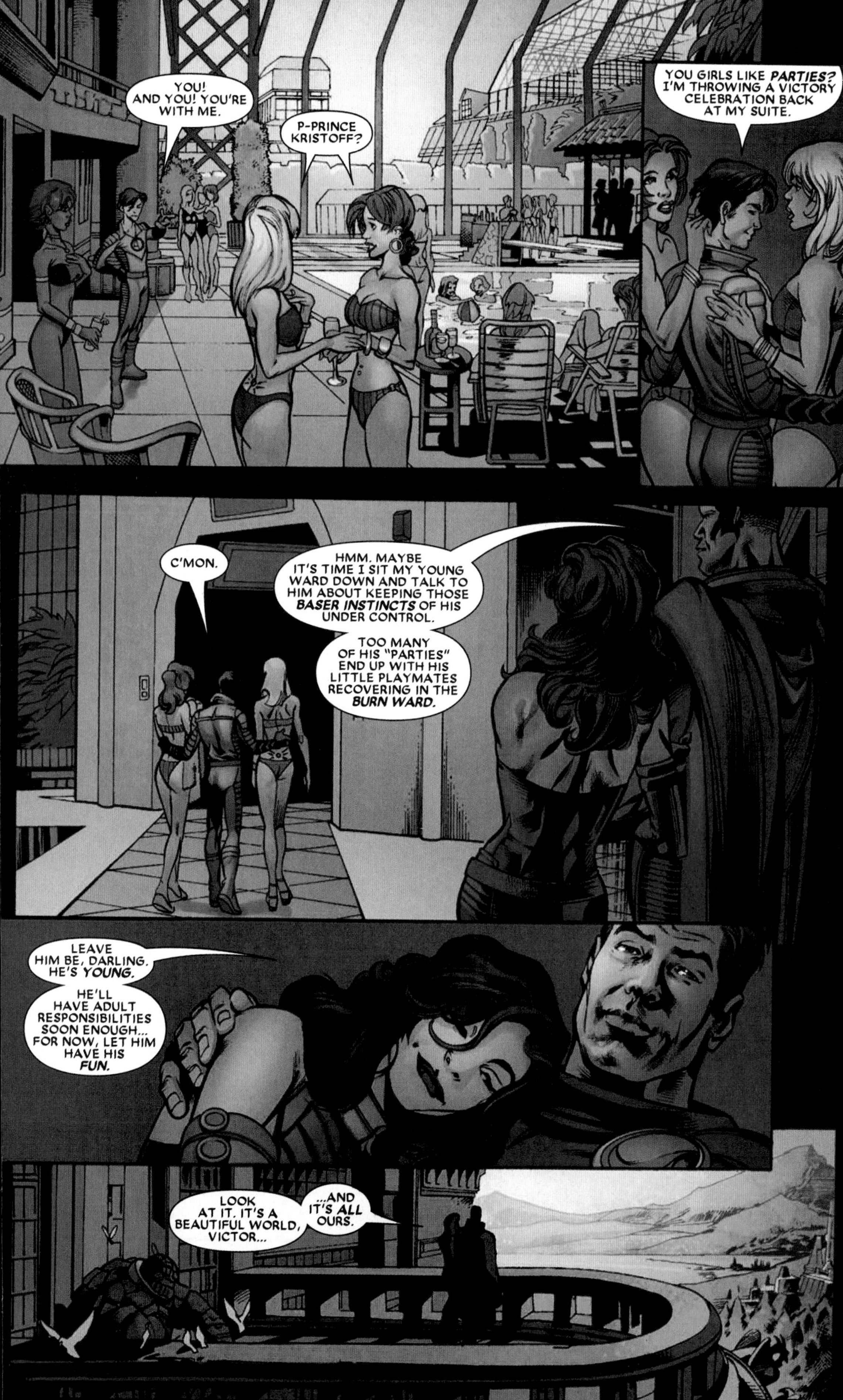
YOU! AND YOU! YOU'RE WITH ME.
P-PRINCE KRISTOFF?
YOU GIRLS LIKE PARTIES? I'M THROWING A VICTORY CELEBRATION BACK AT MY SUITE.
C'MON.
HMM. MAYBE IT'S TIME I SIT MY YOUNG WARD DOWN AND TALK TO HIM ABOUT KEEPING THOSE BASER INSTINCTS OF HIS UNDER CONTROL.
TOO MANY OF HIS "PARTIES" END UP WITH HIS LITTLE PLAYMATES RECOVERING IN THE BURN WARD.
LEAVE HIM BE, DARLING. HE'S YOUNG.
HE'LL HAVE ADULT RESPONSIBILITIES SOON ENOUGH... FOR NOW, LET HIM HAVE HIS FUN.
LOOK AT IT. IT'S A BEAUTIFUL WORLD, VICTOR...
...AND IT'S ALL OURS.

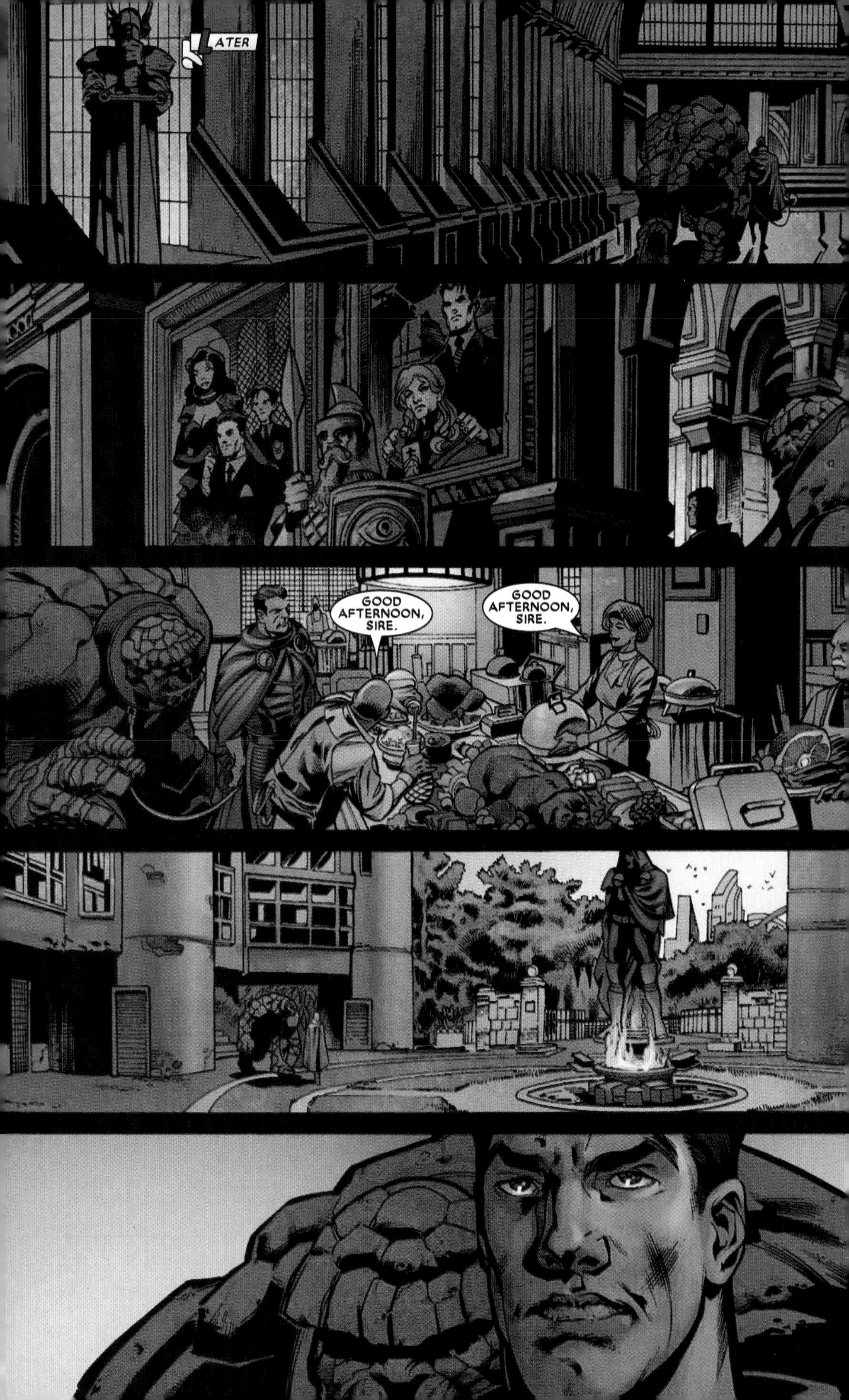
LATER
GOOD AFTERNOON, SIRE.
GOOD AFTERNOON, SIRE.

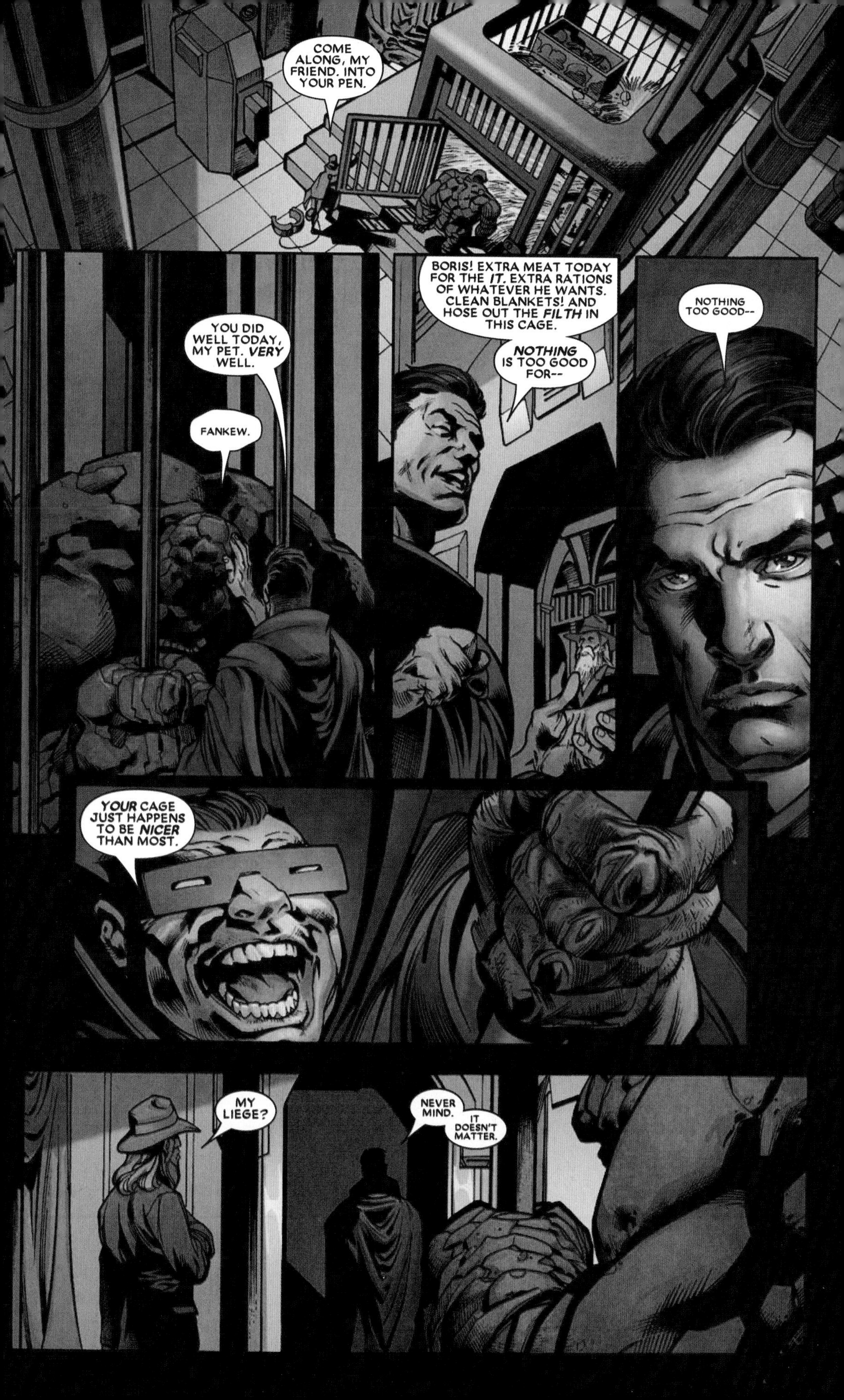
COME ALONG, MY FRIEND. INTO YOUR PEN.
YOU DID WELL TODAY, MY PET. VERY WELL.
FANKEW.
BORIS! EXTRA MEAT TODAY FOR THE IT. EXTRA RATIONS OF WHATEVER HE WANTS. CLEAN BLANKETS! AND HOSE OUT THE FILTH IN THIS CAGE.
NOTHING IS TOO GOOD FOR--
NOTHING TOO GOOD--
YOUR CAGE JUST HAPPENS TO BE NICER THAN MOST.
MY LIEGE?
NEVER MIND.
IT DOESN'T MATTER.

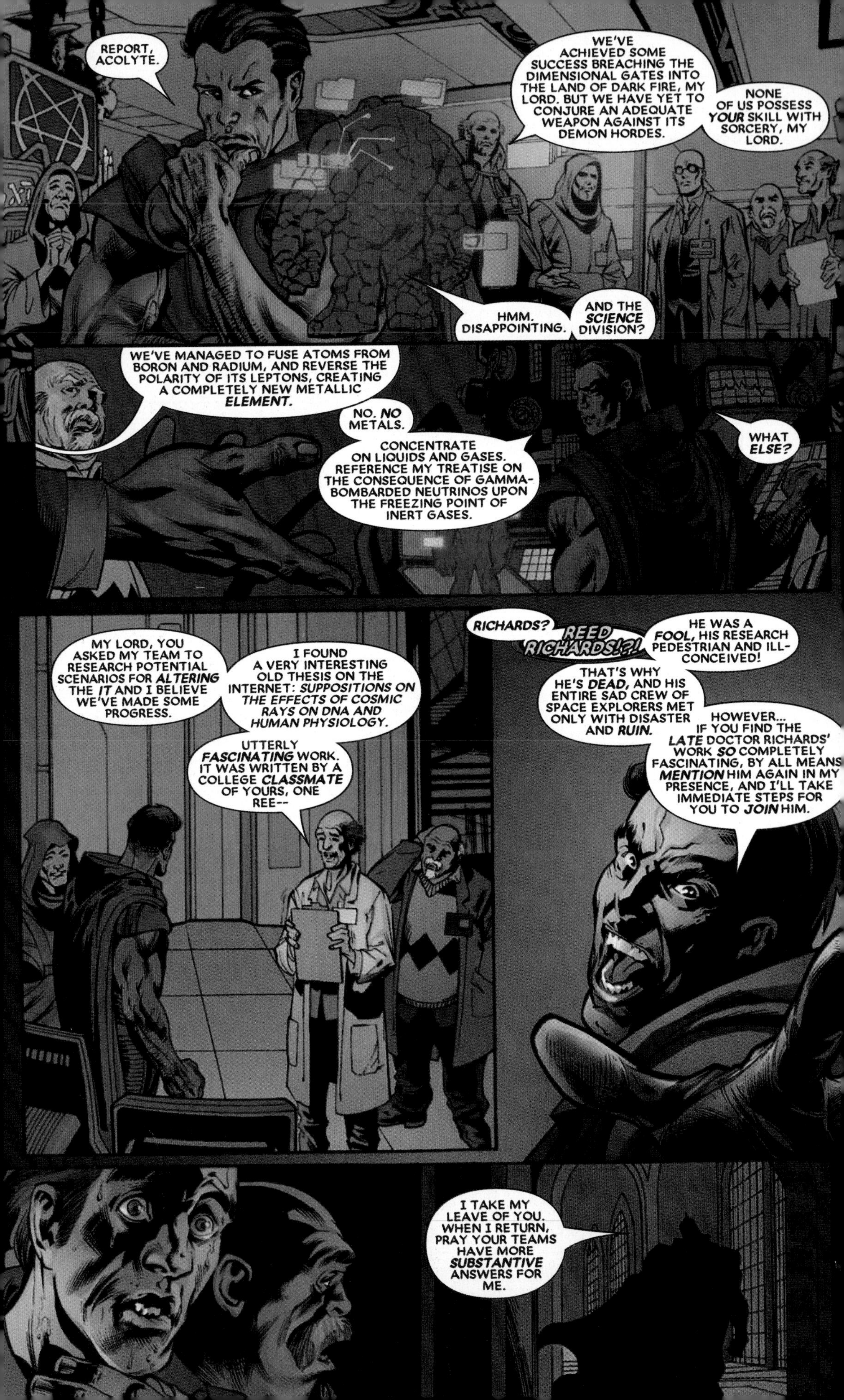
REPORT, ACOLYTE.
WE'VE ACHIEVED SOME SUCCESS BREACHING THE DIMENSIONAL GATES INTO THE LAND OF DARK FIRE, MY LORD. BUT WE HAVE YET TO CONJURE AN ADEQUATE WEAPON AGAINST ITS DEMON HORDES.
NONE OF US POSSESS *YOUR* SKILL WITH SORCERY, MY LORD.
HMM. DISAPPOINTING.
AND THE *SCIENCE* DIVISION?
WE'VE MANAGED TO FUSE ATOMS FROM BORON AND RADIUM, AND REVERSE THE POLARITY OF ITS LEPTONS, CREATING A COMPLETELY NEW METALLIC *ELEMENT.*
NO. *NO* METALS.
CONCENTRATE ON LIQUIDS AND GASES. REFERENCE MY TREATISE ON THE CONSEQUENCE OF GAMMA-BOMBARDED NEUTRINOS UPON THE FREEZING POINT OF INERT GASES.
WHAT *ELSE?*
MY LORD, YOU ASKED MY TEAM TO RESEARCH POTENTIAL SCENARIOS FOR *ALTERING* THE *IT* AND I BELIEVE WE'VE MADE SOME PROGRESS.
I FOUND A VERY INTERESTING OLD THESIS ON THE INTERNET: *SUPPOSITIONS ON THE EFFECTS OF COSMIC RAYS ON DNA AND HUMAN PHYSIOLOGY.*
UTTERLY *FASCINATING* WORK. IT WAS WRITTEN BY A COLLEGE *CLASSMATE* OF YOURS, ONE REE--
RICHARDS?
REED RICHARDS!?!
HE WAS A *FOOL,* HIS RESEARCH PEDESTRIAN AND ILL-CONCEIVED!
THAT'S WHY HE'S *DEAD,* AND HIS ENTIRE SAD CREW OF SPACE EXPLORERS MET ONLY WITH DISASTER AND *RUIN.*
HOWEVER... IF YOU FIND THE *LATE* DOCTOR RICHARDS' WORK *SO* COMPLETELY FASCINATING, BY ALL MEANS *MENTION* HIM AGAIN IN MY PRESENCE, AND I'LL TAKE IMMEDIATE STEPS FOR YOU TO *JOIN* HIM.
I TAKE MY LEAVE OF YOU. WHEN I RETURN, PRAY YOUR TEAMS HAVE MORE *SUBSTANTIVE* ANSWERS FOR ME.

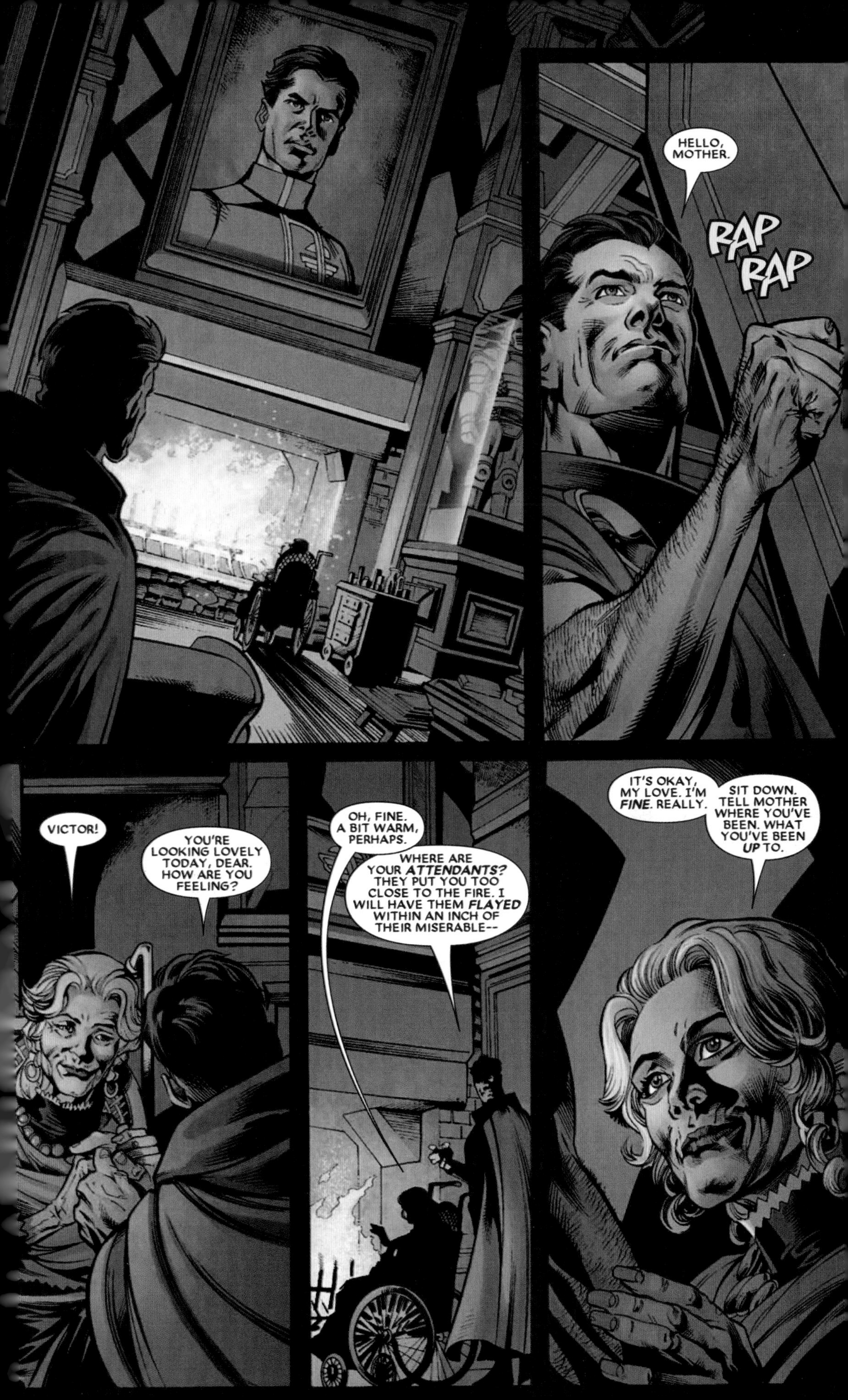
HELLO, MOTHER.
RAP RAP
VICTOR!
YOU'RE LOOKING LOVELY TODAY, DEAR. HOW ARE YOU FEELING?
OH, FINE. A BIT WARM, PERHAPS.
WHERE ARE YOUR *ATTENDANTS?* THEY PUT YOU TOO CLOSE TO THE FIRE. I WILL HAVE THEM *FLAYED* WITHIN AN INCH OF THEIR MISERABLE--
IT'S OKAY, MY LOVE. I'M *FINE*. REALLY.
SIT DOWN. TELL MOTHER WHERE YOU'VE BEEN. WHAT YOU'VE BEEN *UP* TO.

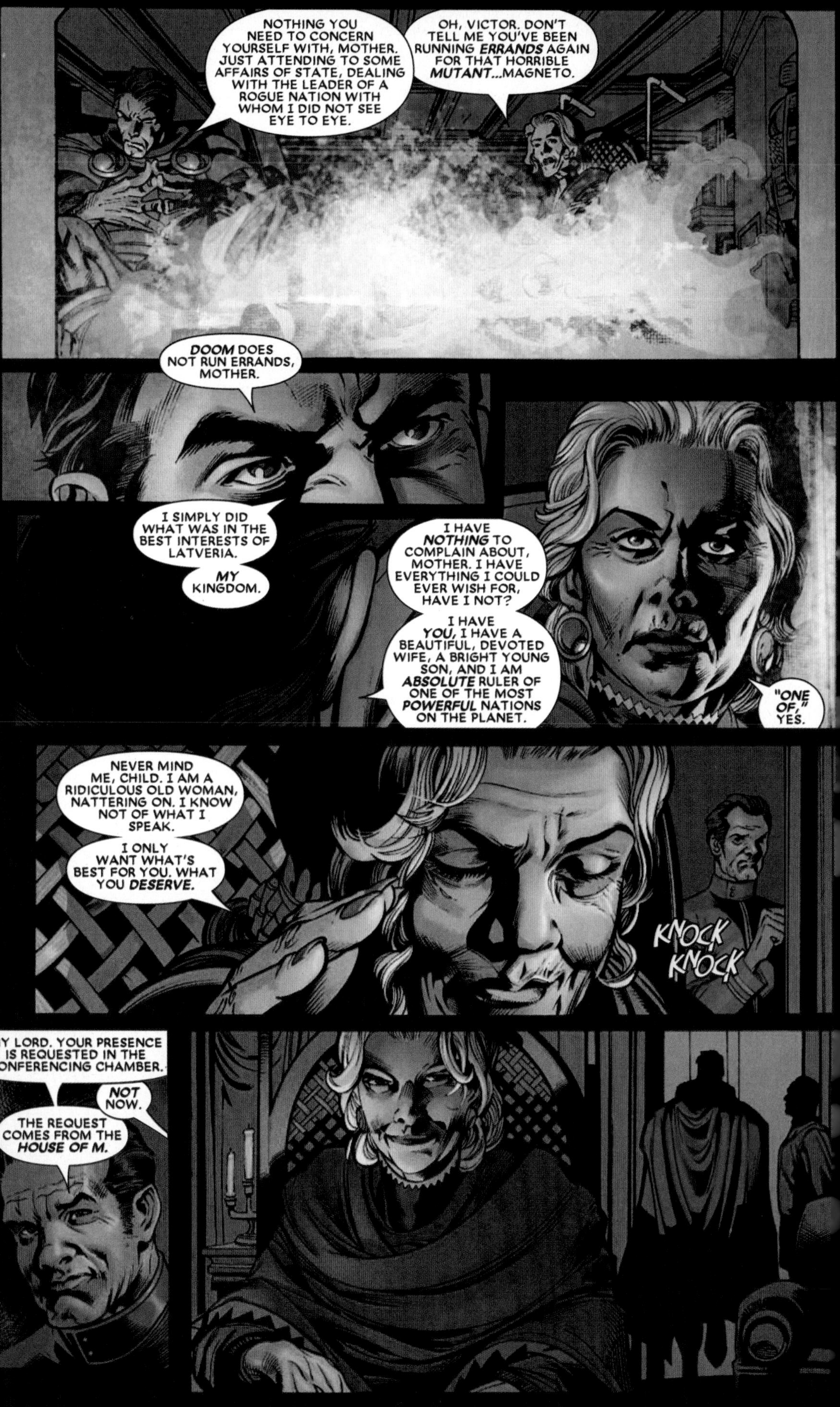

NOTHING YOU NEED TO CONCERN YOURSELF WITH, MOTHER. JUST ATTENDING TO SOME AFFAIRS OF STATE, DEALING WITH THE LEADER OF A ROGUE NATION WITH WHOM I DID NOT SEE EYE TO EYE.
OH, VICTOR. DON'T TELL ME YOU'VE BEEN RUNNING ERRANDS AGAIN FOR THAT HORRIBLE MUTANT...MAGNETO.
DOOM DOES NOT RUN ERRANDS, MOTHER.
I SIMPLY DID WHAT WAS IN THE BEST INTERESTS OF LATVERIA.
MY KINGDOM.
I HAVE NOTHING TO COMPLAIN ABOUT, MOTHER. I HAVE EVERYTHING I COULD EVER WISH FOR, HAVE I NOT?
I HAVE YOU, I HAVE A BEAUTIFUL, DEVOTED WIFE, A BRIGHT YOUNG SON, AND I AM ABSOLUTE RULER OF ONE OF THE MOST POWERFUL NATIONS ON THE PLANET.
"ONE OF," YES.
NEVER MIND ME, CHILD. I AM A RIDICULOUS OLD WOMAN, NATTERING ON. I KNOW NOT OF WHAT I SPEAK.
I ONLY WANT WHAT'S BEST FOR YOU. WHAT YOU DESERVE.
KNOCK KNOCK
MY LORD. YOUR PRESENCE IS REQUESTED IN THE CONFERENCING CHAMBER.
NOT NOW.
THE REQUEST COMES FROM THE HOUSE OF M.

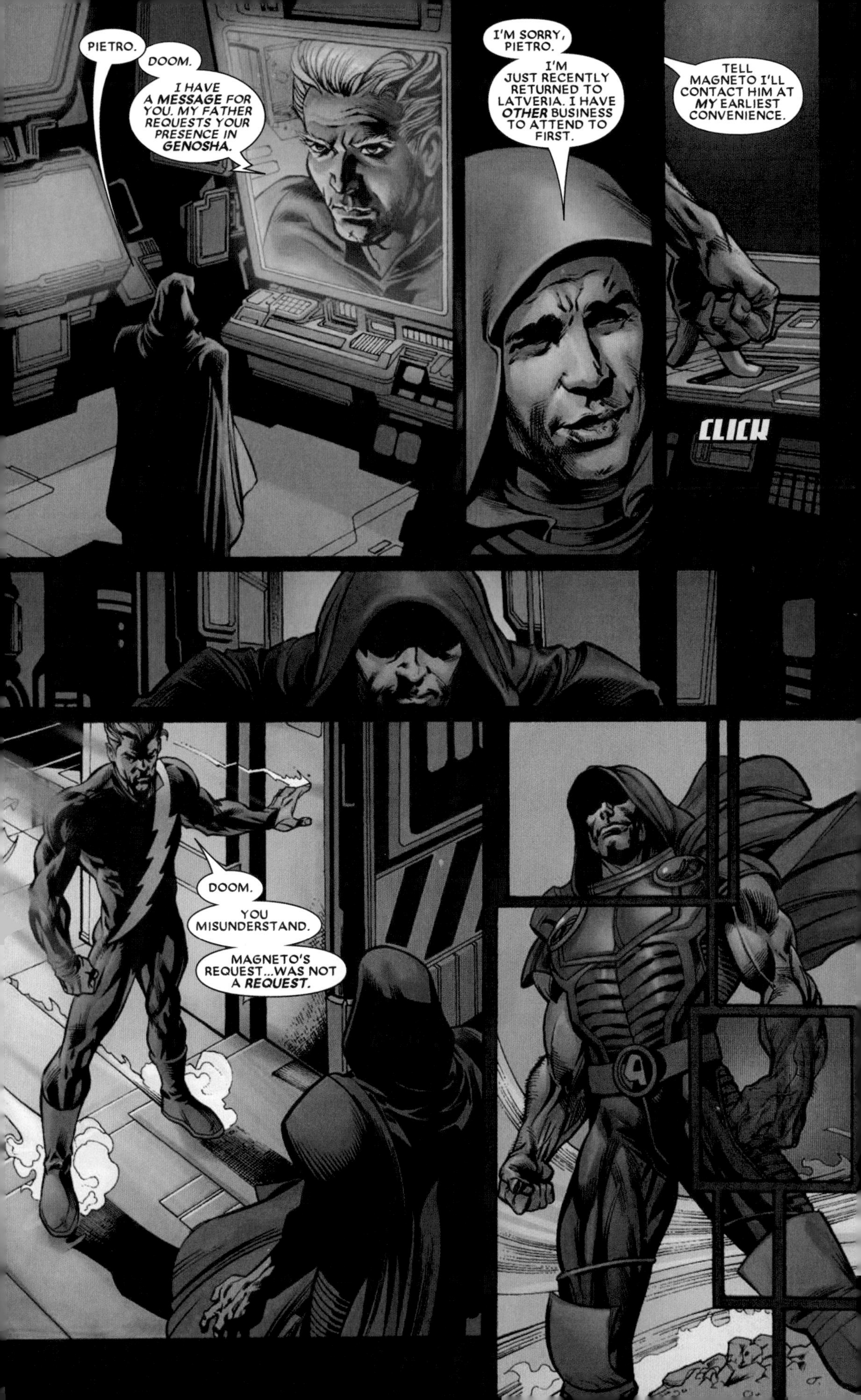
PIETRO.
DOOM.
I HAVE A MESSAGE FOR YOU. MY FATHER REQUESTS YOUR PRESENCE IN GENOSHA.
I'M SORRY, PIETRO.
I'M JUST RECENTLY RETURNED TO LATVERIA. I HAVE OTHER BUSINESS TO ATTEND TO FIRST.
TELL MAGNETO I'LL CONTACT HIM AT MY EARLIEST CONVENIENCE.
CLICK
DOOM.
YOU MISUNDERSTAND.
MAGNETO'S REQUEST...WAS NOT A REQUEST.

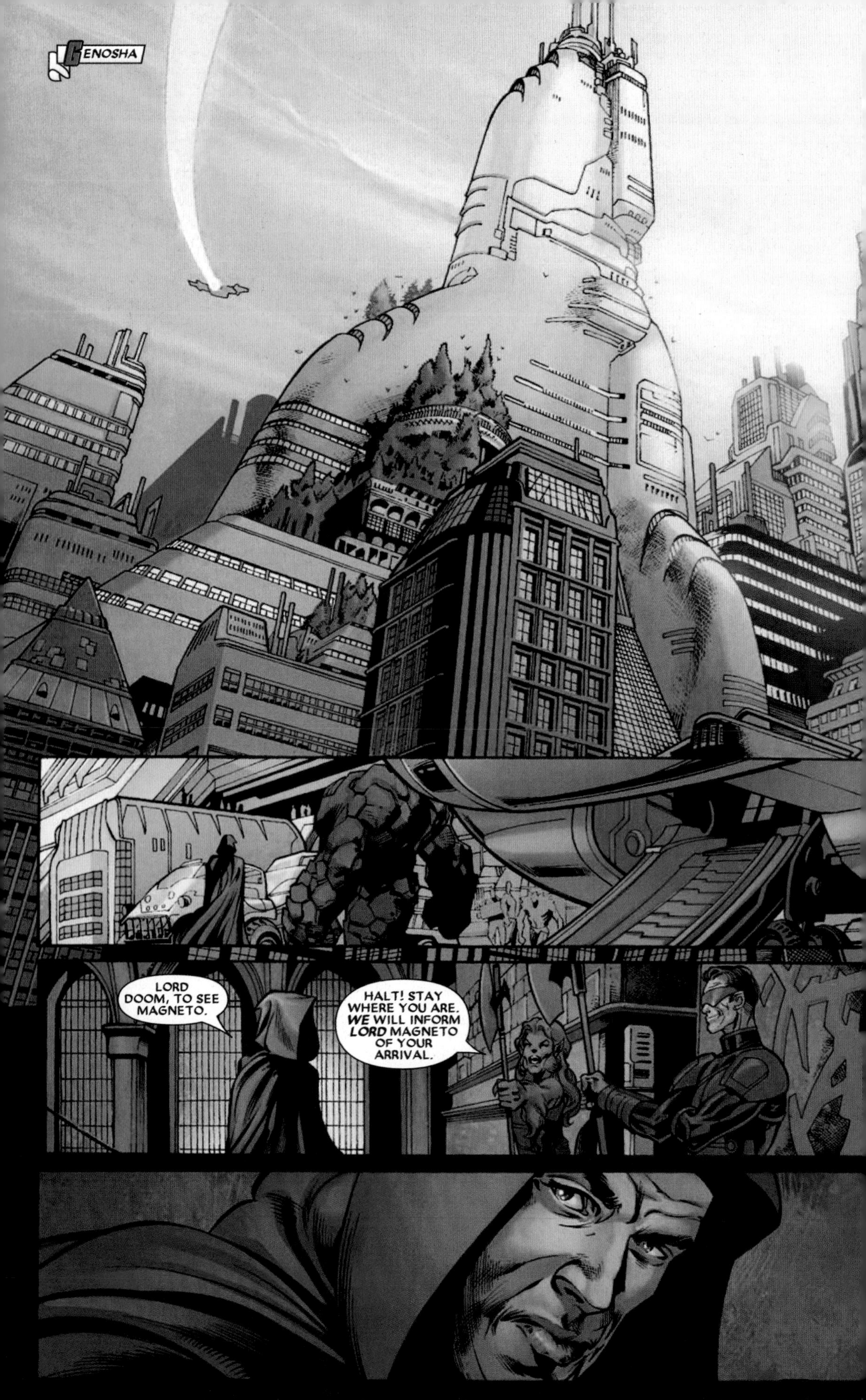
GENOSHA
LORD DOOM, TO SEE MAGNETO.
HALT! STAY WHERE YOU ARE. WE WILL INFORM LORD MAGNETO OF YOUR ARRIVAL.

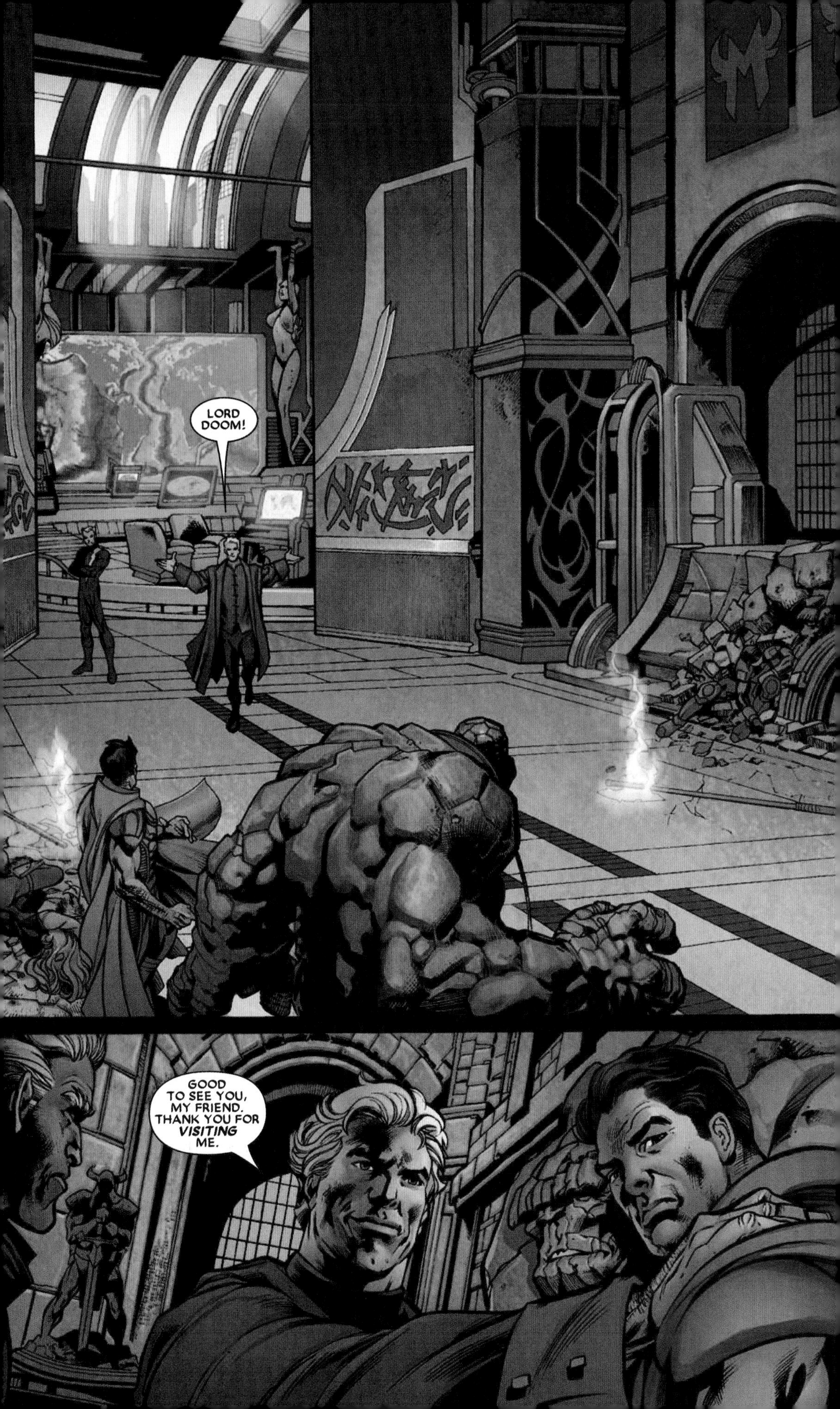
LORD DOOM!
GOOD TO SEE YOU, MY FRIEND. THANK YOU FOR *VISITING* ME.

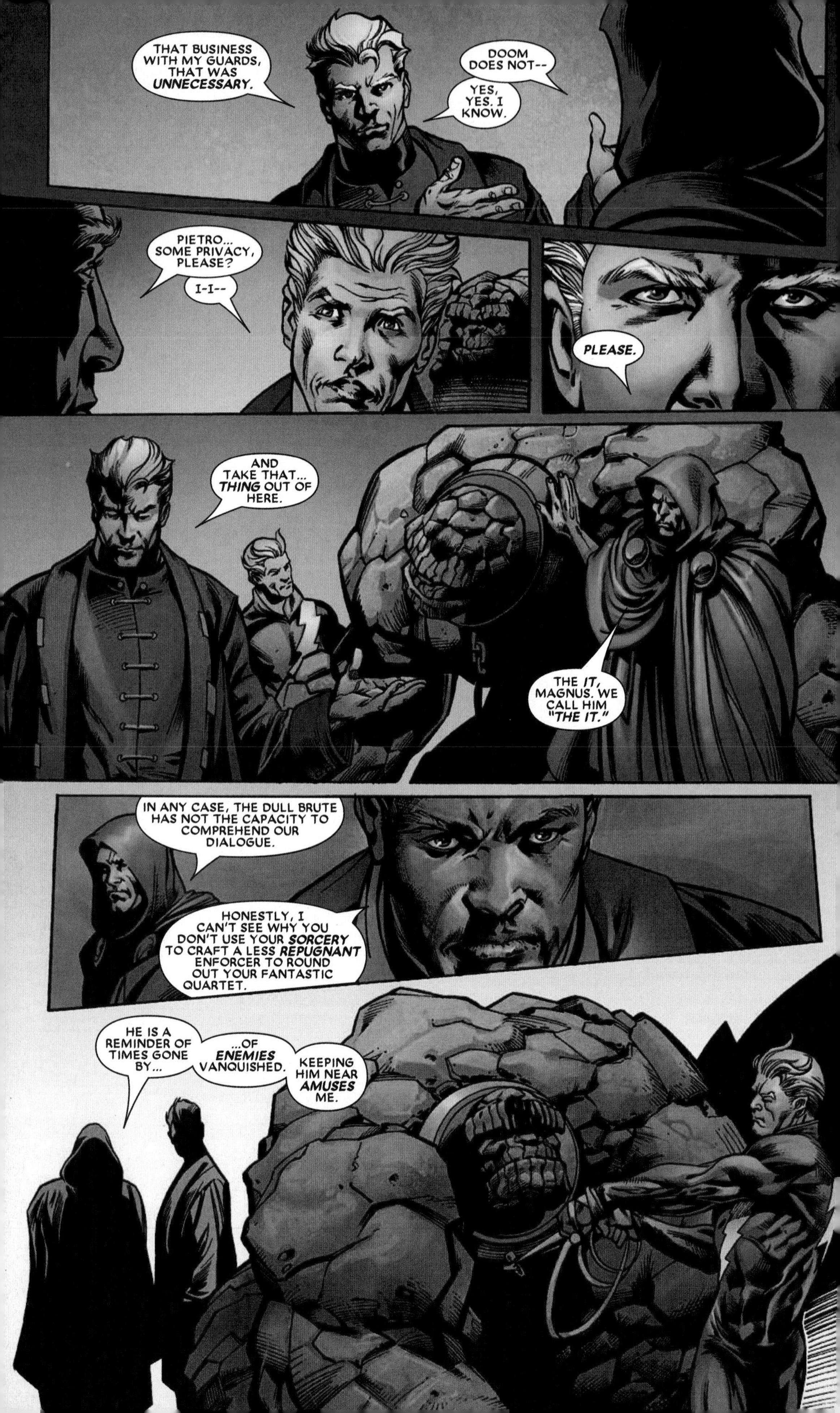
THAT BUSINESS WITH MY GUARDS, THAT WAS UNNECESSARY.
DOOM DOES NOT--
YES, YES. I KNOW.
PIETRO... SOME PRIVACY, PLEASE?
I-I--
PLEASE.
AND TAKE THAT... THING OUT OF HERE.
THE IT, MAGNUS. WE CALL HIM "THE IT."
IN ANY CASE, THE DULL BRUTE HAS NOT THE CAPACITY TO COMPREHEND OUR DIALOGUE.
HONESTLY, I CAN'T SEE WHY YOU DON'T USE YOUR SORCERY TO CRAFT A LESS REPUGNANT ENFORCER TO ROUND OUT YOUR FANTASTIC QUARTET.
HE IS A REMINDER OF TIMES GONE BY...
...OF ENEMIES VANQUISHED.
KEEPING HIM NEAR AMUSES ME.

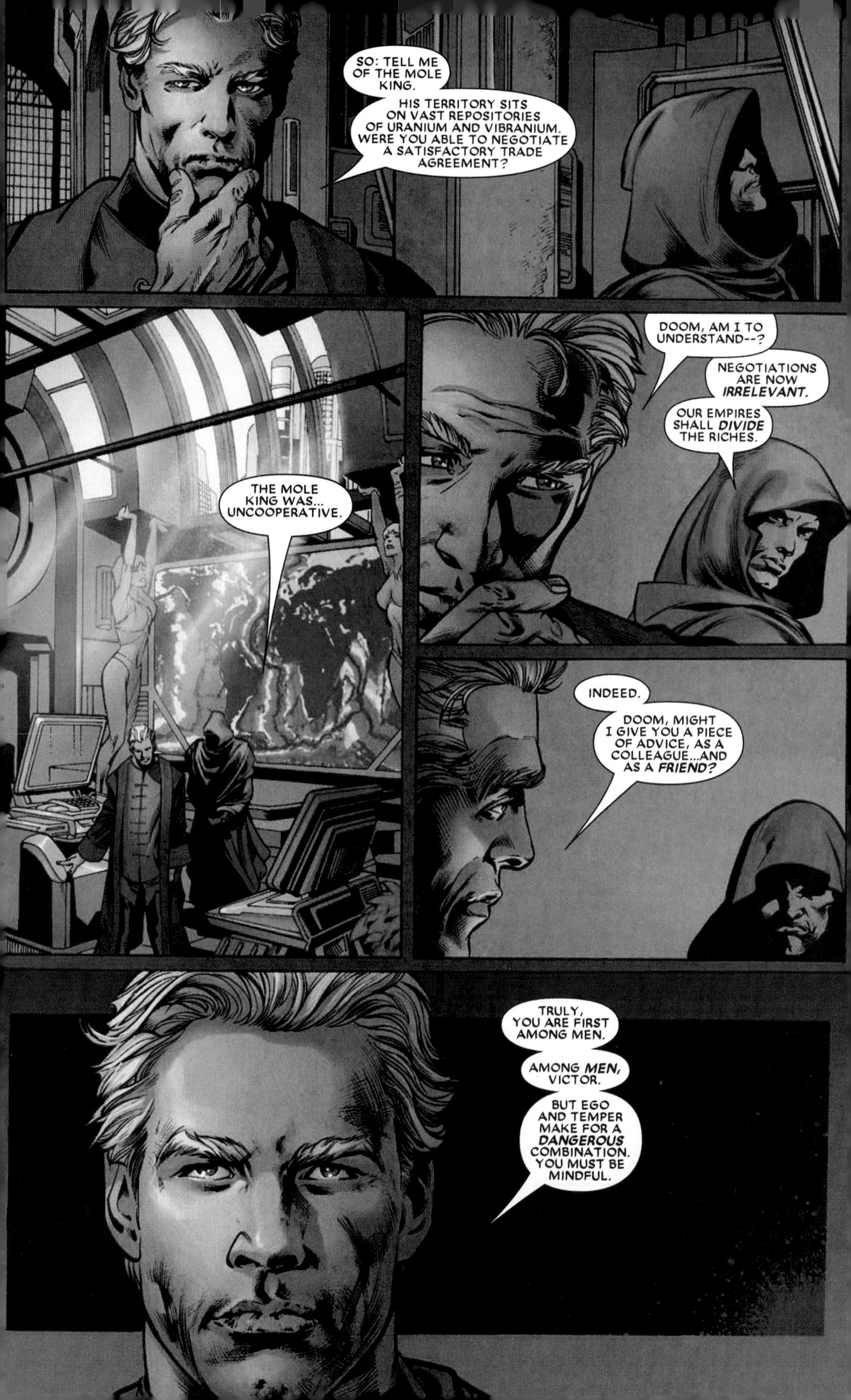
SO: TELL ME OF THE MOLE KING.
HIS TERRITORY SITS ON VAST REPOSITORIES OF URANIUM AND VIBRANIUM. WERE YOU ABLE TO NEGOTIATE A SATISFACTORY TRADE AGREEMENT?
THE MOLE KING WAS... UNCOOPERATIVE.
DOOM, AM I TO UNDERSTAND--?
NEGOTIATIONS ARE NOW IRRELEVANT.
OUR EMPIRES SHALL DIVIDE THE RICHES.
INDEED.
DOOM, MIGHT I GIVE YOU A PIECE OF ADVICE, AS A COLLEAGUE...AND AS A FRIEND?
TRULY, YOU ARE FIRST AMONG MEN.
AMONG MEN, VICTOR.
BUT EGO AND TEMPER MAKE FOR A DANGEROUS COMBINATION. YOU MUST BE MINDFUL.

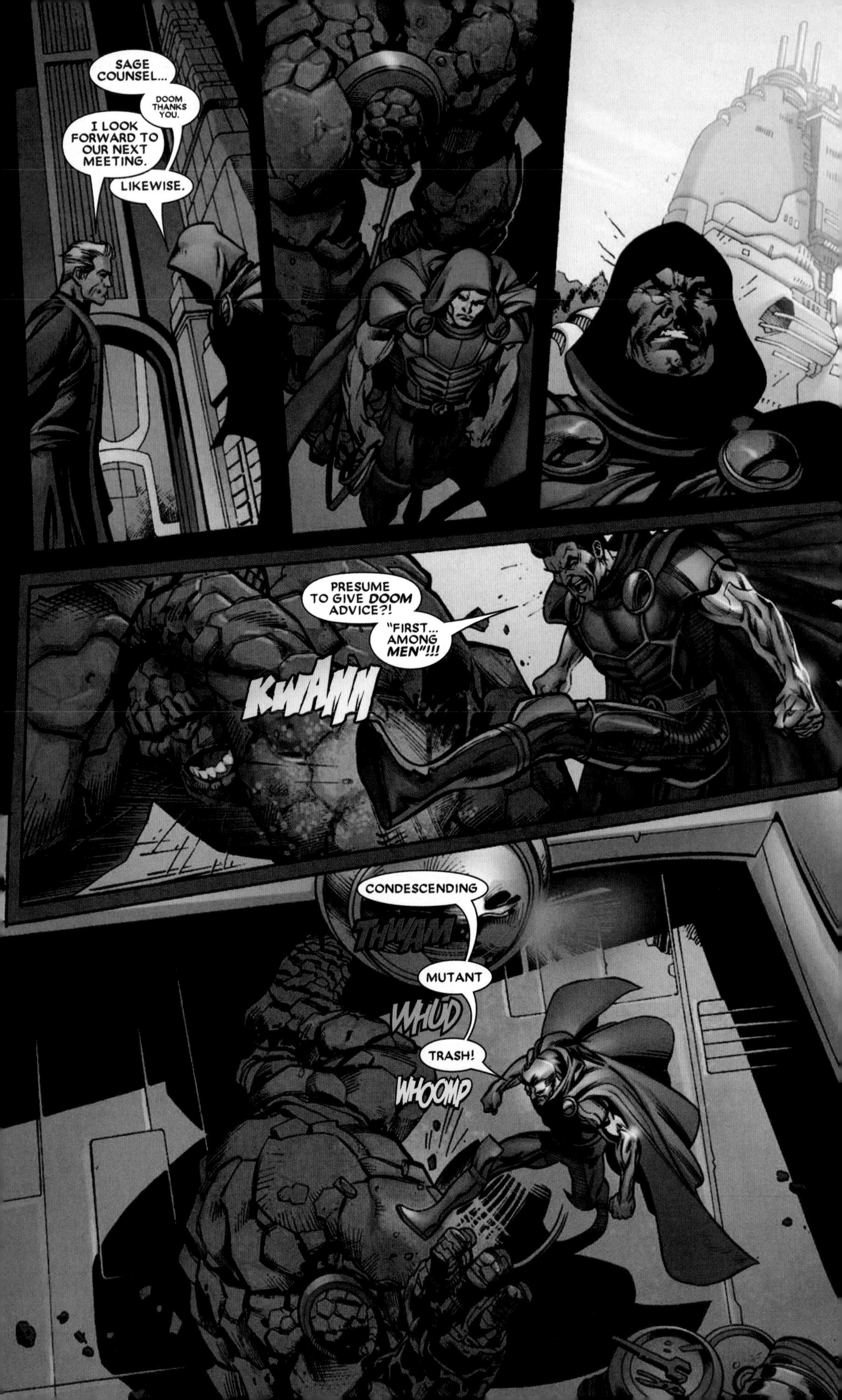

SAGE COUNSEL...
DOOM THANKS YOU.
I LOOK FORWARD TO OUR NEXT MEETING.
LIKEWISE.
PRESUME TO GIVE DOOM ADVICE?!
"FIRST... AMONG MEN"!!!
KWAMM
CONDESCENDING
THWAM
MUTANT
WHUD
TRASH!
WHOOMP

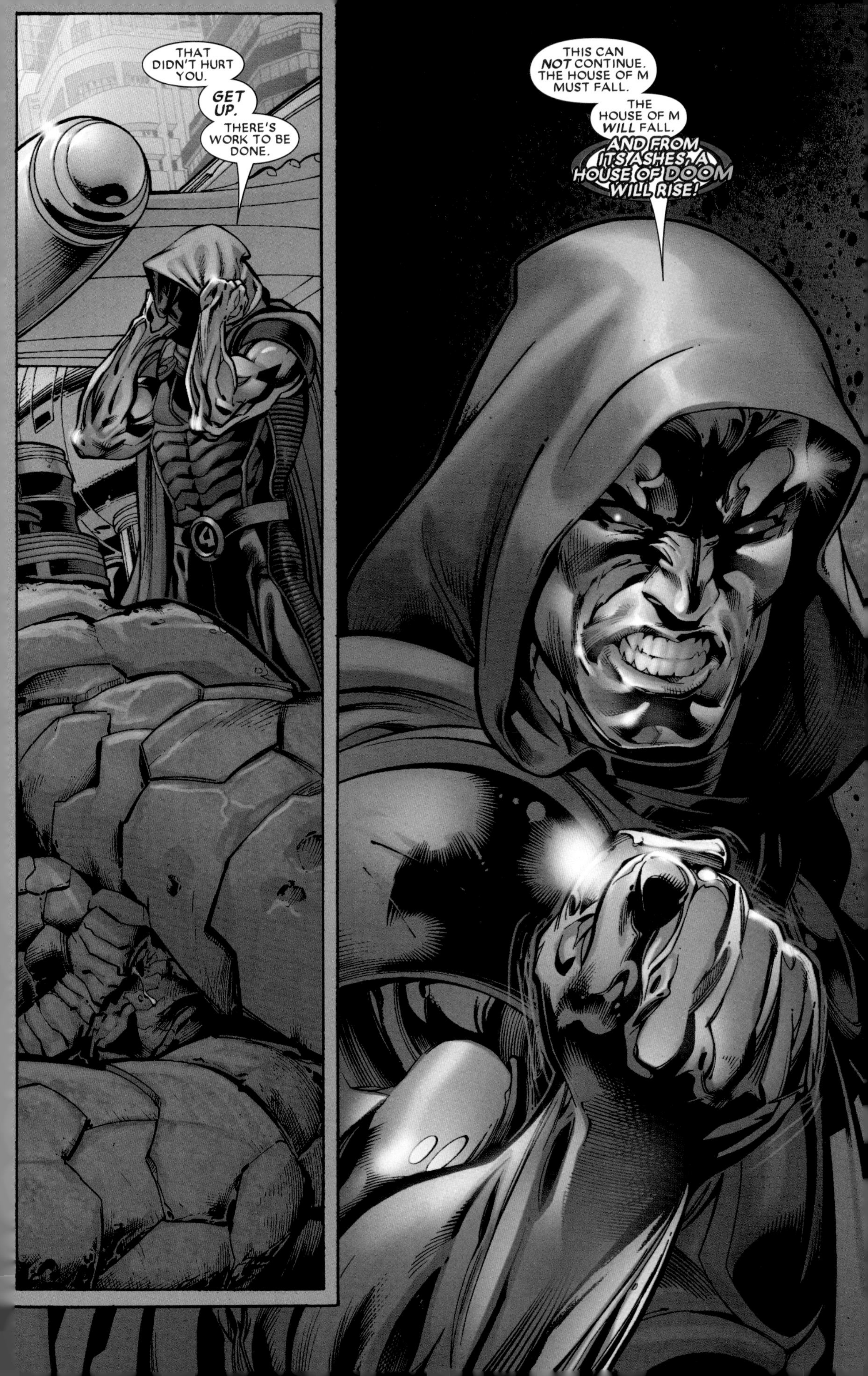
THAT DIDN'T HURT YOU.
GET UP.
THERE'S WORK TO BE DONE.
THIS CAN NOT CONTINUE. THE HOUSE OF M MUST FALL.
THE HOUSE OF M WILL FALL.
AND FROM ITS ASHES, A HOUSE OF DOOM WILL RISE!

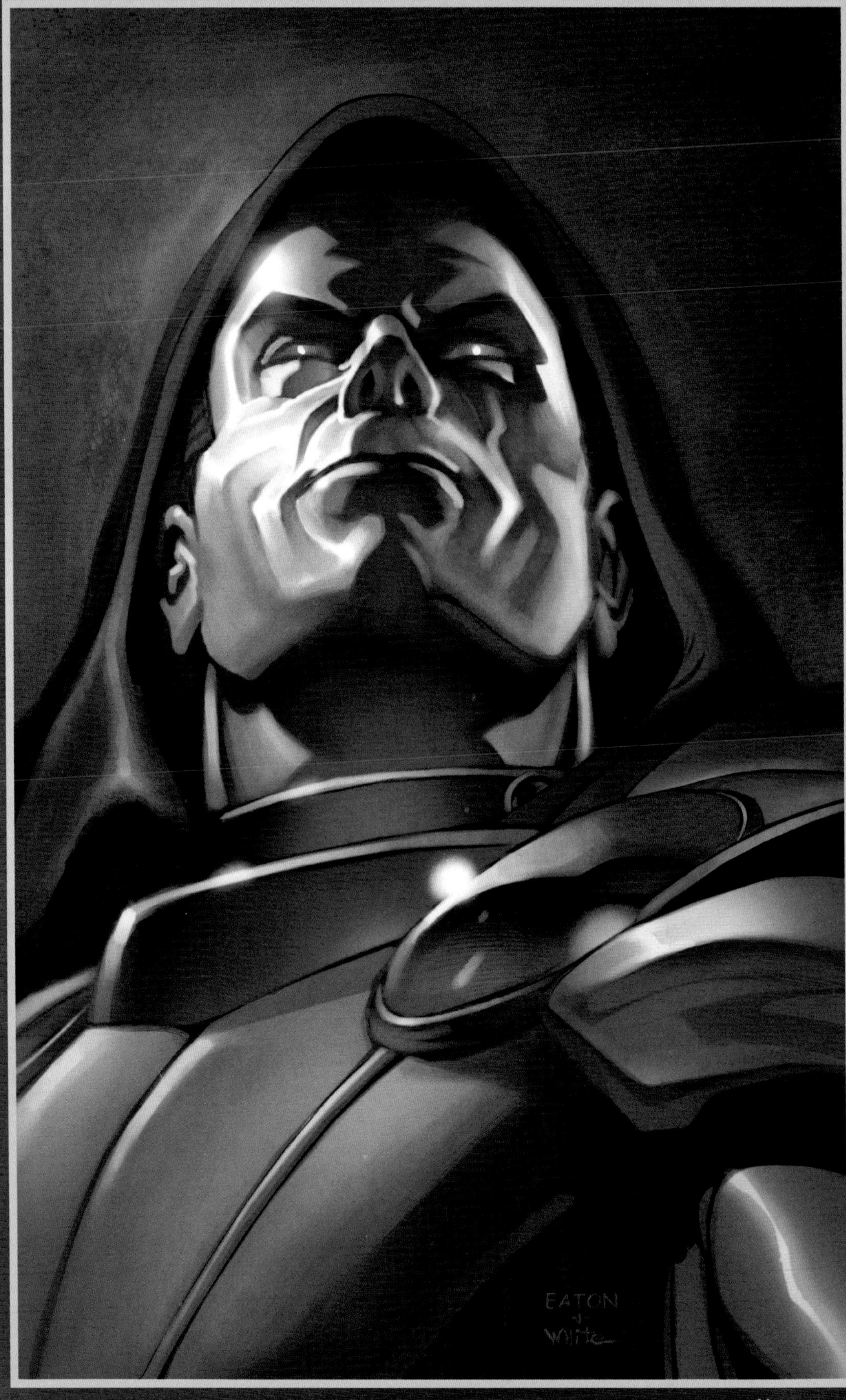
EATON
WHITE

FANTASTIC FOUR: HOUSE OF M #2

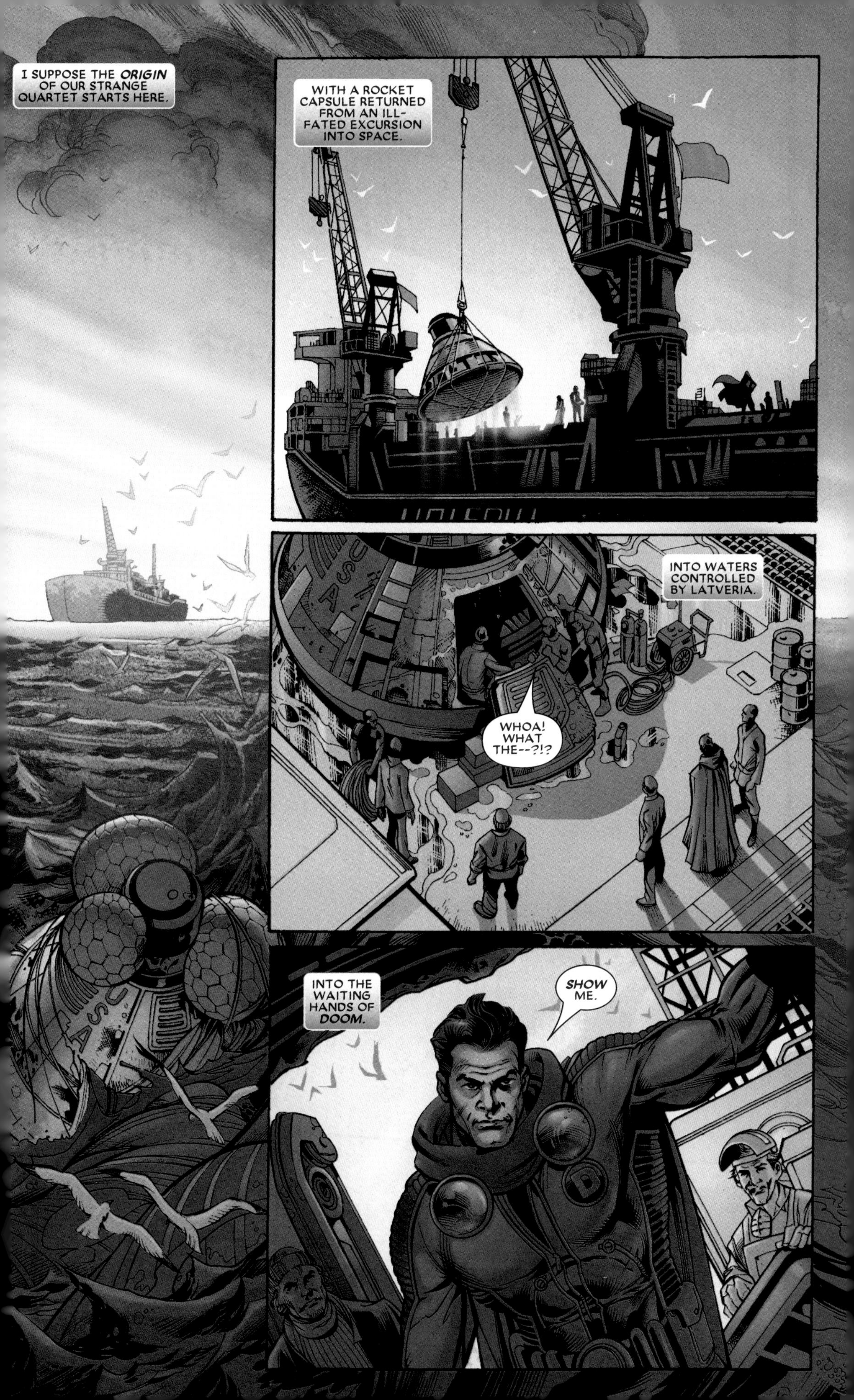
I SUPPOSE THE *ORIGIN* OF OUR STRANGE QUARTET STARTS HERE.
WITH A ROCKET CAPSULE RETURNED FROM AN ILL-FATED EXCURSION INTO SPACE.
INTO WATERS CONTROLLED BY LATVERIA.
WHOA! WHAT THE--?!?
INTO THE WAITING HANDS OF *DOOM.*
SHOW ME.

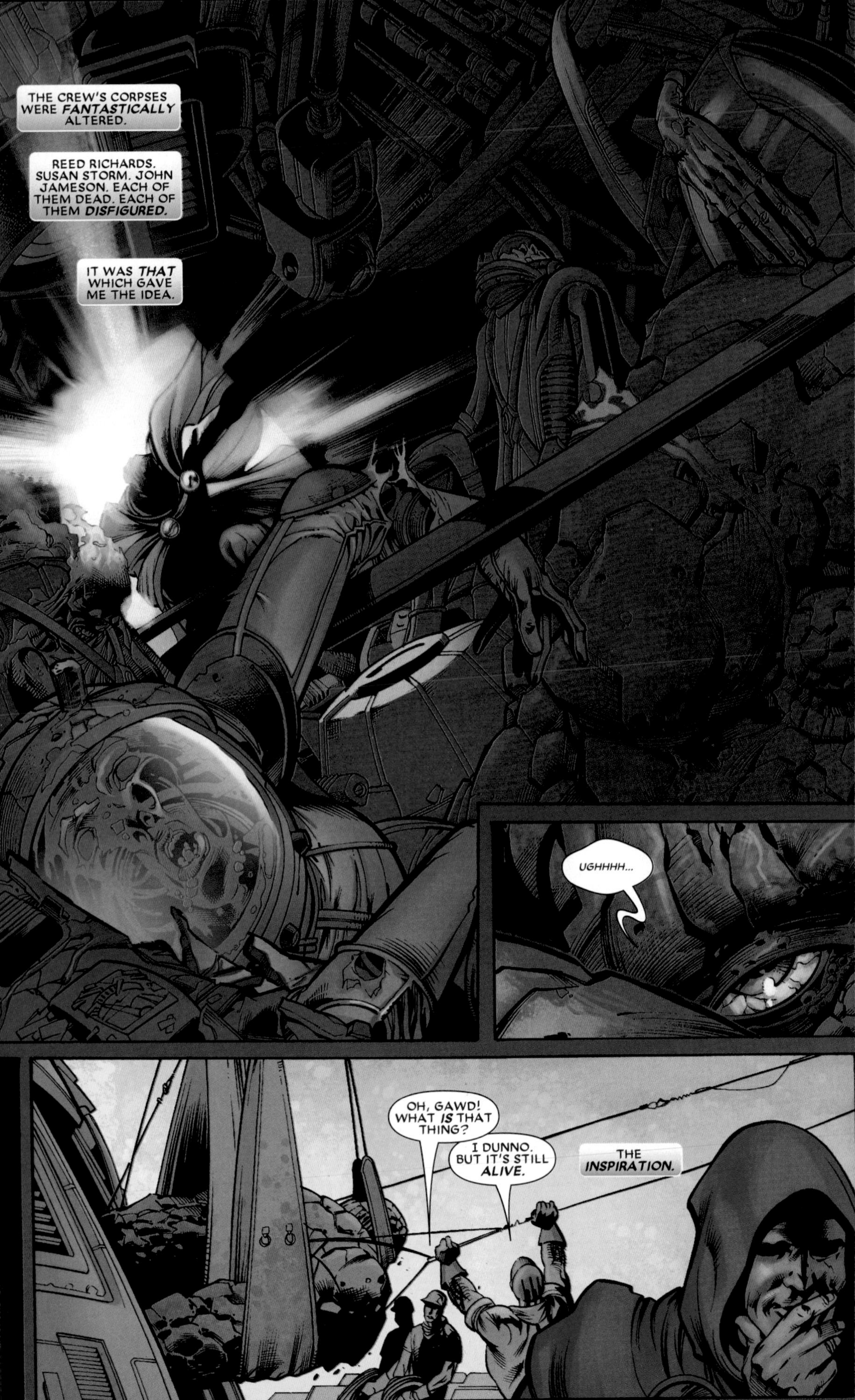

THE CREW'S CORPSES WERE *FANTASTICALLY* ALTERED.
REED RICHARDS. SUSAN STORM. JOHN JAMESON. EACH OF THEM DEAD. EACH OF THEM *DISFIGURED.*
IT WAS *THAT* WHICH GAVE ME THE IDEA.
UGHHHH...
OH, GAWD! WHAT *IS* THAT THING?
I DUNNO. BUT IT'S STILL *ALIVE.*
THE *INSPIRATION.*

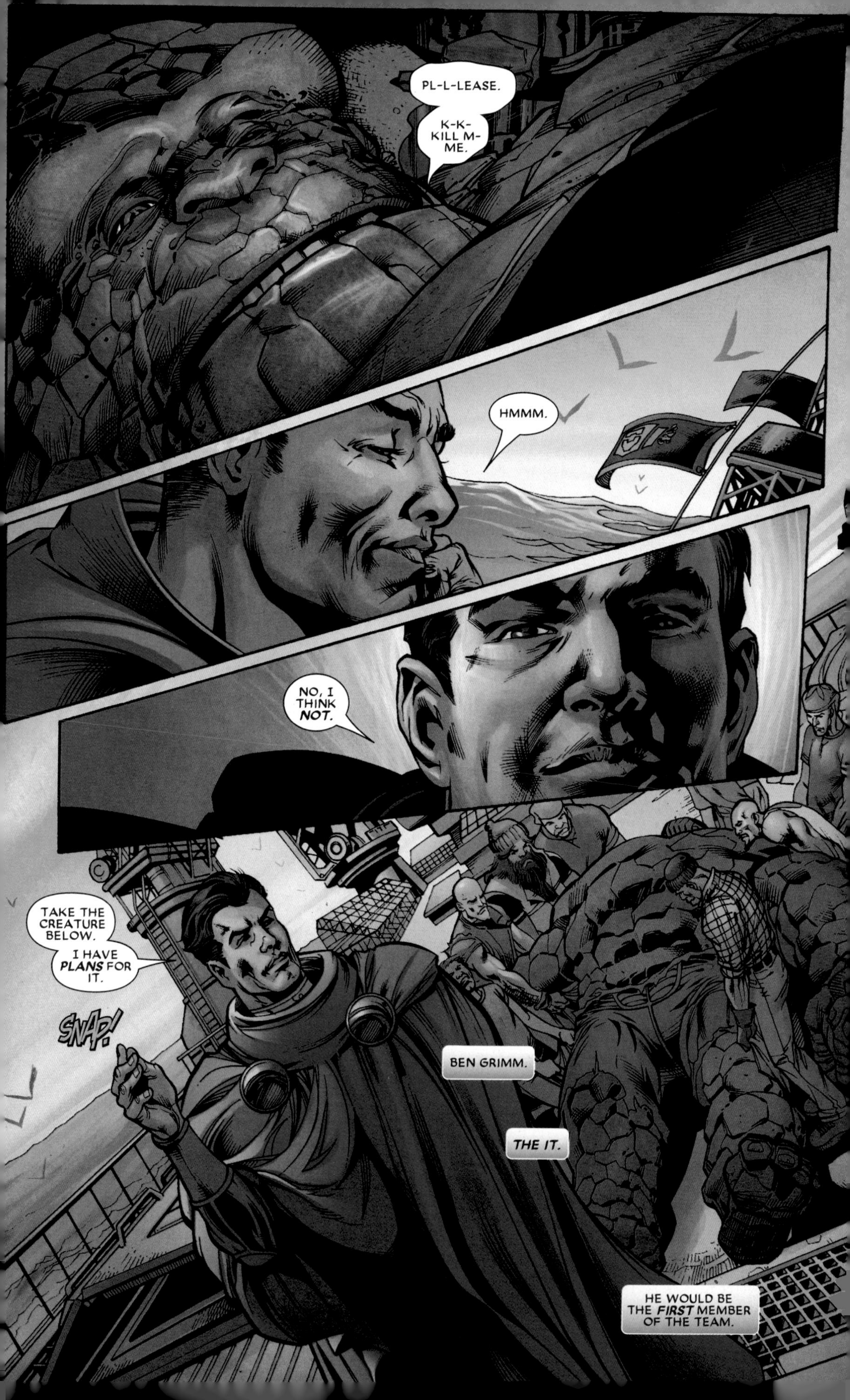
PL-L-LEASE.
K-K-KILL M-ME.
HMMM.
NO, I THINK NOT.
TAKE THE CREATURE BELOW.
I HAVE PLANS FOR IT.
SNAP!
BEN GRIMM.
THE IT.
HE WOULD BE THE FIRST MEMBER OF THE TEAM.

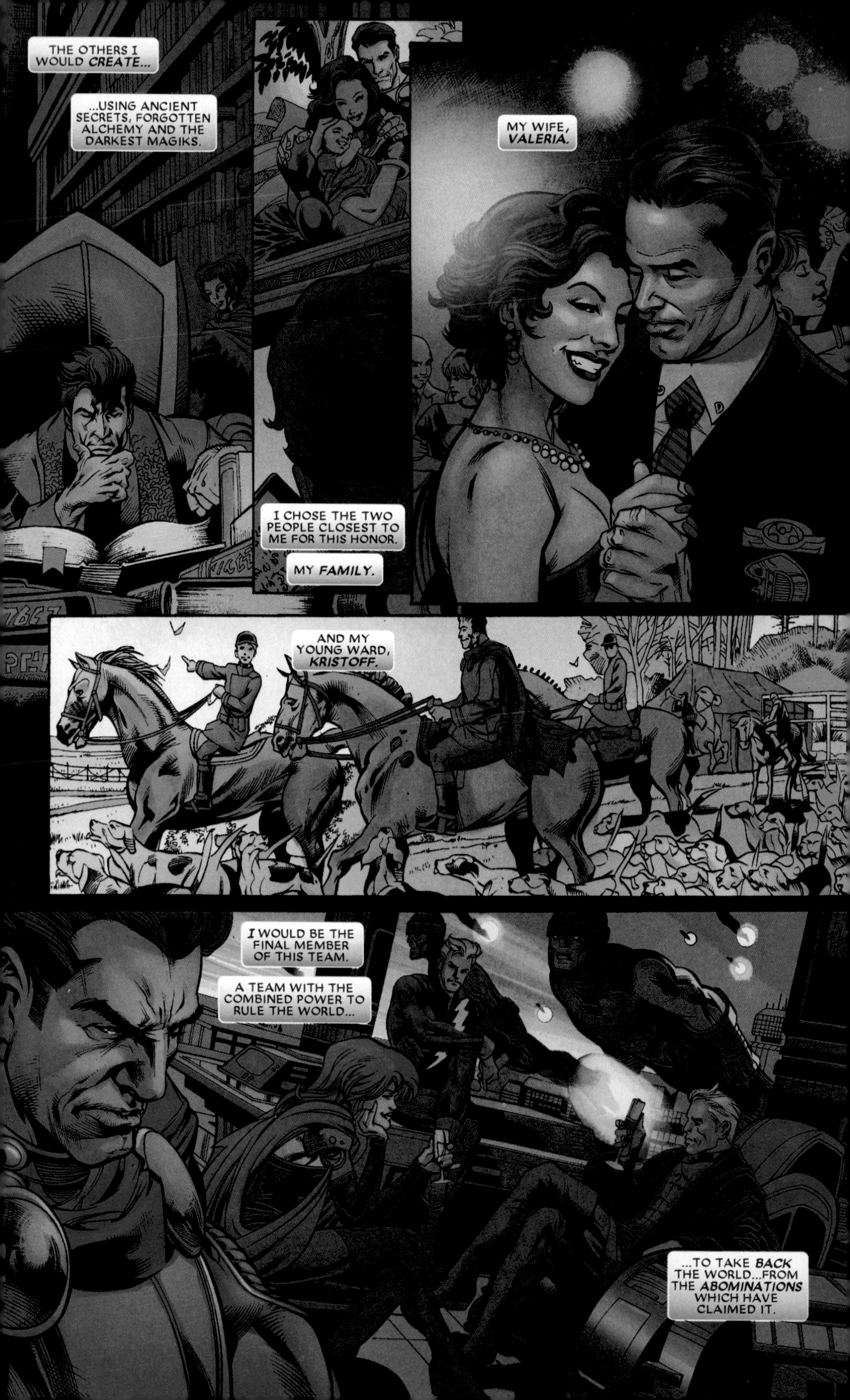
THE OTHERS I WOULD CREATE...
...USING ANCIENT SECRETS, FORGOTTEN ALCHEMY AND THE DARKEST MAGIKS.
I CHOSE THE TWO PEOPLE CLOSEST TO ME FOR THIS HONOR.
MY FAMILY.
MY WIFE, VALERIA.
AND MY YOUNG WARD, KRISTOFF.
I WOULD BE THE FINAL MEMBER OF THIS TEAM.
A TEAM WITH THE COMBINED POWER TO RULE THE WORLD...
...TO TAKE BACK THE WORLD...FROM THE ABOMINATIONS WHICH HAVE CLAIMED IT.

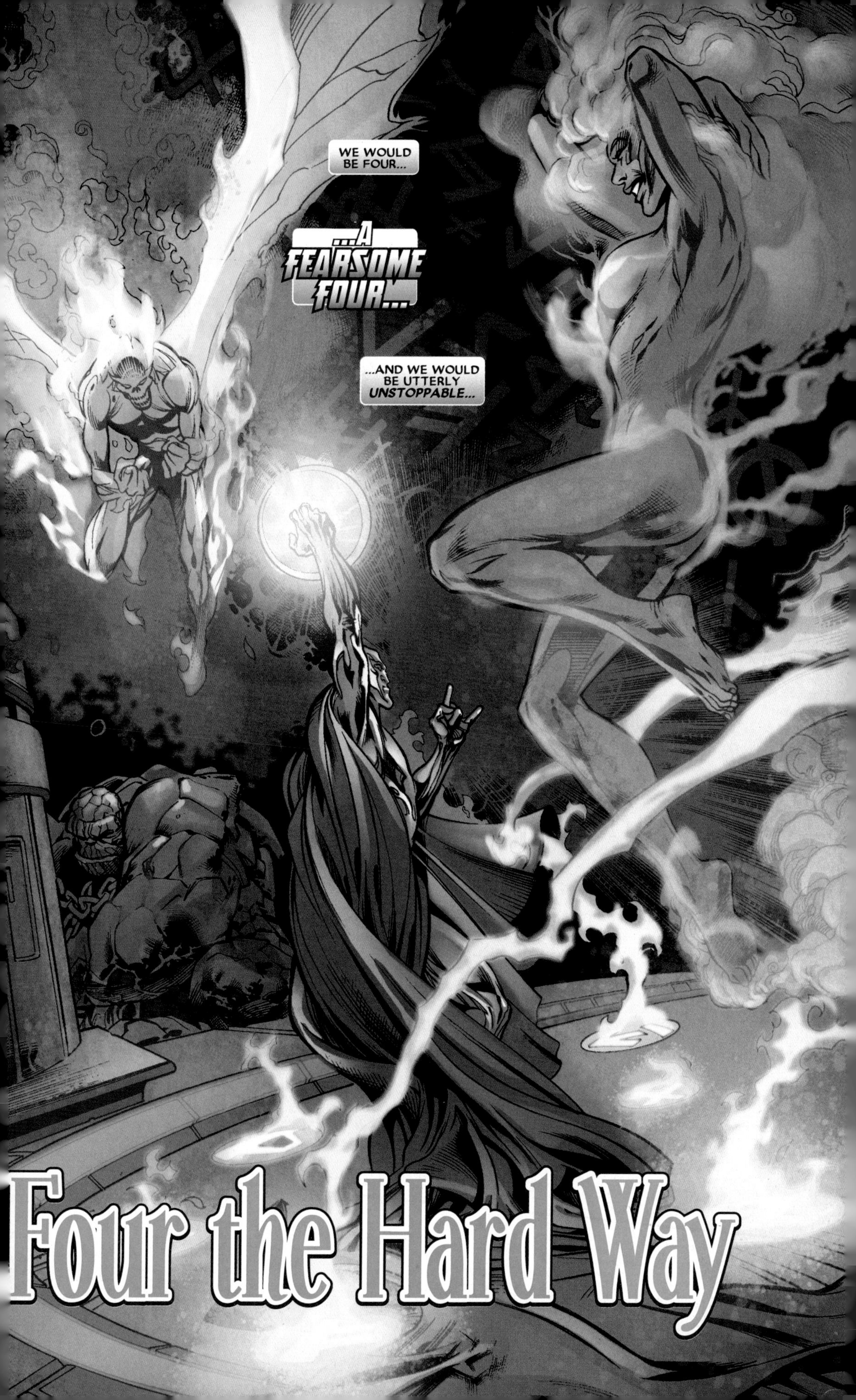
WE WOULD BE FOUR...
...A FEARSOME FOUR...
...AND WE WOULD BE UTTERLY UNSTOPPABLE...
Four the Hard Way

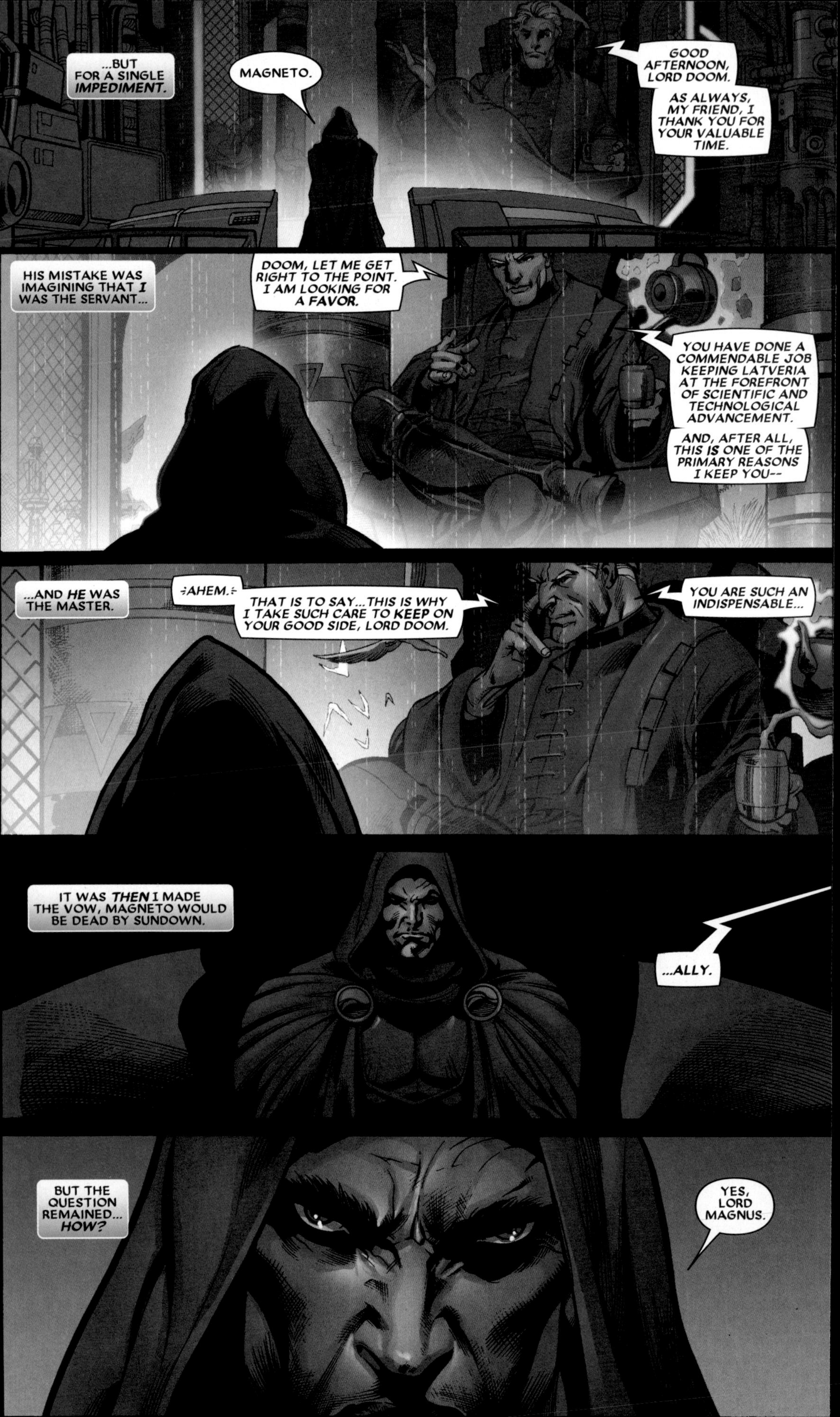
...BUT FOR A SINGLE IMPEDIMENT.
MAGNETO.
GOOD AFTERNOON, LORD DOOM.
AS ALWAYS, MY FRIEND, I THANK YOU FOR YOUR VALUABLE TIME.
HIS MISTAKE WAS IMAGINING THAT I WAS THE SERVANT...
DOOM, LET ME GET RIGHT TO THE POINT. I AM LOOKING FOR A FAVOR.
YOU HAVE DONE A COMMENDABLE JOB KEEPING LATVERIA AT THE FOREFRONT OF SCIENTIFIC AND TECHNOLOGICAL ADVANCEMENT.
AND, AFTER ALL, THIS IS ONE OF THE PRIMARY REASONS I KEEP YOU--
...AND HE WAS THE MASTER.
AHEM.
THAT IS TO SAY... THIS IS WHY I TAKE SUCH CARE TO KEEP ON YOUR GOOD SIDE, LORD DOOM.
YOU ARE SUCH AN INDISPENSABLE...
IT WAS THEN I MADE THE VOW, MAGNETO WOULD BE DEAD BY SUNDOWN.
...ALLY.
BUT THE QUESTION REMAINED... HOW?
YES, LORD MAGNUS.

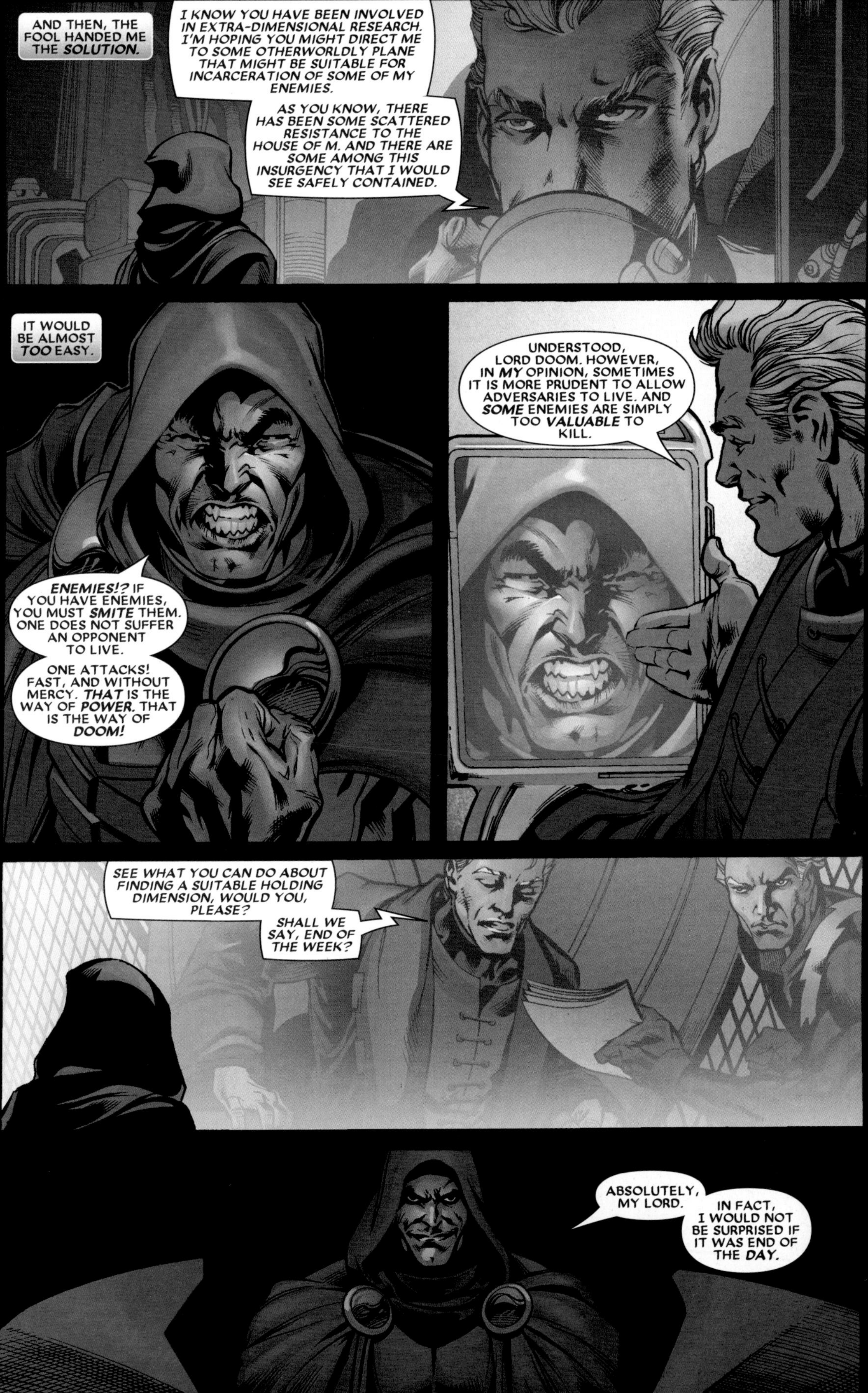
AND THEN, THE FOOL HANDED ME THE SOLUTION.
I KNOW YOU HAVE BEEN INVOLVED IN EXTRA-DIMENSIONAL RESEARCH. I'M HOPING YOU MIGHT DIRECT ME TO SOME OTHERWORLDLY PLANE THAT MIGHT BE SUITABLE FOR INCARCERATION OF SOME OF MY ENEMIES.
AS YOU KNOW, THERE HAS BEEN SOME SCATTERED RESISTANCE TO THE HOUSE OF M. AND THERE ARE SOME AMONG THIS INSURGENCY THAT I WOULD SEE SAFELY CONTAINED.
IT WOULD BE ALMOST TOO EASY.
ENEMIES!? IF YOU HAVE ENEMIES, YOU MUST SMITE THEM. ONE DOES NOT SUFFER AN OPPONENT TO LIVE.
ONE ATTACKS! FAST, AND WITHOUT MERCY. THAT IS THE WAY OF POWER. THAT IS THE WAY OF DOOM!
UNDERSTOOD, LORD DOOM. HOWEVER, IN MY OPINION, SOMETIMES IT IS MORE PRUDENT TO ALLOW ADVERSARIES TO LIVE. AND SOME ENEMIES ARE SIMPLY TOO VALUABLE TO KILL.
SEE WHAT YOU CAN DO ABOUT FINDING A SUITABLE HOLDING DIMENSION, WOULD YOU, PLEASE?
SHALL WE SAY, END OF THE WEEK?
ABSOLUTELY, MY LORD.
IN FACT, I WOULD NOT BE SURPRISED IF IT WAS END OF THE DAY.

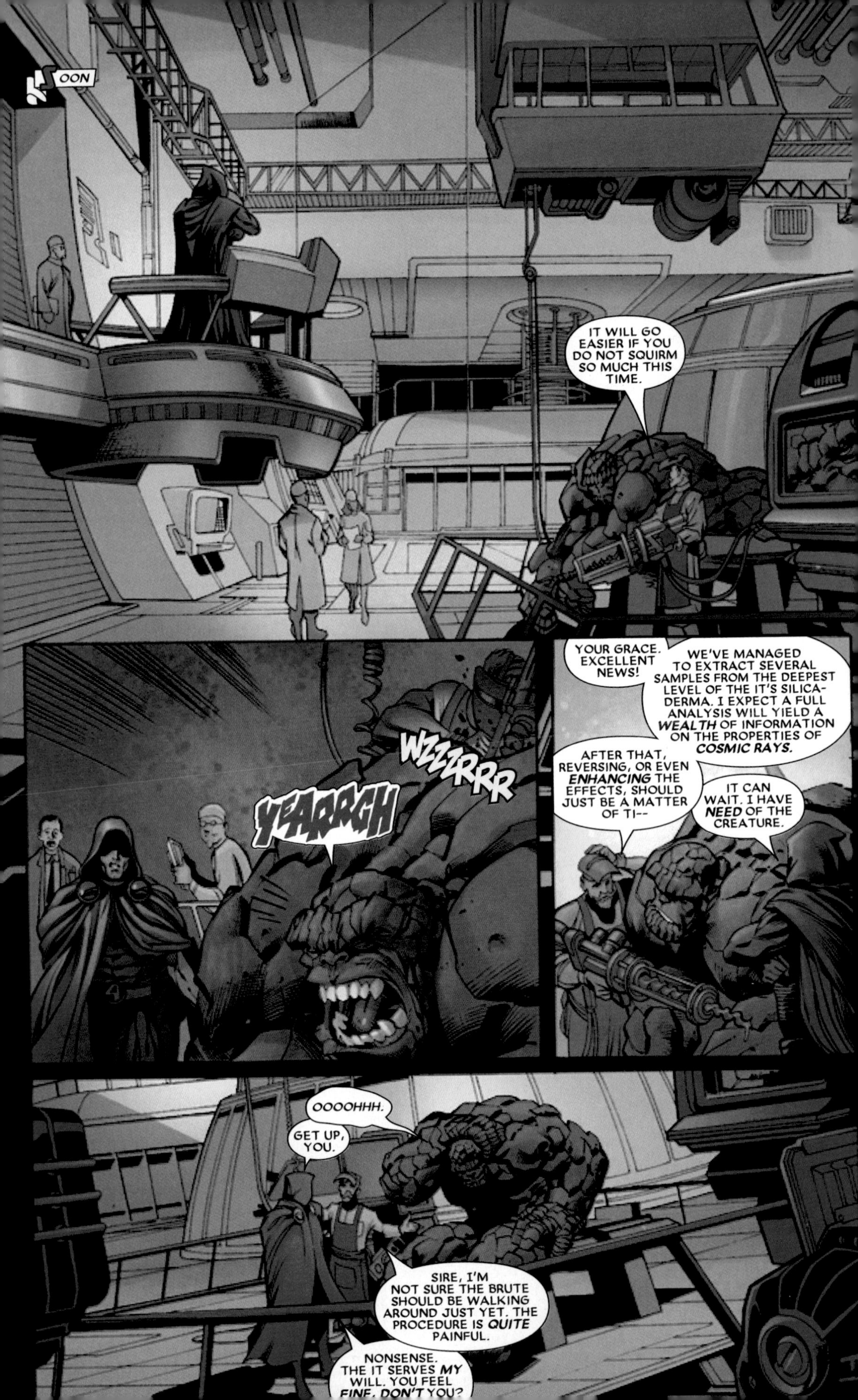
SOON
IT WILL GO EASIER IF YOU DO NOT SQUIRM SO MUCH THIS TIME.
WZZZRRR
YEARRGH
YOUR GRACE. EXCELLENT NEWS!
WE'VE MANAGED TO EXTRACT SEVERAL SAMPLES FROM THE DEEPEST LEVEL OF THE IT'S SILICA-DERMA. I EXPECT A FULL ANALYSIS WILL YIELD A WEALTH OF INFORMATION ON THE PROPERTIES OF COSMIC RAYS.
AFTER THAT, REVERSING, OR EVEN ENHANCING THE EFFECTS, SHOULD JUST BE A MATTER OF TI--
IT CAN WAIT. I HAVE NEED OF THE CREATURE.
OOOOHHH.
GET UP, YOU.
SIRE, I'M NOT SURE THE BRUTE SHOULD BE WALKING AROUND JUST YET. THE PROCEDURE IS QUITE PAINFUL.
NONSENSE. THE IT SERVES MY WILL. YOU FEEL FINE, DON'T YOU?

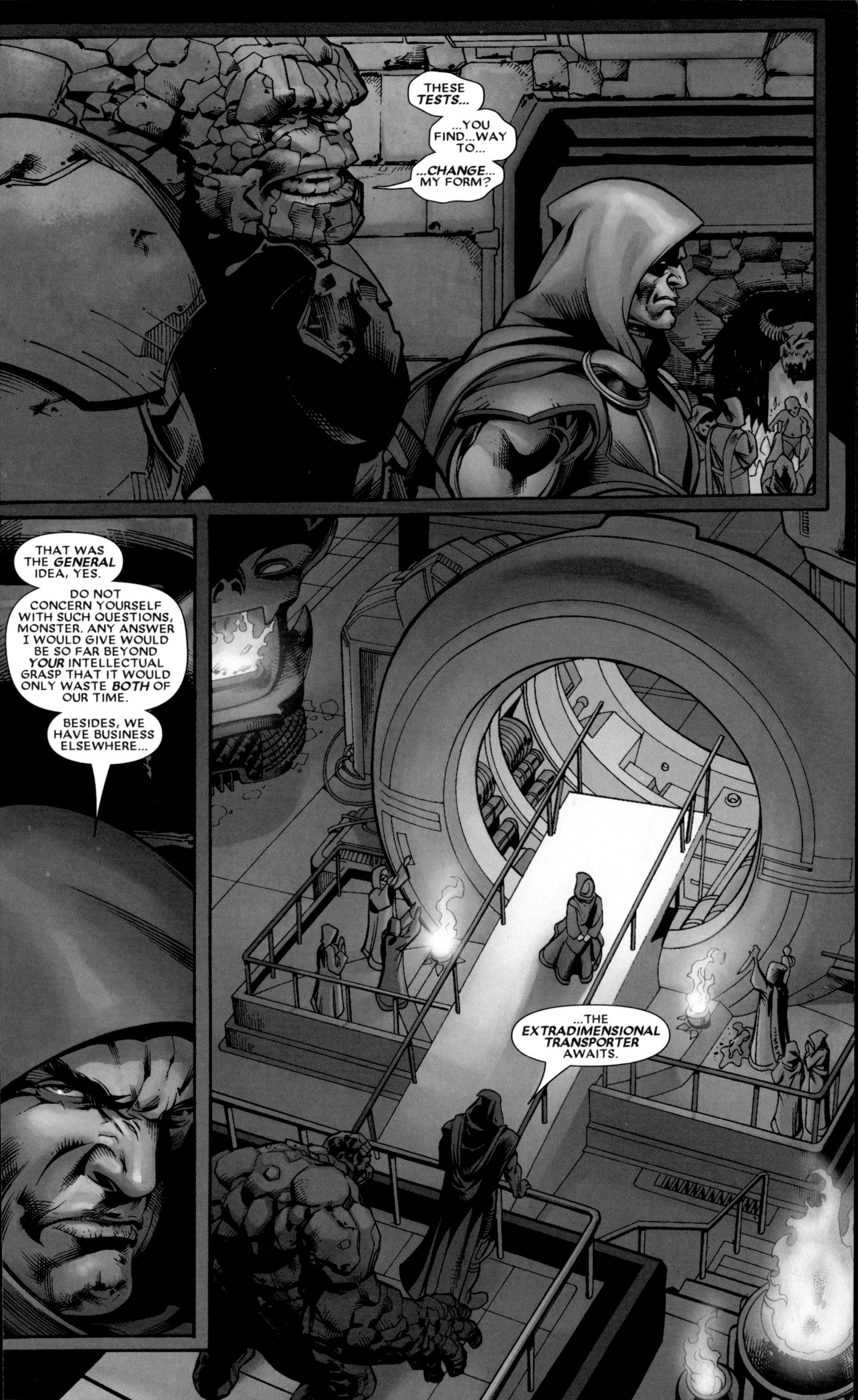
THESE TESTS...
...YOU FIND...WAY TO...
...CHANGE... MY FORM?
THAT WAS THE GENERAL IDEA, YES.
DO NOT CONCERN YOURSELF WITH SUCH QUESTIONS, MONSTER. ANY ANSWER I WOULD GIVE WOULD BE SO FAR BEYOND YOUR INTELLECTUAL GRASP THAT IT WOULD ONLY WASTE BOTH OF OUR TIME.
BESIDES, WE HAVE BUSINESS ELSEWHERE...
...THE EXTRADIMENSIONAL TRANSPORTER AWAITS.

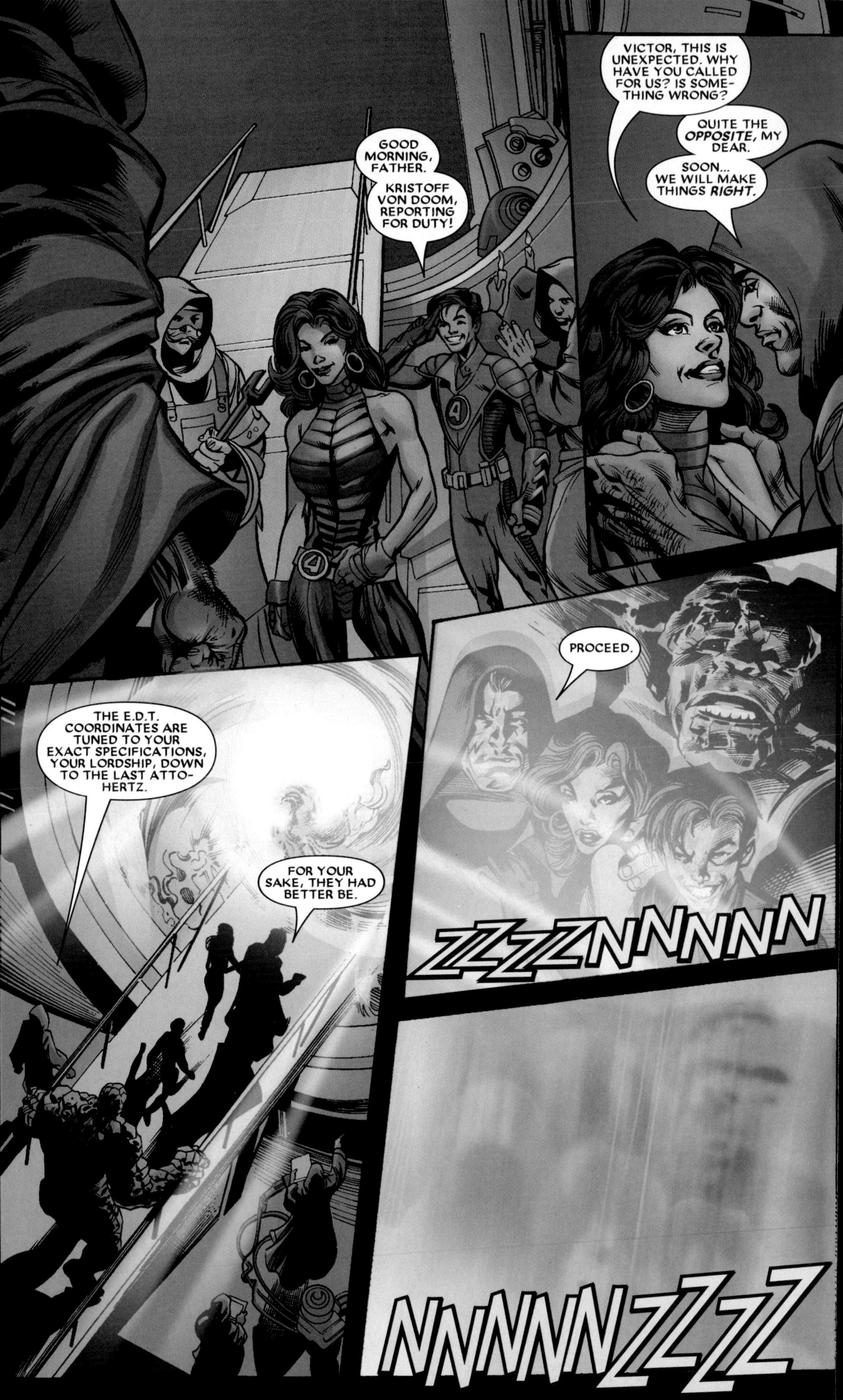
GOOD MORNING, FATHER.
KRISTOFF VON DOOM, REPORTING FOR DUTY!
VICTOR, THIS IS UNEXPECTED. WHY HAVE YOU CALLED FOR US? IS SOME-THING WRONG?
QUITE THE *OPPOSITE*, MY DEAR.
SOON... WE WILL MAKE THINGS *RIGHT*.
THE E.D.T. COORDINATES ARE TUNED TO YOUR EXACT SPECIFICATIONS, YOUR LORDSHIP, DOWN TO THE LAST ATTO-HERTZ.
FOR YOUR SAKE, THEY HAD BETTER BE.
PROCEED.
ZZZZNNNNNN
NNNNNZZZ

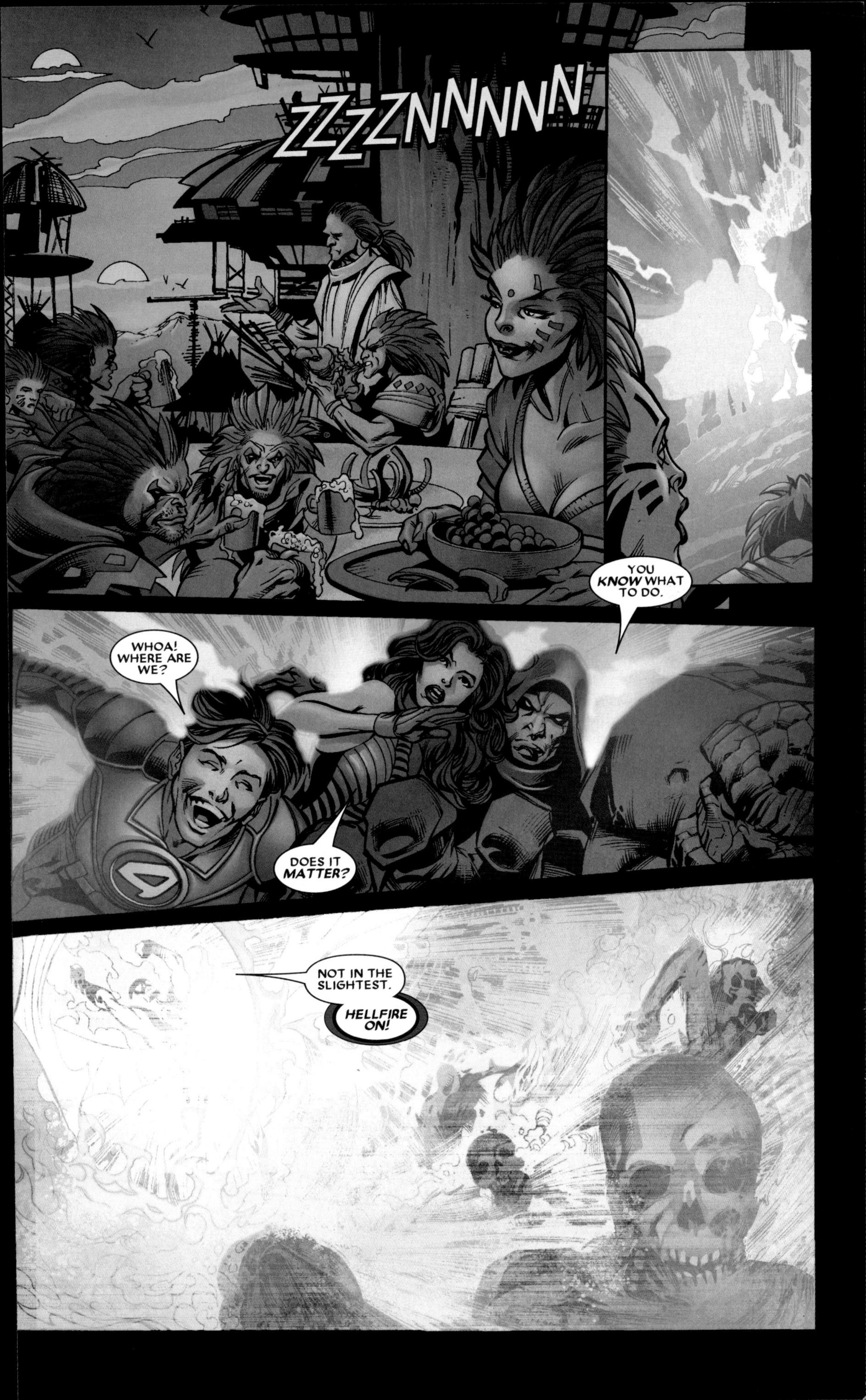
ZZZZNNNNNN
YOU KNOW WHAT TO DO.
WHOA! WHERE ARE WE?
DOES IT MATTER?
NOT IN THE SLIGHTEST.
HELLFIRE ON!

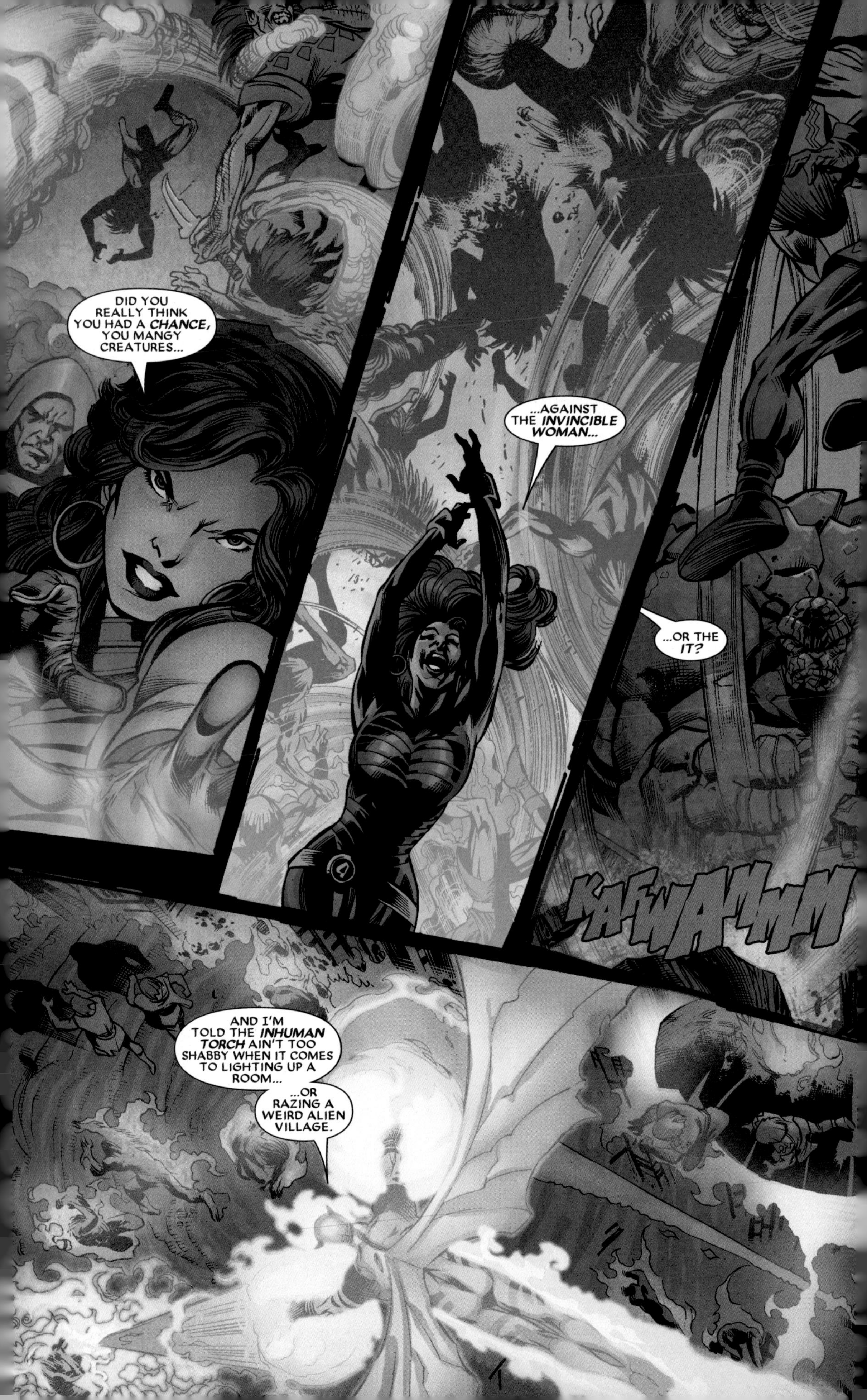
DID YOU REALLY THINK YOU HAD A *CHANCE,* YOU MANGY CREATURES...
...AGAINST THE *INVINCIBLE WOMAN...*
...OR THE *IT?*
KA-WAMMM
AND I'M TOLD THE *INHUMAN TORCH* AIN'T TOO SHABBY WHEN IT COMES TO LIGHTING UP A ROOM...
...OR RAZING A WEIRD ALIEN VILLAGE.

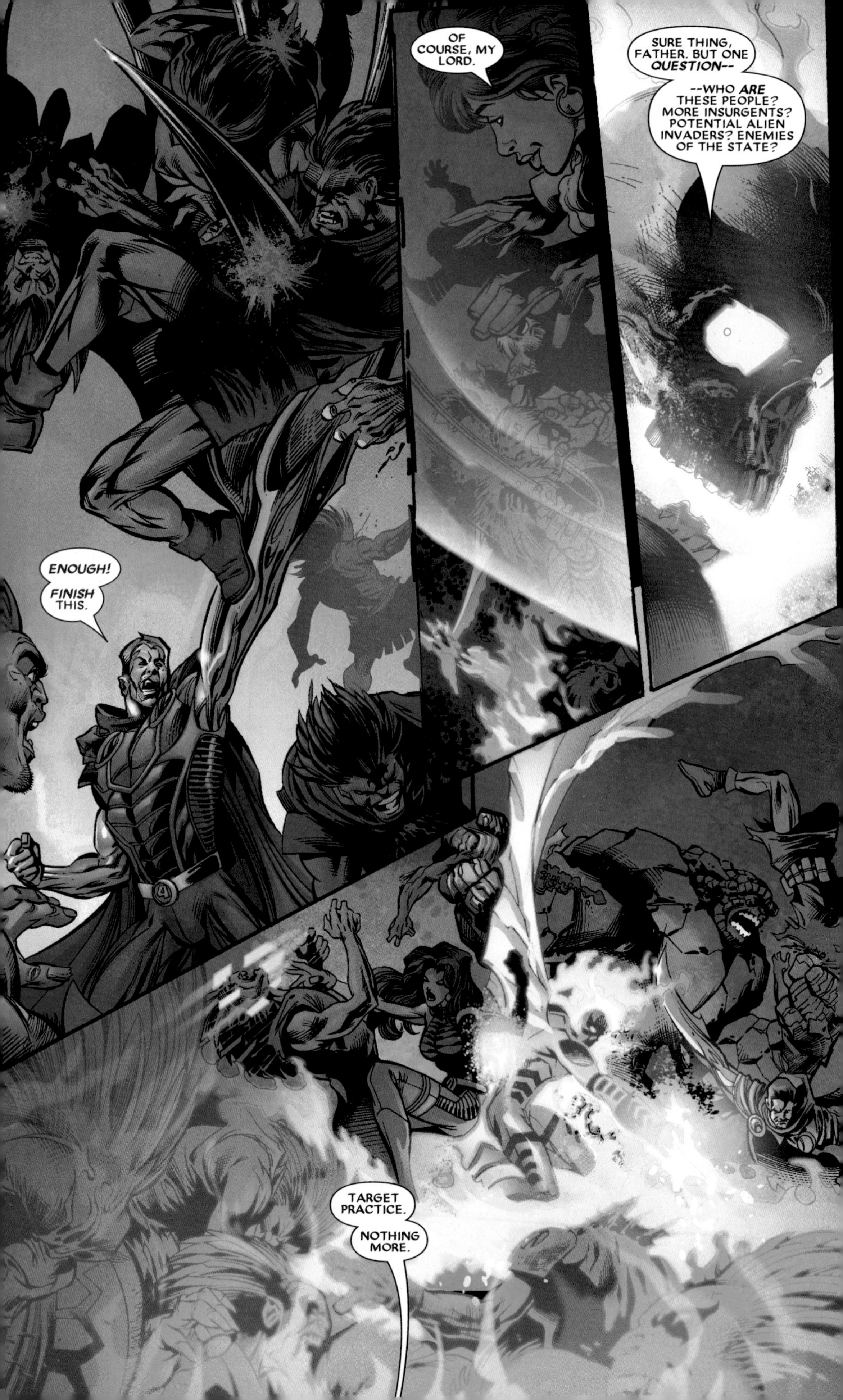
OF COURSE, MY LORD.
SURE THING, FATHER. BUT ONE QUESTION--
--WHO ARE THESE PEOPLE? MORE INSURGENTS? POTENTIAL ALIEN INVADERS? ENEMIES OF THE STATE?
ENOUGH!
FINISH THIS.
TARGET PRACTICE.
NOTHING MORE.

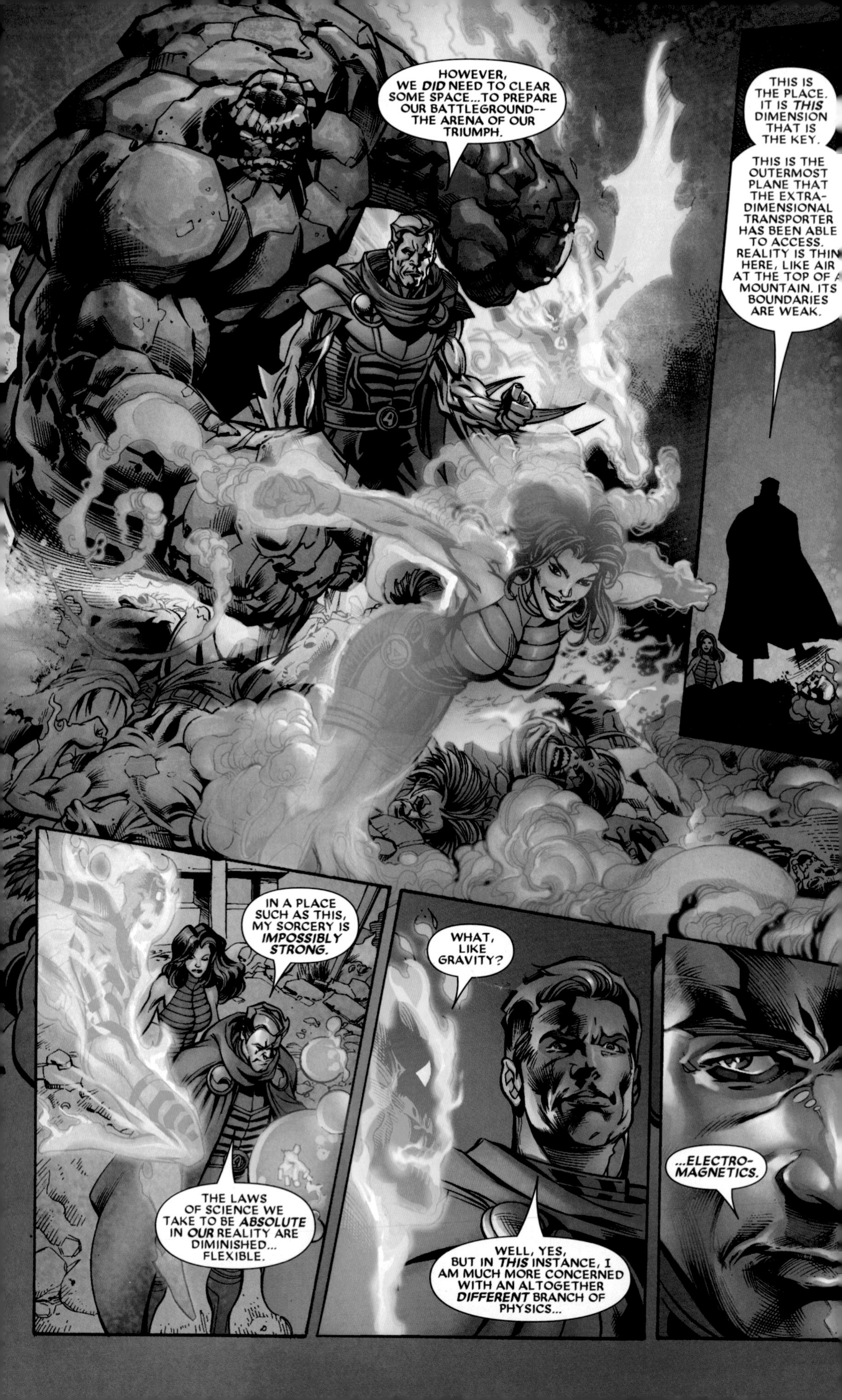
HOWEVER, WE DID NEED TO CLEAR SOME SPACE...TO PREPARE OUR BATTLEGROUND-- THE ARENA OF OUR TRIUMPH.
THIS IS THE PLACE. IT IS THIS DIMENSION THAT IS THE KEY.
THIS IS THE OUTERMOST PLANE THAT THE EXTRA-DIMENSIONAL TRANSPORTER HAS BEEN ABLE TO ACCESS. REALITY IS THIN HERE, LIKE AIR AT THE TOP OF A MOUNTAIN. ITS BOUNDARIES ARE WEAK.
IN A PLACE SUCH AS THIS, MY SORCERY IS IMPOSSIBLY STRONG.
THE LAWS OF SCIENCE WE TAKE TO BE ABSOLUTE IN OUR REALITY ARE DIMINISHED... FLEXIBLE.
WHAT, LIKE GRAVITY?
WELL, YES, BUT IN THIS INSTANCE, I AM MUCH MORE CONCERNED WITH AN ALTOGETHER DIFFERENT BRANCH OF PHYSICS...
...ELECTRO-MAGNETICS.

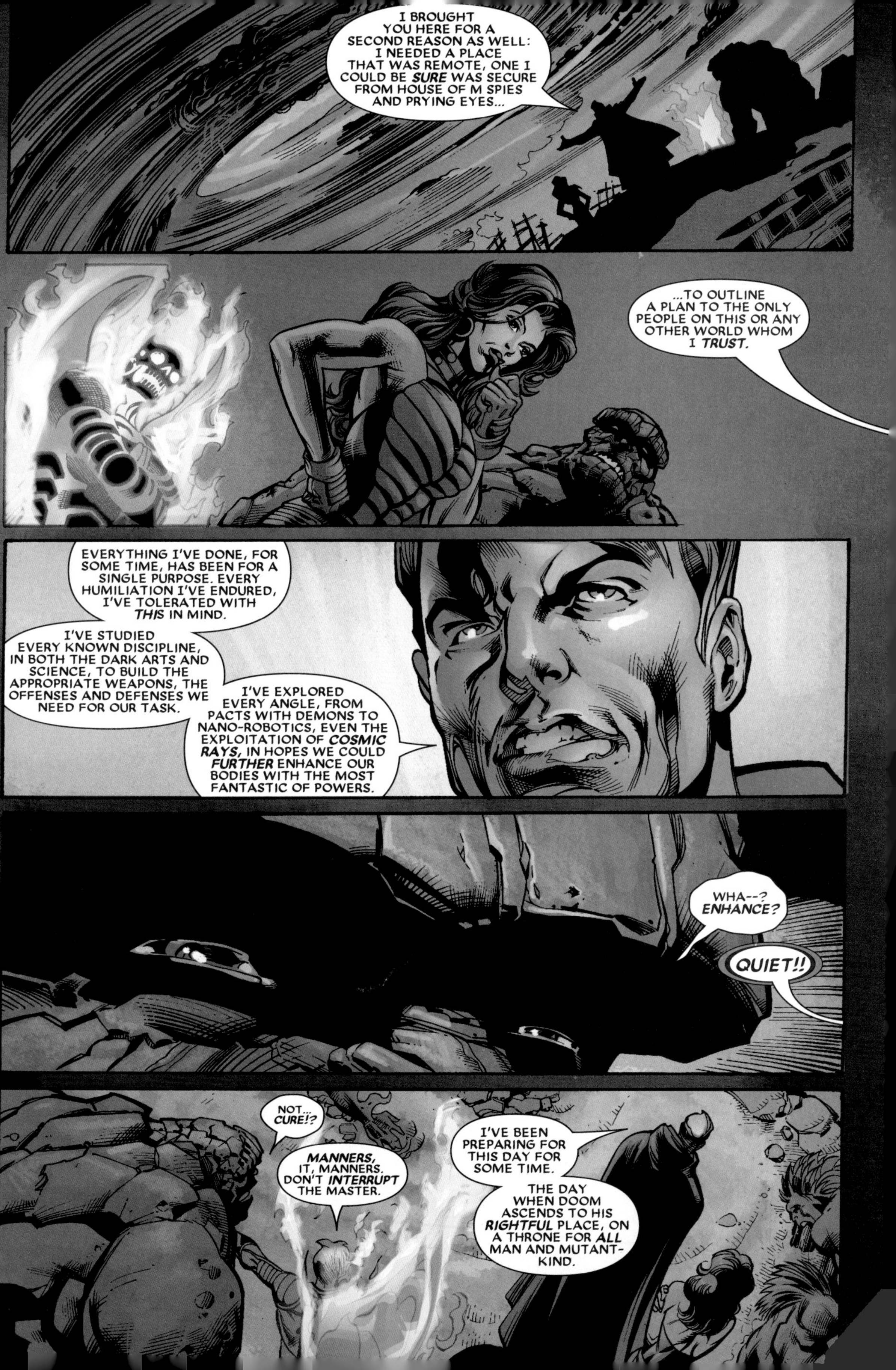

I BROUGHT YOU HERE FOR A SECOND REASON AS WELL: I NEEDED A PLACE THAT WAS REMOTE, ONE I COULD BE *SURE* WAS SECURE FROM HOUSE OF M SPIES AND PRYING EYES...
...TO OUTLINE A PLAN TO THE ONLY PEOPLE ON THIS OR ANY OTHER WORLD WHOM I *TRUST.*
EVERYTHING I'VE DONE, FOR SOME TIME, HAS BEEN FOR A SINGLE PURPOSE. EVERY HUMILIATION I'VE ENDURED, I'VE TOLERATED WITH *THIS* IN MIND.
I'VE STUDIED EVERY KNOWN DISCIPLINE, IN BOTH THE DARK ARTS AND SCIENCE, TO BUILD THE APPROPRIATE WEAPONS, THE OFFENSES AND DEFENSES WE NEED FOR OUR TASK.
I'VE EXPLORED EVERY ANGLE, FROM PACTS WITH DEMONS TO NANO-ROBOTICS, EVEN THE EXPLOITATION OF *COSMIC RAYS,* IN HOPES WE COULD *FURTHER* ENHANCE OUR BODIES WITH THE MOST FANTASTIC OF POWERS.
WHA--? *ENHANCE?*
QUIET!!
NOT... *CURE!?*
MANNERS, IT, MANNERS. DON'T *INTERRUPT* THE MASTER.
I'VE BEEN PREPARING FOR THIS DAY FOR SOME TIME.
THE DAY WHEN DOOM ASCENDS TO HIS *RIGHTFUL* PLACE, ON A THRONE FOR *ALL* MAN AND MUTANT-KIND.

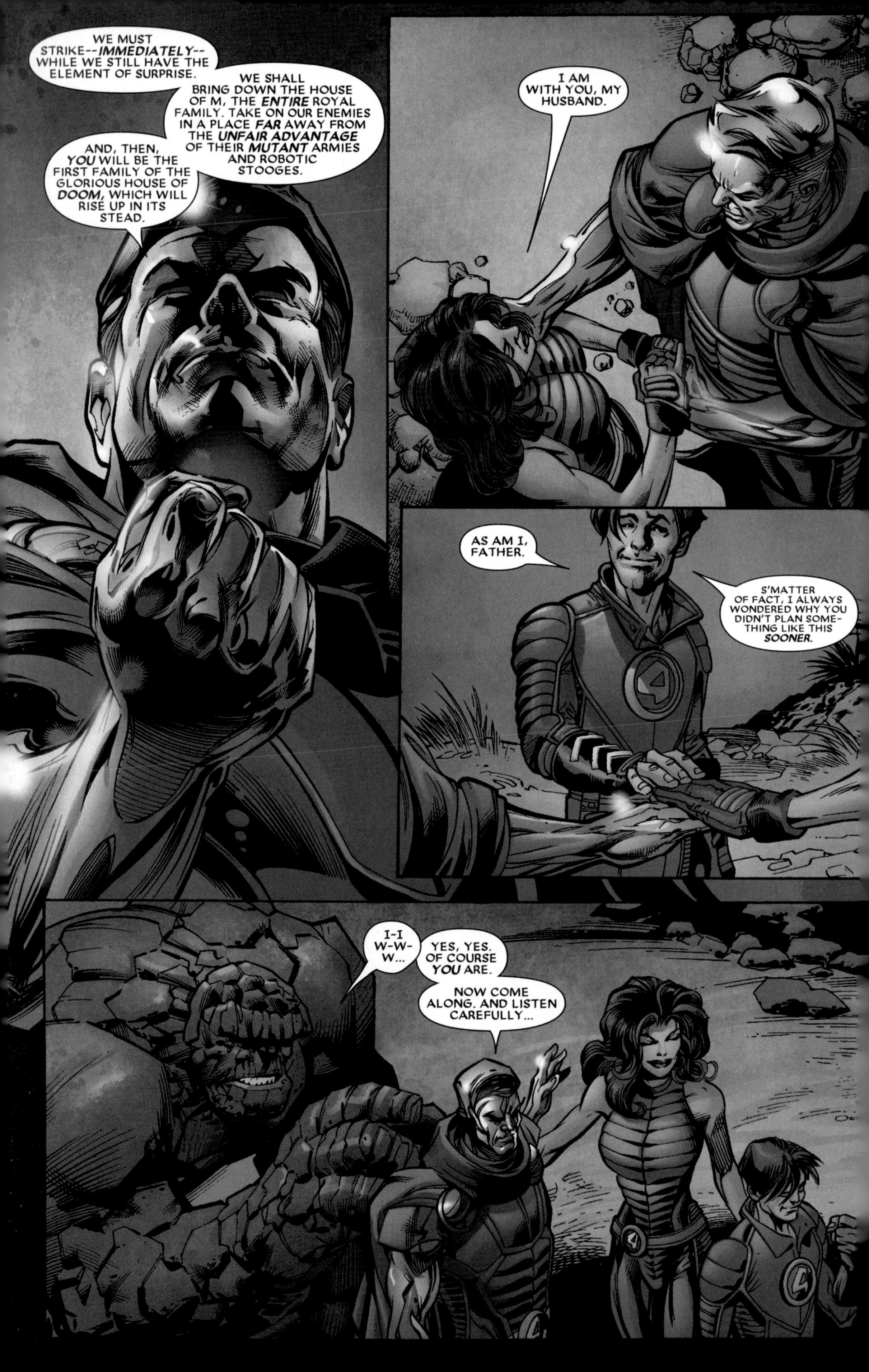

WE MUST STRIKE--IMMEDIATELY--WHILE WE STILL HAVE THE ELEMENT OF SURPRISE.
WE SHALL BRING DOWN THE HOUSE OF M, THE ENTIRE ROYAL FAMILY. TAKE ON OUR ENEMIES IN A PLACE FAR AWAY FROM THE UNFAIR ADVANTAGE OF THEIR MUTANT ARMIES AND ROBOTIC STOOGES.
AND, THEN, YOU WILL BE THE FIRST FAMILY OF THE GLORIOUS HOUSE OF DOOM, WHICH WILL RISE UP IN ITS STEAD.
I AM WITH YOU, MY HUSBAND.
AS AM I, FATHER.
S'MATTER OF FACT, I ALWAYS WONDERED WHY YOU DIDN'T PLAN SOME-THING LIKE THIS SOONER.
I-I W-W-W...
YES, YES. OF COURSE YOU ARE.
NOW COME ALONG. AND LISTEN CAREFULLY...

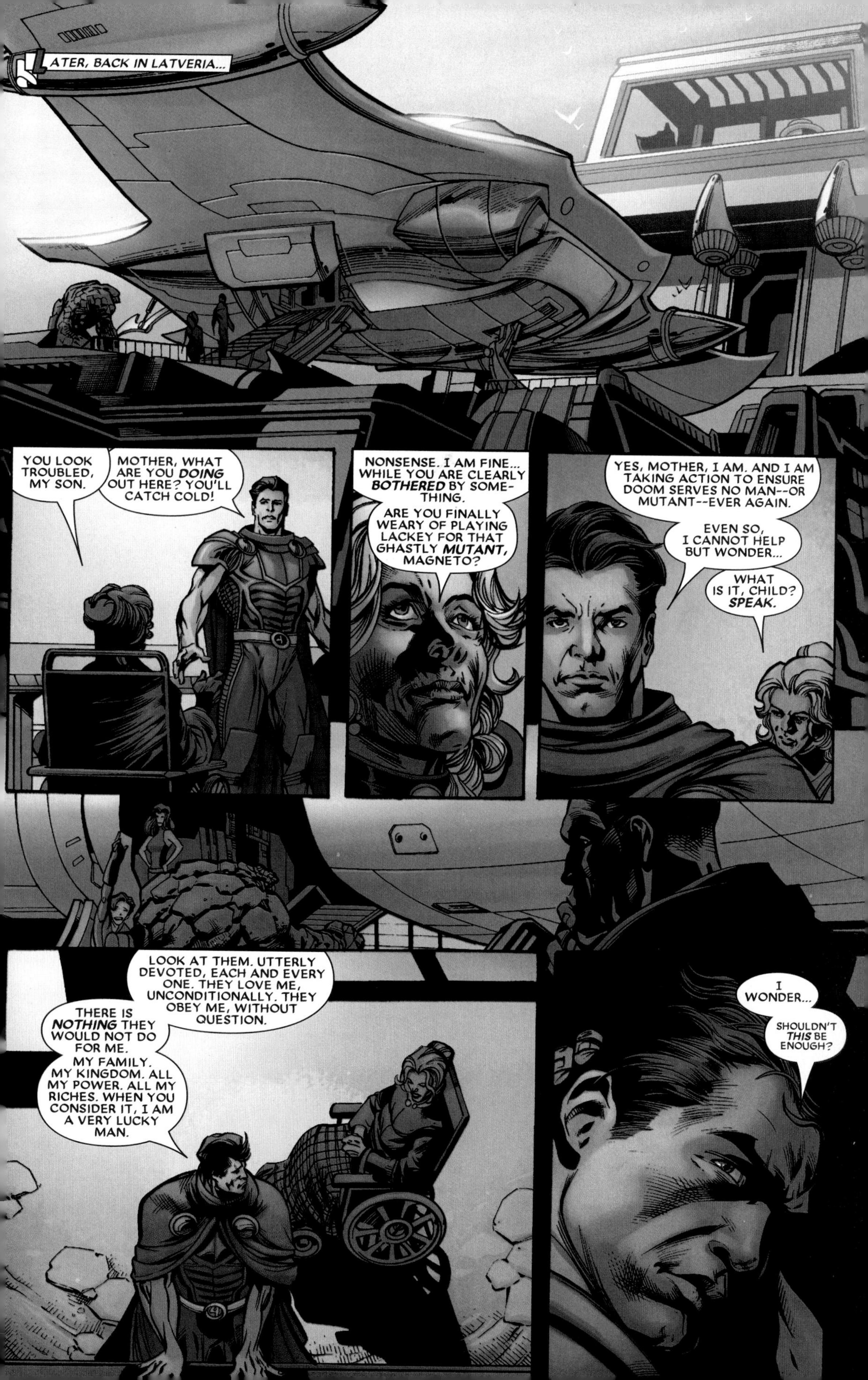
LATER, BACK IN LATVERIA...
YOU LOOK TROUBLED, MY SON.
MOTHER, WHAT ARE YOU DOING OUT HERE? YOU'LL CATCH COLD!
NONSENSE. I AM FINE... WHILE YOU ARE CLEARLY BOTHERED BY SOME-THING.
ARE YOU FINALLY WEARY OF PLAYING LACKEY FOR THAT GHASTLY MUTANT, MAGNETO?
YES, MOTHER, I AM. AND I AM TAKING ACTION TO ENSURE DOOM SERVES NO MAN--OR MUTANT--EVER AGAIN.
EVEN SO, I CANNOT HELP BUT WONDER...
WHAT IS IT, CHILD? SPEAK.
LOOK AT THEM. UTTERLY DEVOTED, EACH AND EVERY ONE. THEY LOVE ME, UNCONDITIONALLY. THEY OBEY ME, WITHOUT QUESTION.
THERE IS NOTHING THEY WOULD NOT DO FOR ME.
MY FAMILY. MY KINGDOM. ALL MY POWER. ALL MY RICHES. WHEN YOU CONSIDER IT, I AM A VERY LUCKY MAN.
I WONDER...
SHOULDN'T THIS BE ENOUGH?

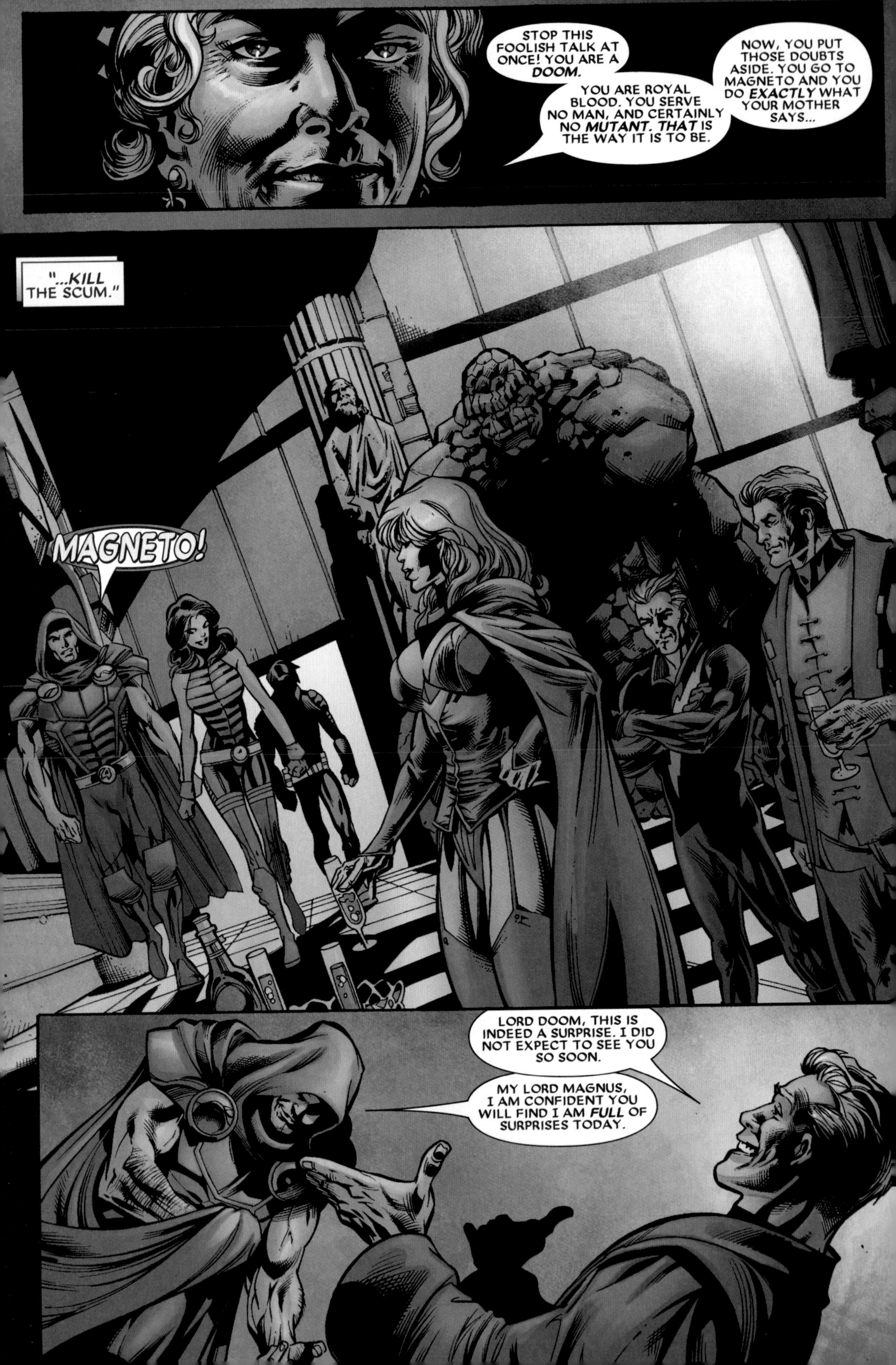
STOP THIS FOOLISH TALK AT ONCE! YOU ARE A *DOOM.*
YOU ARE ROYAL BLOOD. YOU SERVE NO MAN, AND CERTAINLY NO *MUTANT. THAT* IS THE WAY IT IS TO BE.
NOW, YOU PUT THOSE DOUBTS ASIDE. YOU GO TO MAGNETO AND YOU DO *EXACTLY* WHAT YOUR MOTHER SAYS...
"...*KILL* THE SCUM."
MAGNETO!
LORD DOOM, THIS IS INDEED A SURPRISE. I DID NOT EXPECT TO SEE YOU SO SOON.
MY LORD MAGNUS, I AM CONFIDENT YOU WILL FIND I AM *FULL* OF SURPRISES TODAY.

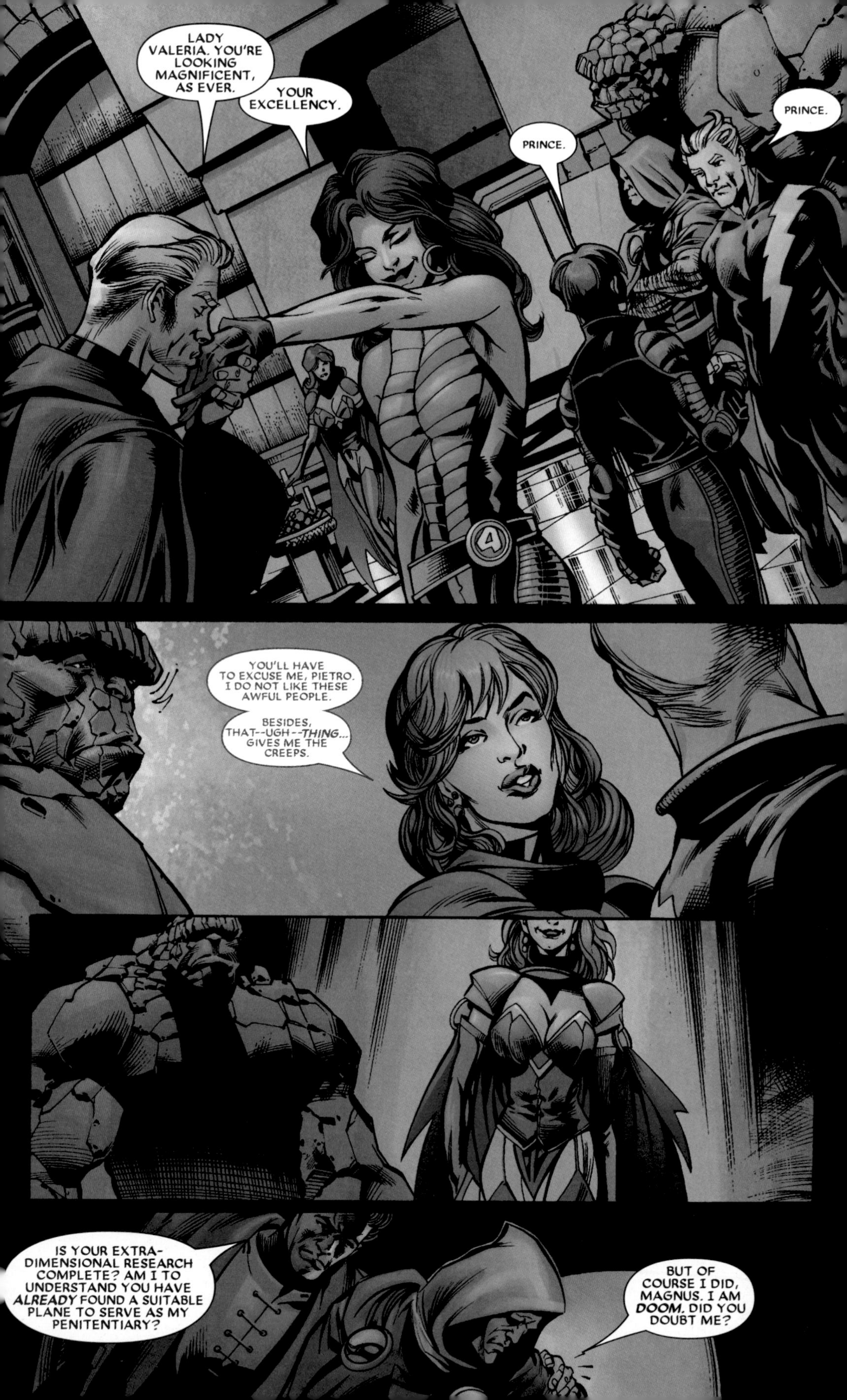
LADY VALERIA. YOU'RE LOOKING MAGNIFICENT, AS EVER.
YOUR EXCELLENCY.
PRINCE.
PRINCE.
YOU'LL HAVE TO EXCUSE ME, PIETRO. I DO NOT LIKE THESE AWFUL PEOPLE.
BESIDES, THAT--UGH--*THING*... GIVES ME THE CREEPS.
IS YOUR EXTRA-DIMENSIONAL RESEARCH COMPLETE? AM I TO UNDERSTAND YOU HAVE *ALREADY* FOUND A SUITABLE PLANE TO SERVE AS MY PENITENTIARY?
BUT OF COURSE I DID, MAGNUS. I AM ***DOOM.*** DID YOU DOUBT ME?

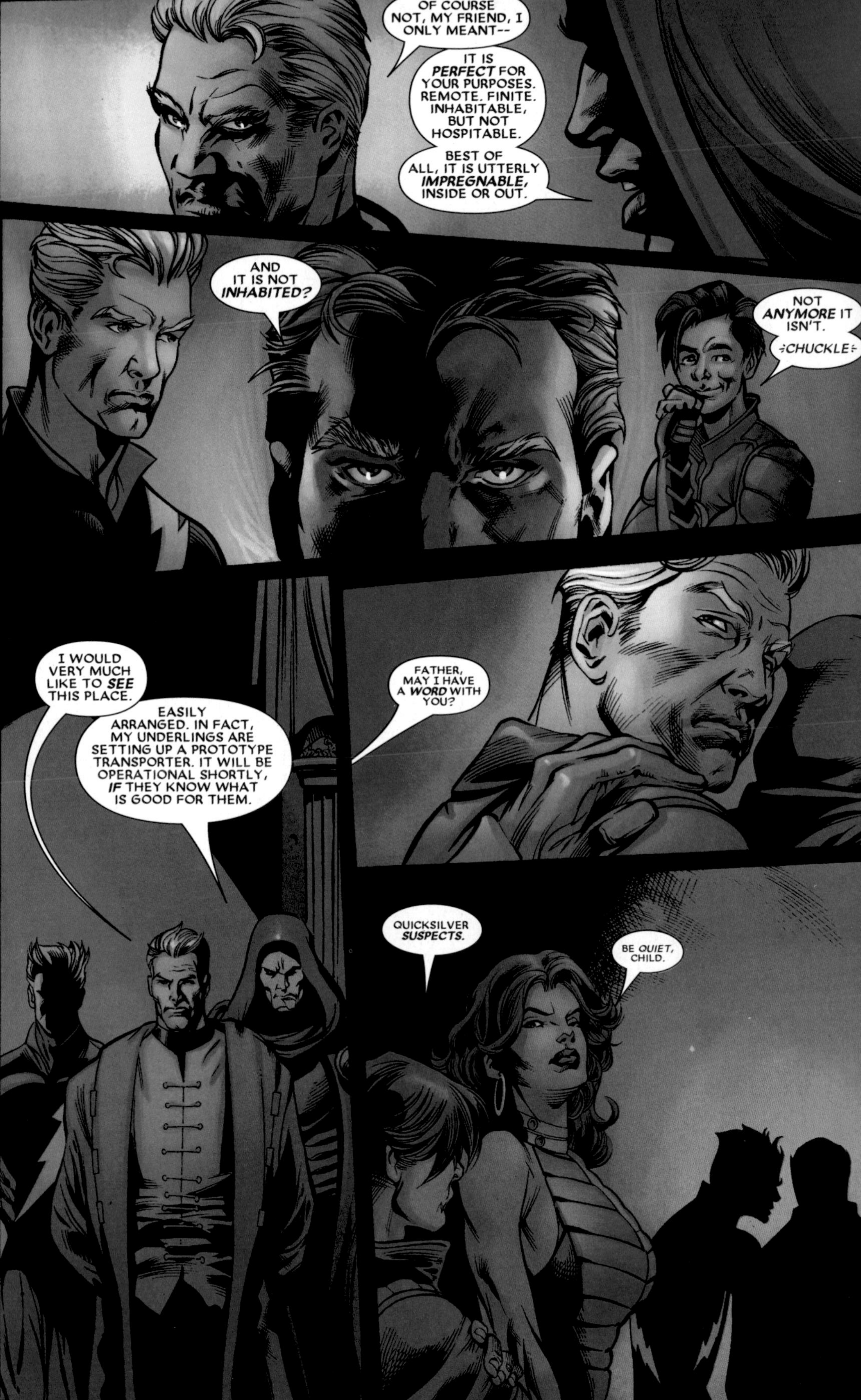
OF COURSE NOT, MY FRIEND, I ONLY MEANT--
IT IS PERFECT FOR YOUR PURPOSES. REMOTE. FINITE. INHABITABLE, BUT NOT HOSPITABLE.
BEST OF ALL, IT IS UTTERLY IMPREGNABLE, INSIDE OR OUT.
AND IT IS NOT INHABITED?
NOT ANYMORE IT ISN'T.
=CHUCKLE=
FATHER, MAY I HAVE A WORD WITH YOU?
I WOULD VERY MUCH LIKE TO SEE THIS PLACE.
EASILY ARRANGED. IN FACT, MY UNDERLINGS ARE SETTING UP A PROTOTYPE TRANSPORTER. IT WILL BE OPERATIONAL SHORTLY, IF THEY KNOW WHAT IS GOOD FOR THEM.
QUICKSILVER SUSPECTS.
BE QUIET, CHILD.

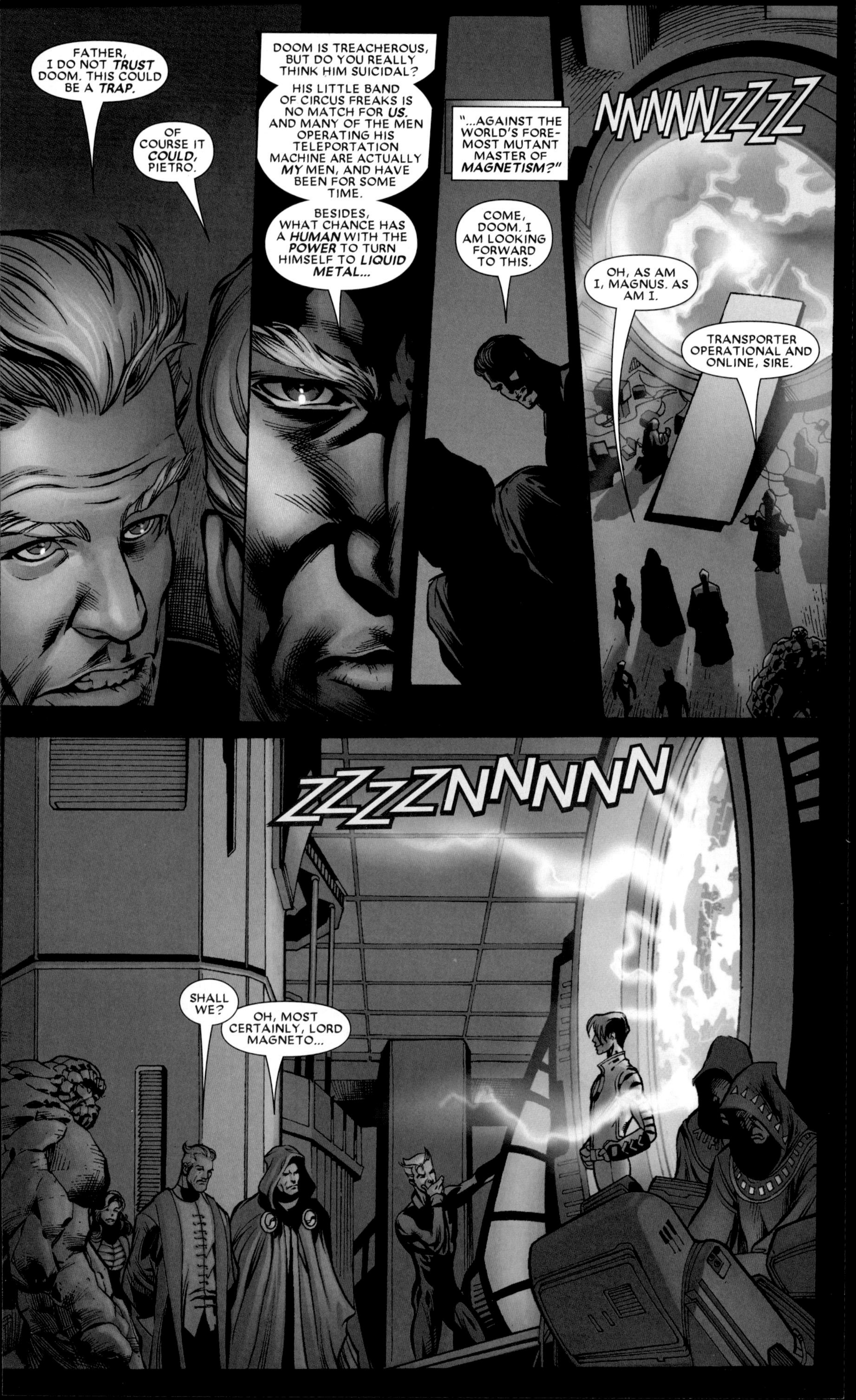
FATHER, I DO NOT TRUST DOOM. THIS COULD BE A TRAP.
OF COURSE IT COULD, PIETRO.
DOOM IS TREACHEROUS, BUT DO YOU REALLY THINK HIM SUICIDAL?
HIS LITTLE BAND OF CIRCUS FREAKS IS NO MATCH FOR US. AND MANY OF THE MEN OPERATING HIS TELEPORTATION MACHINE ARE ACTUALLY MY MEN, AND HAVE BEEN FOR SOME TIME.
BESIDES, WHAT CHANCE HAS A HUMAN WITH THE POWER TO TURN HIMSELF TO LIQUID METAL...
"...AGAINST THE WORLD'S FORE-MOST MUTANT MASTER OF MAGNETISM?"
COME, DOOM. I AM LOOKING FORWARD TO THIS.
NNNNNZZZZ
OH, AS AM I, MAGNUS. AS AM I.
TRANSPORTER OPERATIONAL AND ONLINE, SIRE.
ZZZZNNNNNN
SHALL WE?
OH, MOST CERTAINLY, LORD MAGNETO...

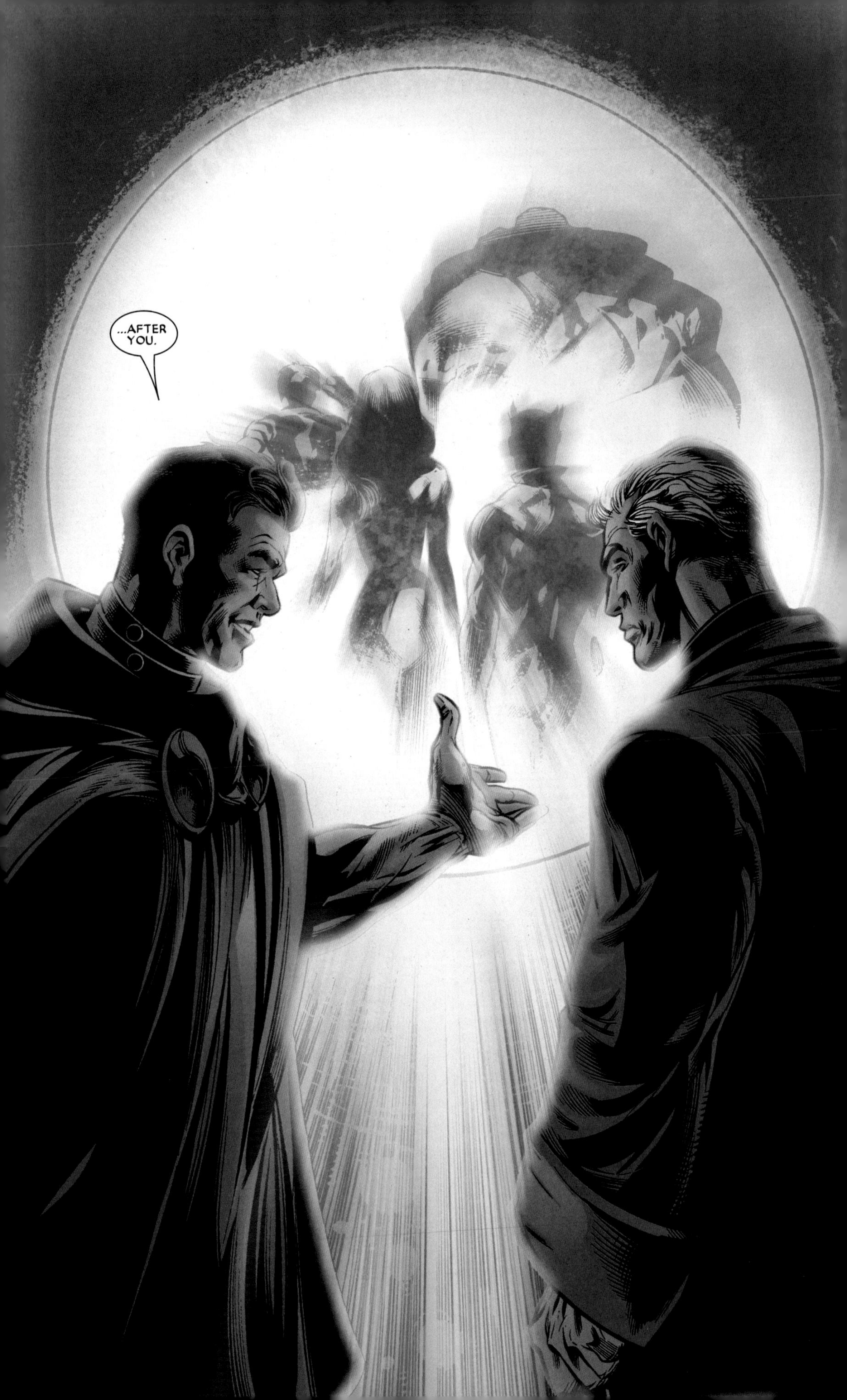
...AFTER YOU.

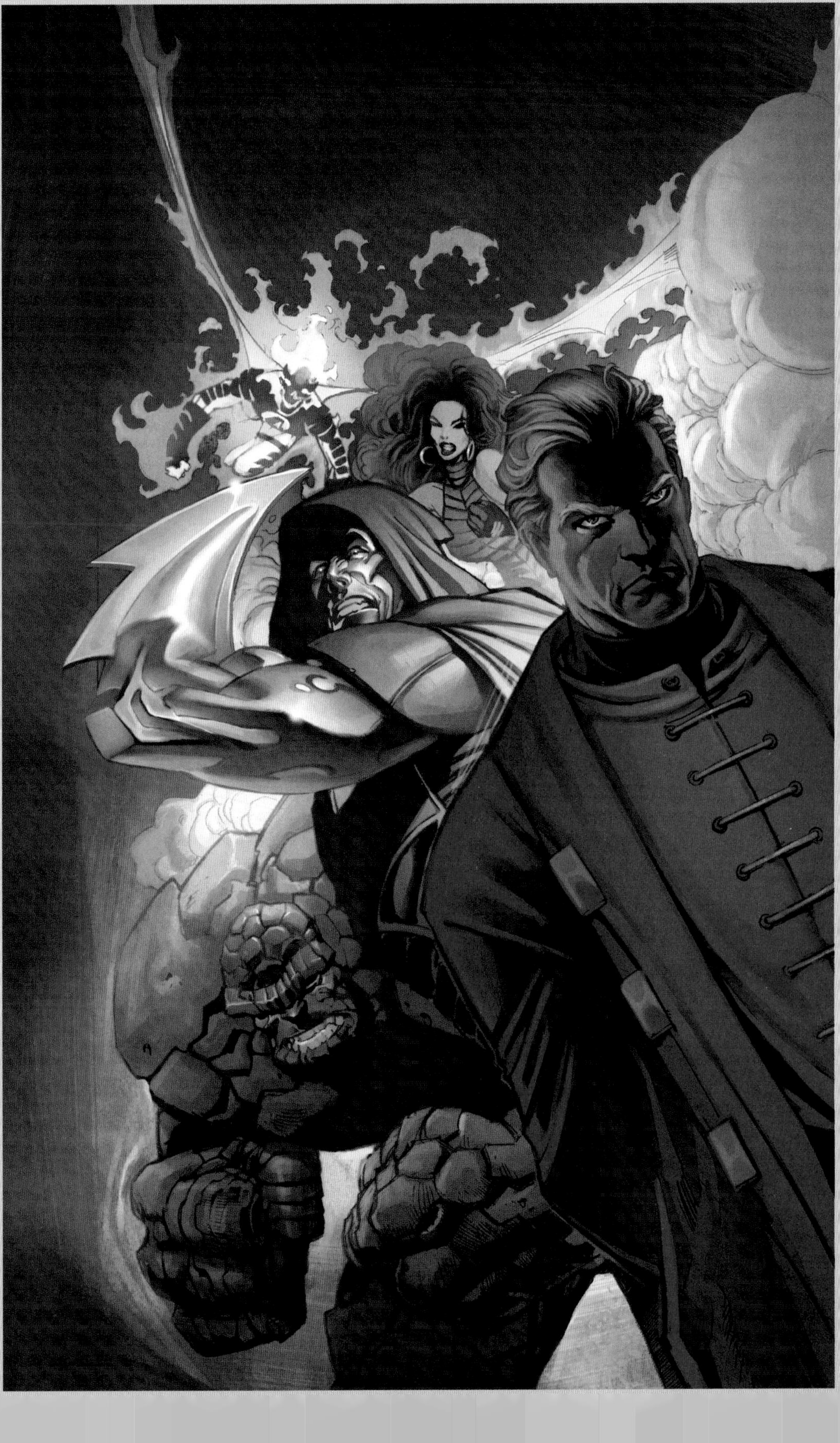

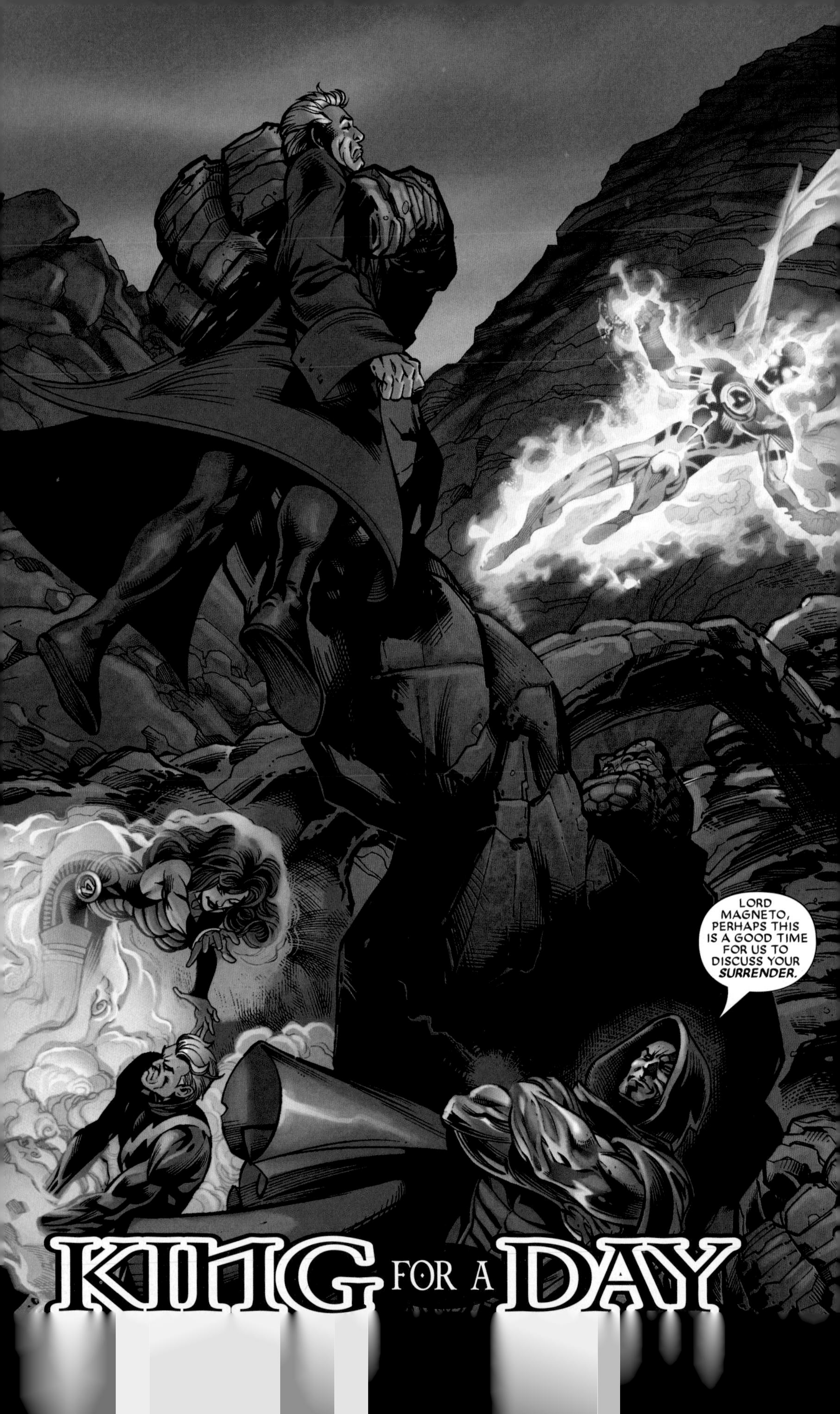
LORD MAGNETO, PERHAPS THIS IS A GOOD TIME FOR US TO DISCUSS YOUR SURRENDER.
KING FOR A DAY

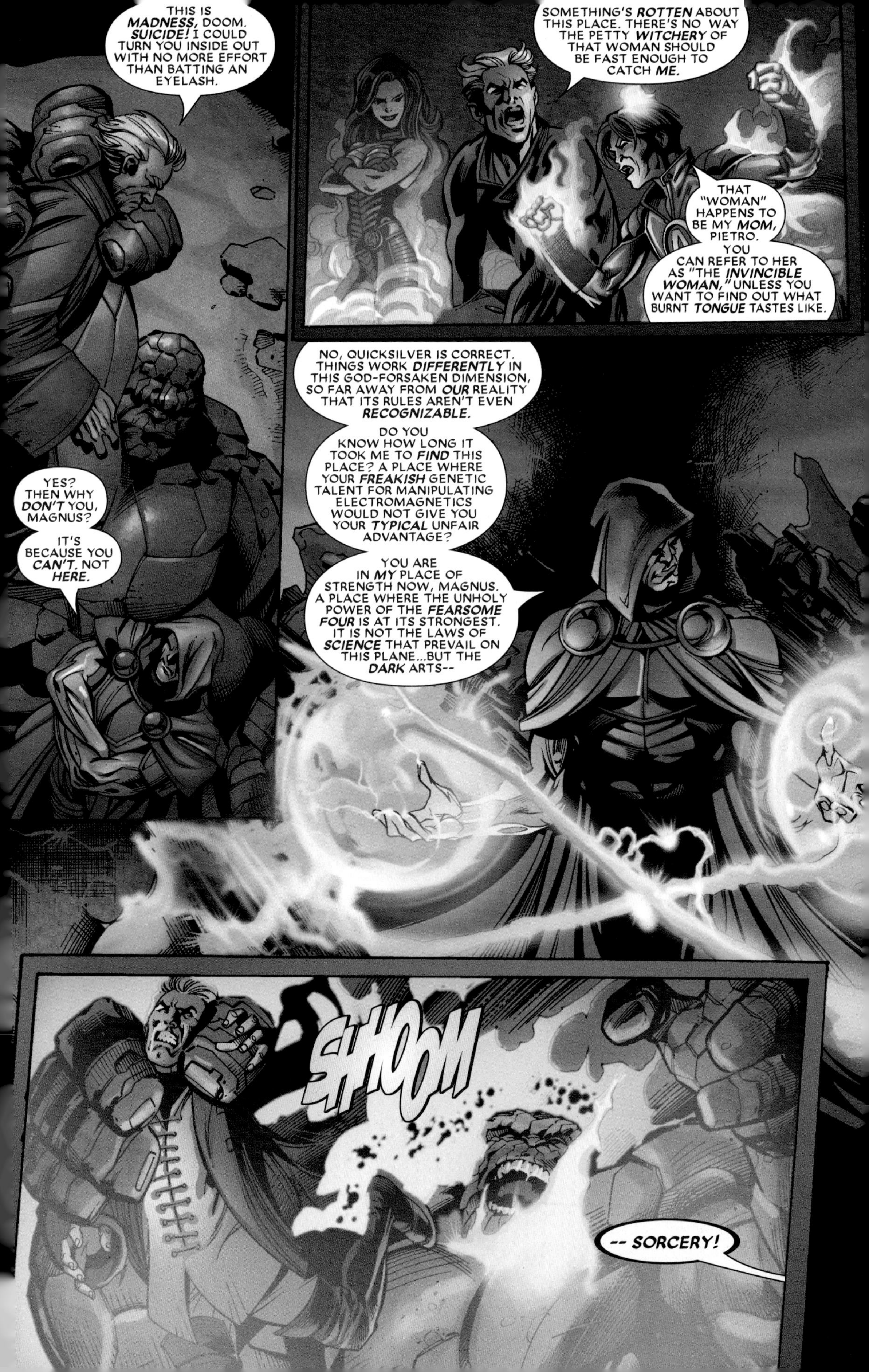
THIS IS MADNESS, DOOM. SUICIDE! I COULD TURN YOU INSIDE OUT WITH NO MORE EFFORT THAN BATTING AN EYELASH.
SOMETHING'S ROTTEN ABOUT THIS PLACE. THERE'S NO WAY THE PETTY WITCHERY OF THAT WOMAN SHOULD BE FAST ENOUGH TO CATCH ME.
THAT "WOMAN" HAPPENS TO BE MY MOM, PIETRO.
YOU CAN REFER TO HER AS "THE INVINCIBLE WOMAN," UNLESS YOU WANT TO FIND OUT WHAT BURNT TONGUE TASTES LIKE.
YES? THEN WHY DON'T YOU, MAGNUS?
IT'S BECAUSE YOU CAN'T. NOT HERE.
NO, QUICKSILVER IS CORRECT. THINGS WORK DIFFERENTLY IN THIS GOD-FORSAKEN DIMENSION, SO FAR AWAY FROM OUR REALITY THAT ITS RULES AREN'T EVEN RECOGNIZABLE.
DO YOU KNOW HOW LONG IT TOOK ME TO FIND THIS PLACE? A PLACE WHERE YOUR FREAKISH GENETIC TALENT FOR MANIPULATING ELECTROMAGNETICS WOULD NOT GIVE YOU YOUR TYPICAL UNFAIR ADVANTAGE?
YOU ARE IN MY PLACE OF STRENGTH NOW, MAGNUS. A PLACE WHERE THE UNHOLY POWER OF THE FEARSOME FOUR IS AT ITS STRONGEST. IT IS NOT THE LAWS OF SCIENCE THAT PREVAIL ON THIS PLANE...BUT THE DARK ARTS--
SHHOOM
-- SORCERY!

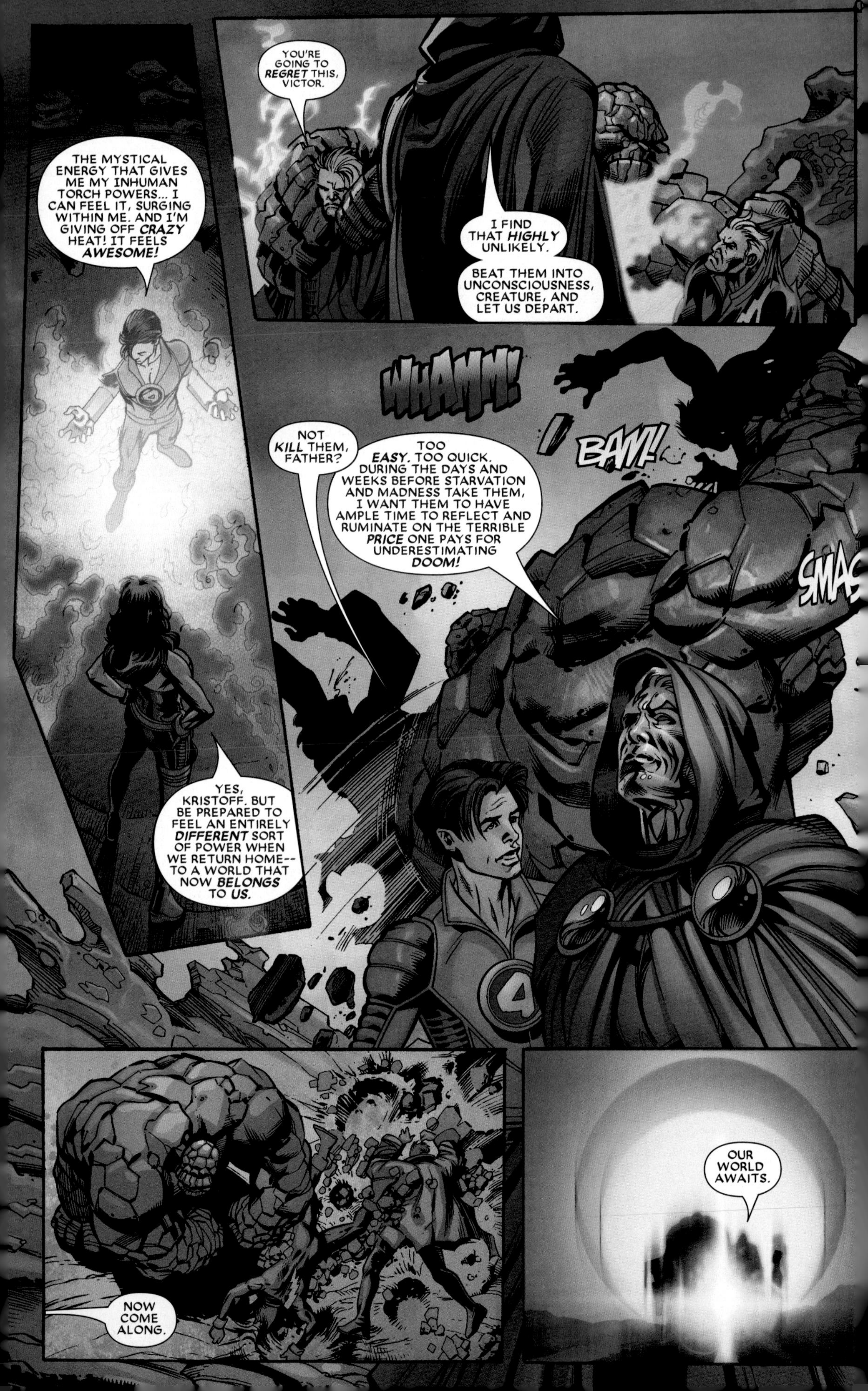
YOU'RE GOING TO REGRET THIS, VICTOR.
I FIND THAT HIGHLY UNLIKELY.
BEAT THEM INTO UNCONSCIOUSNESS, CREATURE, AND LET US DEPART.
THE MYSTICAL ENERGY THAT GIVES ME MY INHUMAN TORCH POWERS... I CAN FEEL IT, SURGING WITHIN ME. AND I'M GIVING OFF CRAZY HEAT! IT FEELS AWESOME!
WHAMM!
BAM!
SMAS
NOT KILL THEM, FATHER?
TOO EASY. TOO QUICK. DURING THE DAYS AND WEEKS BEFORE STARVATION AND MADNESS TAKE THEM, I WANT THEM TO HAVE AMPLE TIME TO REFLECT AND RUMINATE ON THE TERRIBLE PRICE ONE PAYS FOR UNDERESTIMATING DOOM!
YES, KRISTOFF. BUT BE PREPARED TO FEEL AN ENTIRELY DIFFERENT SORT OF POWER WHEN WE RETURN HOME-- TO A WORLD THAT NOW BELONGS TO US.
NOW COME ALONG.
OUR WORLD AWAITS.

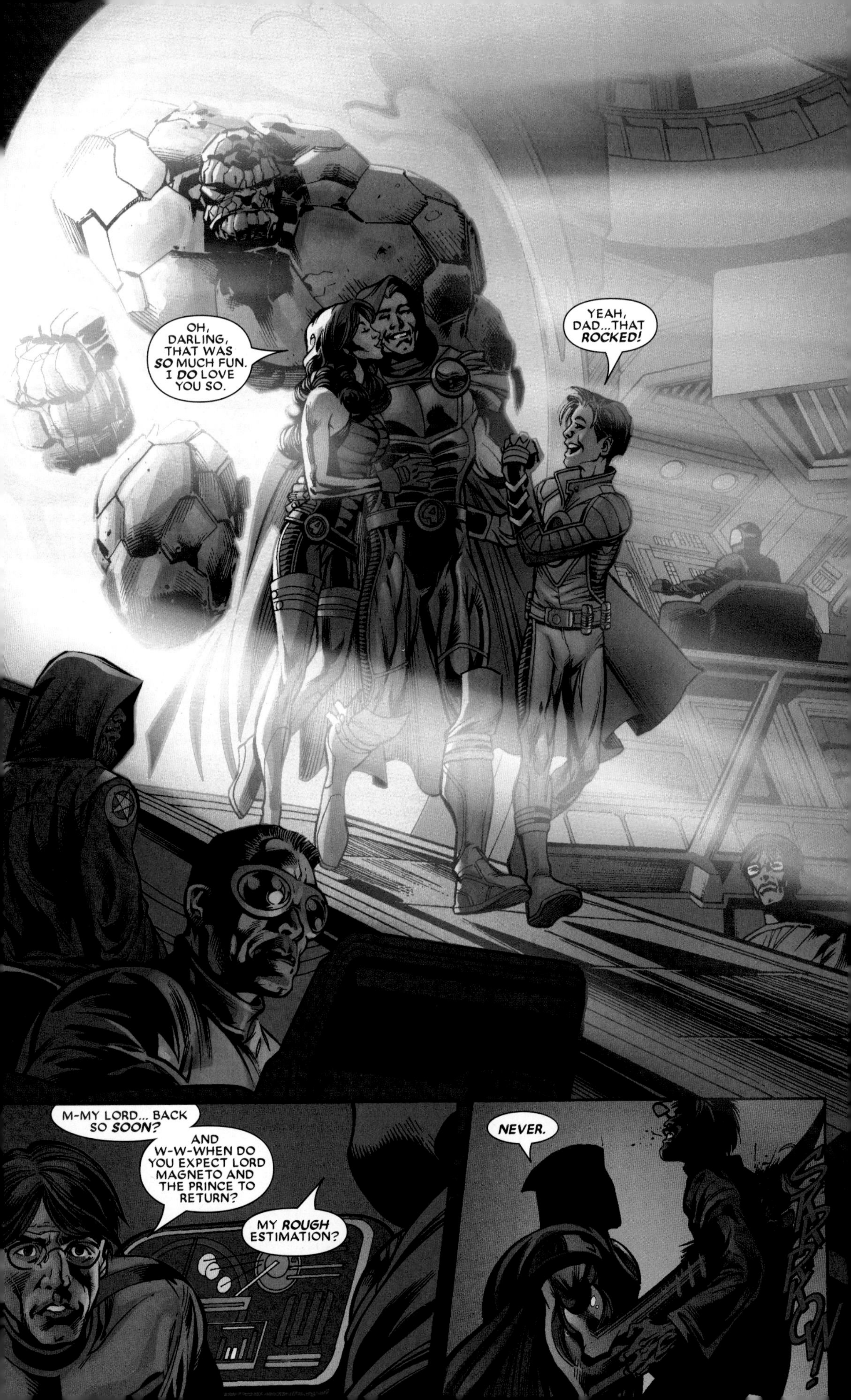

OH, DARLING, THAT WAS SO MUCH FUN. I DO LOVE YOU SO.
YEAH, DAD...THAT ROCKED!
M-MY LORD... BACK SO SOON?
AND W-W-WHEN DO YOU EXPECT LORD MAGNETO AND THE PRINCE TO RETURN?
MY ROUGH ESTIMATION?
NEVER.

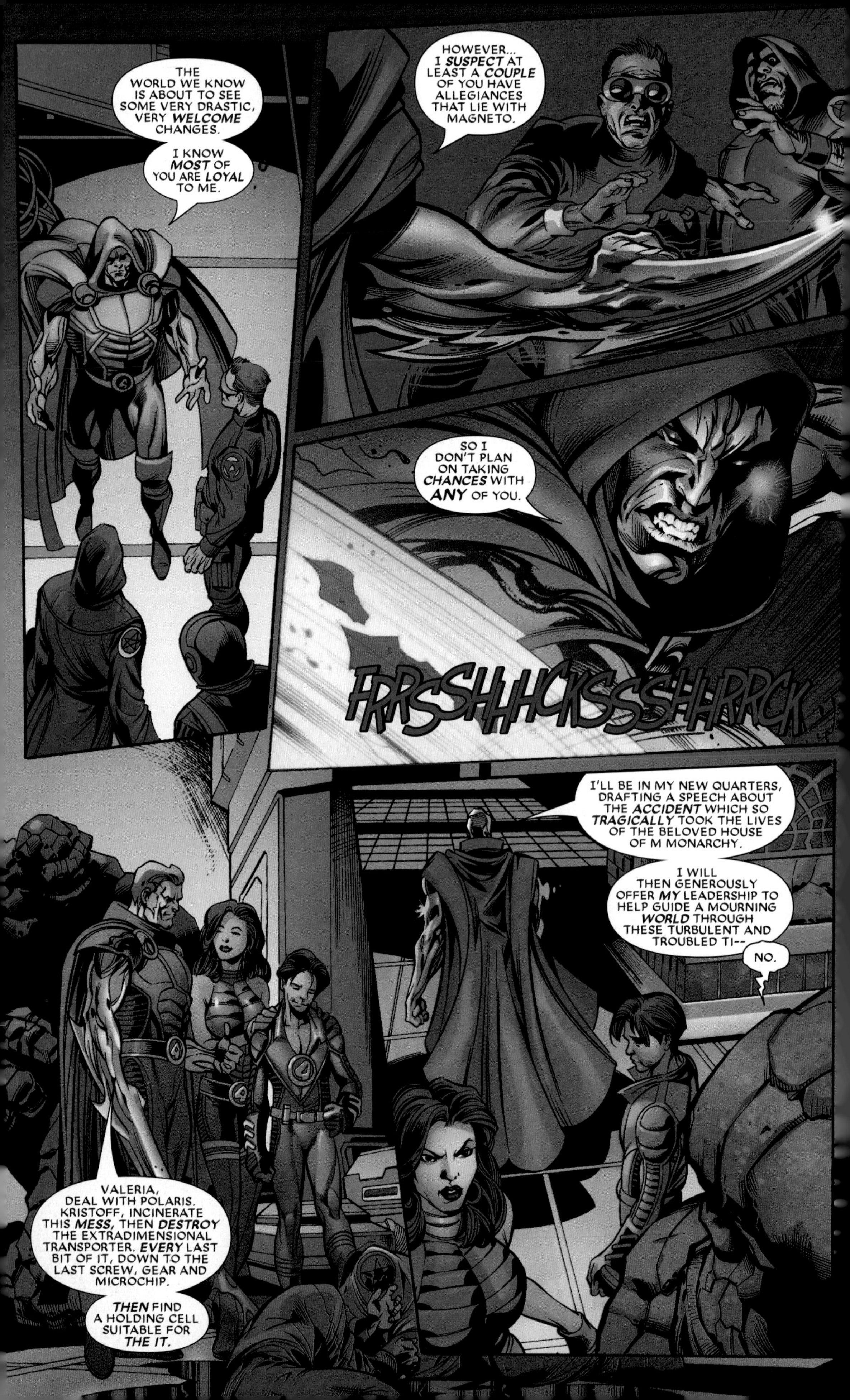
THE WORLD WE KNOW IS ABOUT TO SEE SOME VERY DRASTIC, VERY WELCOME CHANGES.
I KNOW MOST OF YOU ARE LOYAL TO ME.
HOWEVER... I SUSPECT AT LEAST A COUPLE OF YOU HAVE ALLEGIANCES THAT LIE WITH MAGNETO.
SO I DON'T PLAN ON TAKING CHANCES WITH ANY OF YOU.
FRRSSHHHCKSSSSHHRRCK
I'LL BE IN MY NEW QUARTERS, DRAFTING A SPEECH ABOUT THE ACCIDENT WHICH SO TRAGICALLY TOOK THE LIVES OF THE BELOVED HOUSE OF M MONARCHY.
I WILL THEN GENEROUSLY OFFER MY LEADERSHIP TO HELP GUIDE A MOURNING WORLD THROUGH THESE TURBULENT AND TROUBLED TI--
NO.
VALERIA, DEAL WITH POLARIS. KRISTOFF, INCINERATE THIS MESS, THEN DESTROY THE EXTRADIMENSIONAL TRANSPORTER. EVERY LAST BIT OF IT, DOWN TO THE LAST SCREW, GEAR AND MICROCHIP.
THEN FIND A HOLDING CELL SUITABLE FOR THE IT.

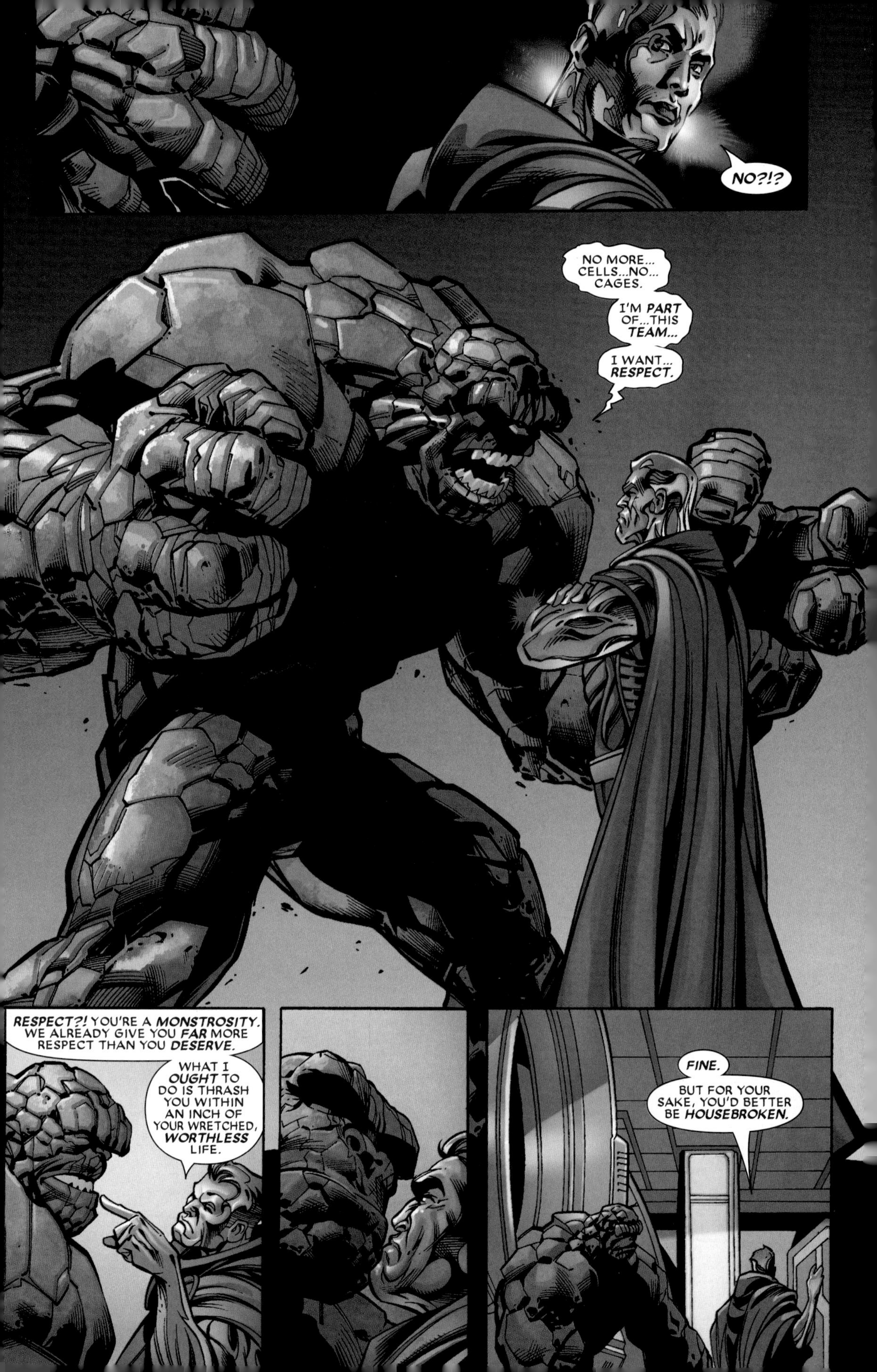
NO?!?
NO MORE... CELLS...NO... CAGES.
I'M PART OF...THIS TEAM...
I WANT... RESPECT.
RESPECT?! YOU'RE A MONSTROSITY. WE ALREADY GIVE YOU FAR MORE RESPECT THAN YOU DESERVE.
WHAT I OUGHT TO DO IS THRASH YOU WITHIN AN INCH OF YOUR WRETCHED, WORTHLESS LIFE.
FINE.
BUT FOR YOUR SAKE, YOU'D BETTER BE HOUSEBROKEN.

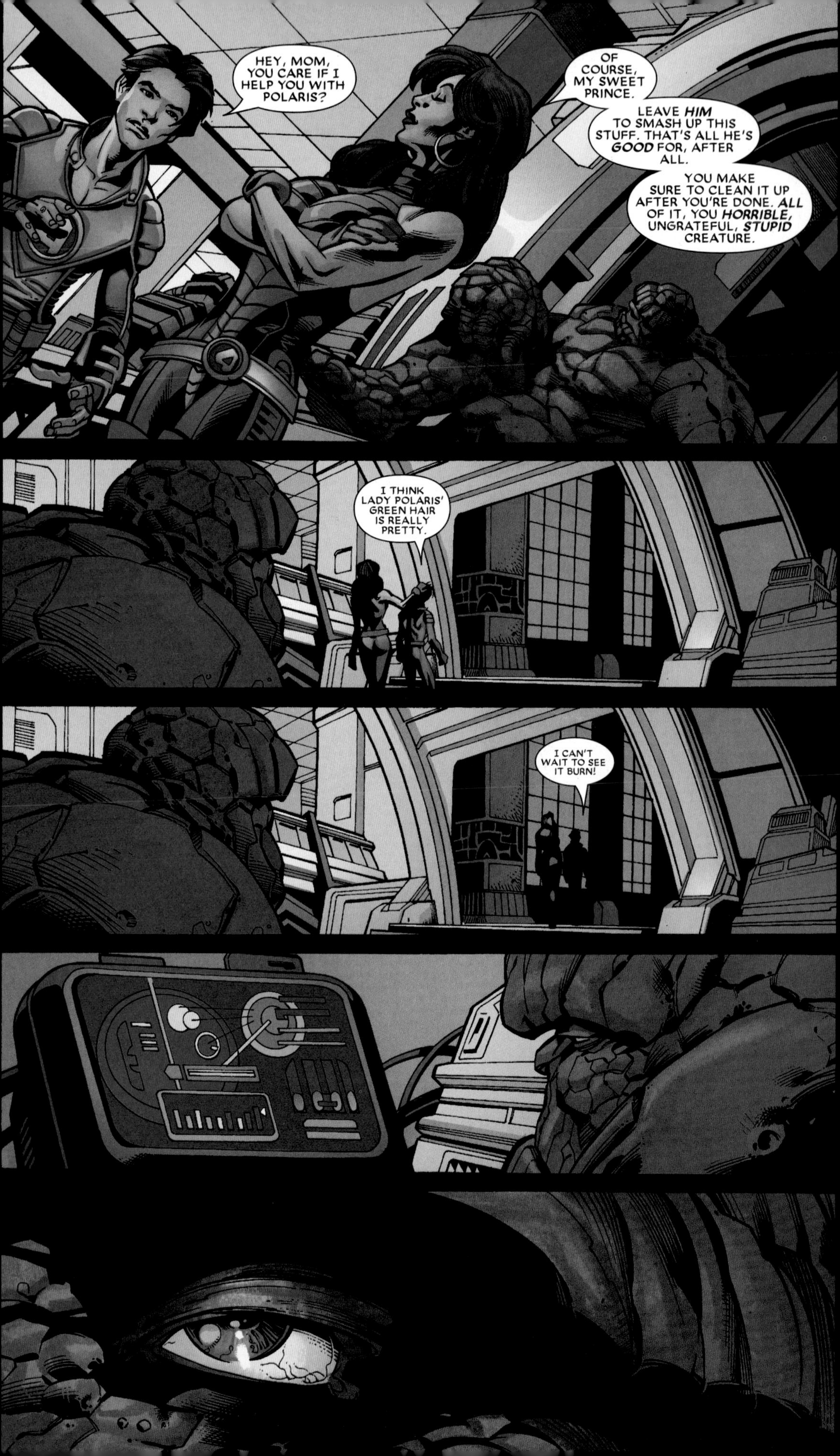
HEY, MOM, YOU CARE IF I HELP YOU WITH POLARIS?
OF COURSE, MY SWEET PRINCE.
LEAVE HIM TO SMASH UP THIS STUFF. THAT'S ALL HE'S GOOD FOR, AFTER ALL.
YOU MAKE SURE TO CLEAN IT UP AFTER YOU'RE DONE. ALL OF IT, YOU HORRIBLE, UNGRATEFUL, STUPID CREATURE.
I THINK LADY POLARIS' GREEN HAIR IS REALLY PRETTY.
I CAN'T WAIT TO SEE IT BURN!

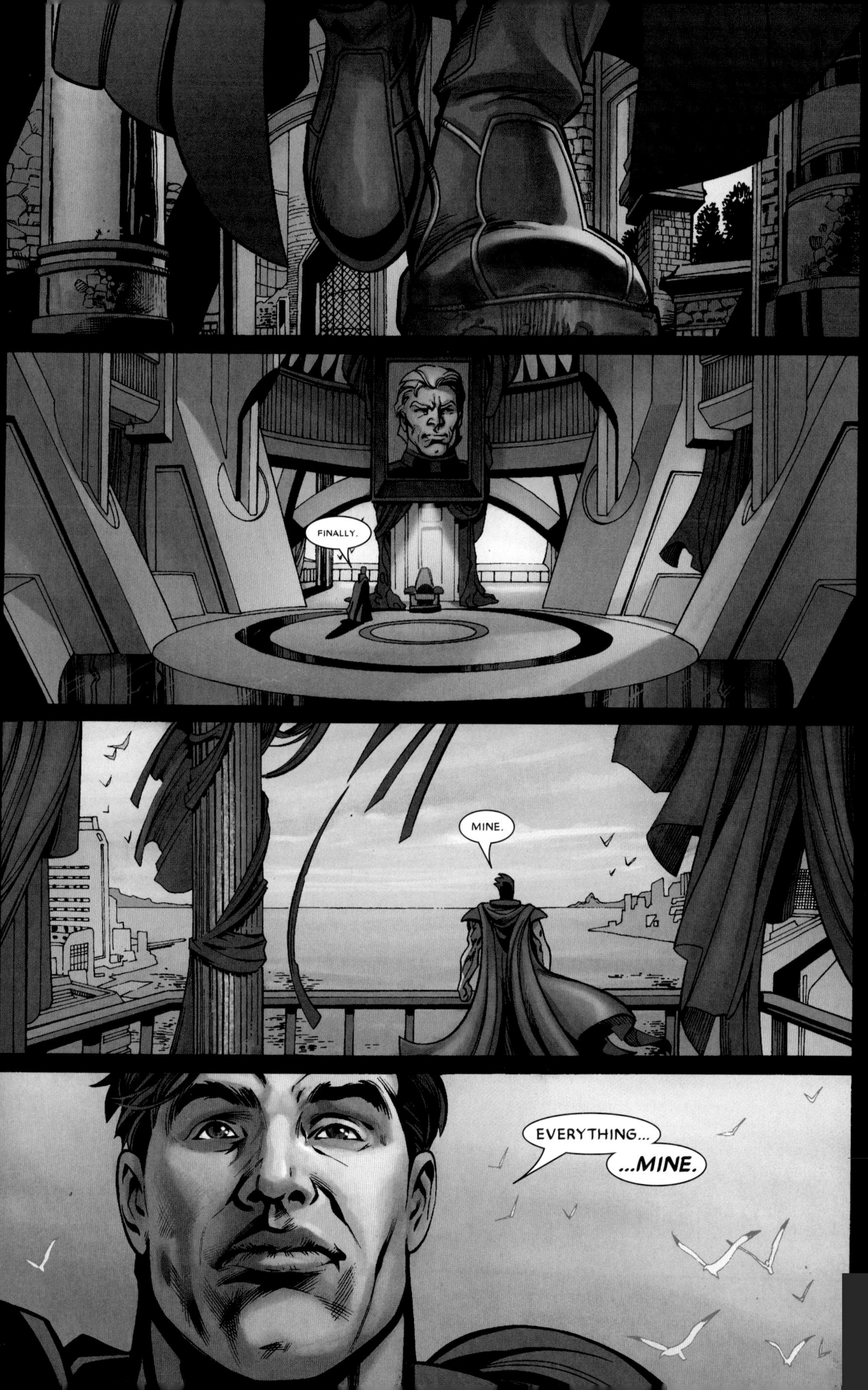
FINALLY.
MINE.
EVERYTHING...
...MINE.

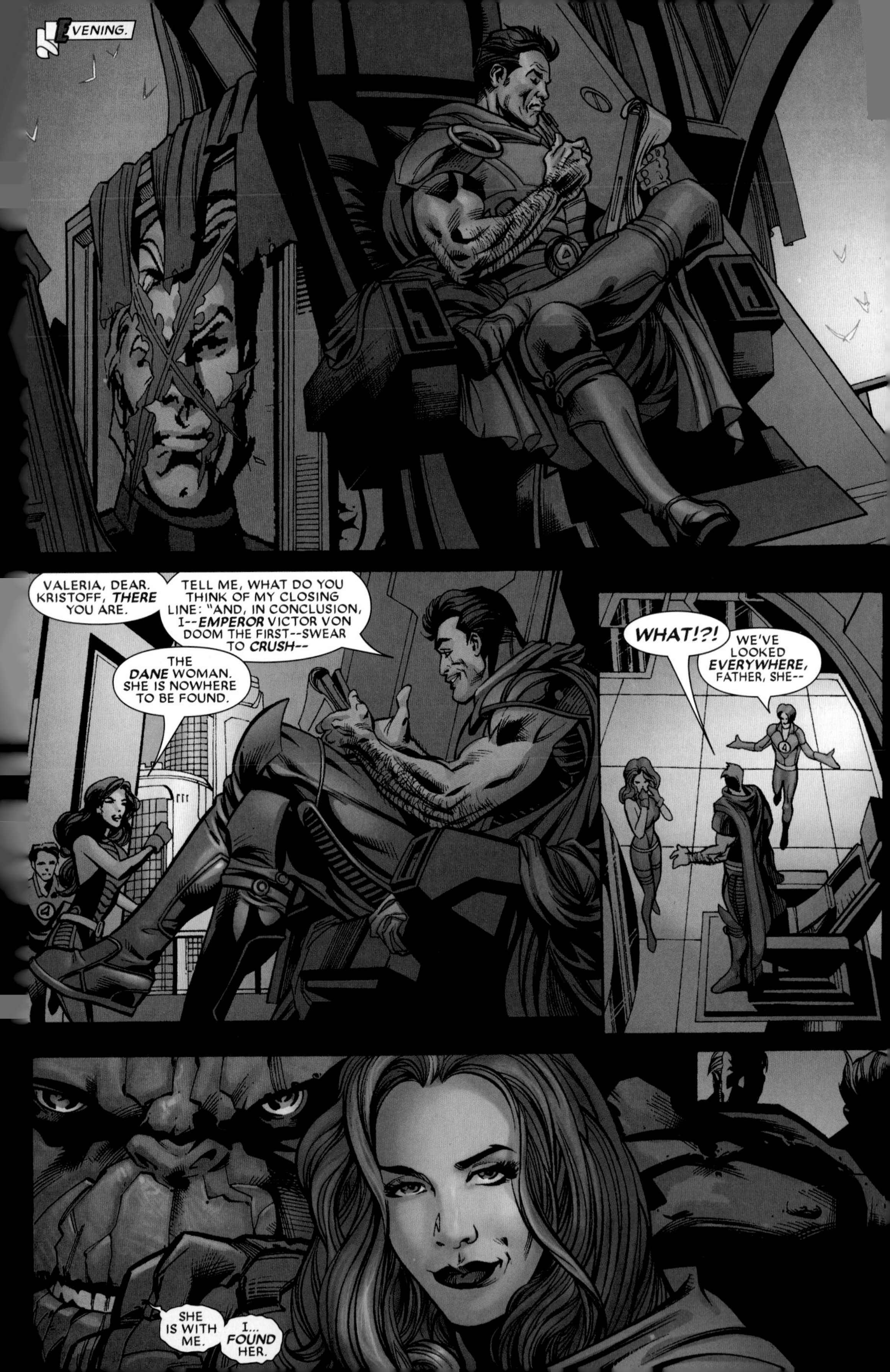
EVENING.
VALERIA, DEAR. KRISTOFF, THERE YOU ARE.
TELL ME, WHAT DO YOU THINK OF MY CLOSING LINE: "AND, IN CONCLUSION, I--EMPEROR VICTOR VON DOOM THE FIRST--SWEAR TO CRUSH--
THE DANE WOMAN. SHE IS NOWHERE TO BE FOUND.
WHAT!?!
WE'VE LOOKED EVERYWHERE, FATHER, SHE--
SHE IS WITH ME.
I... FOUND HER.

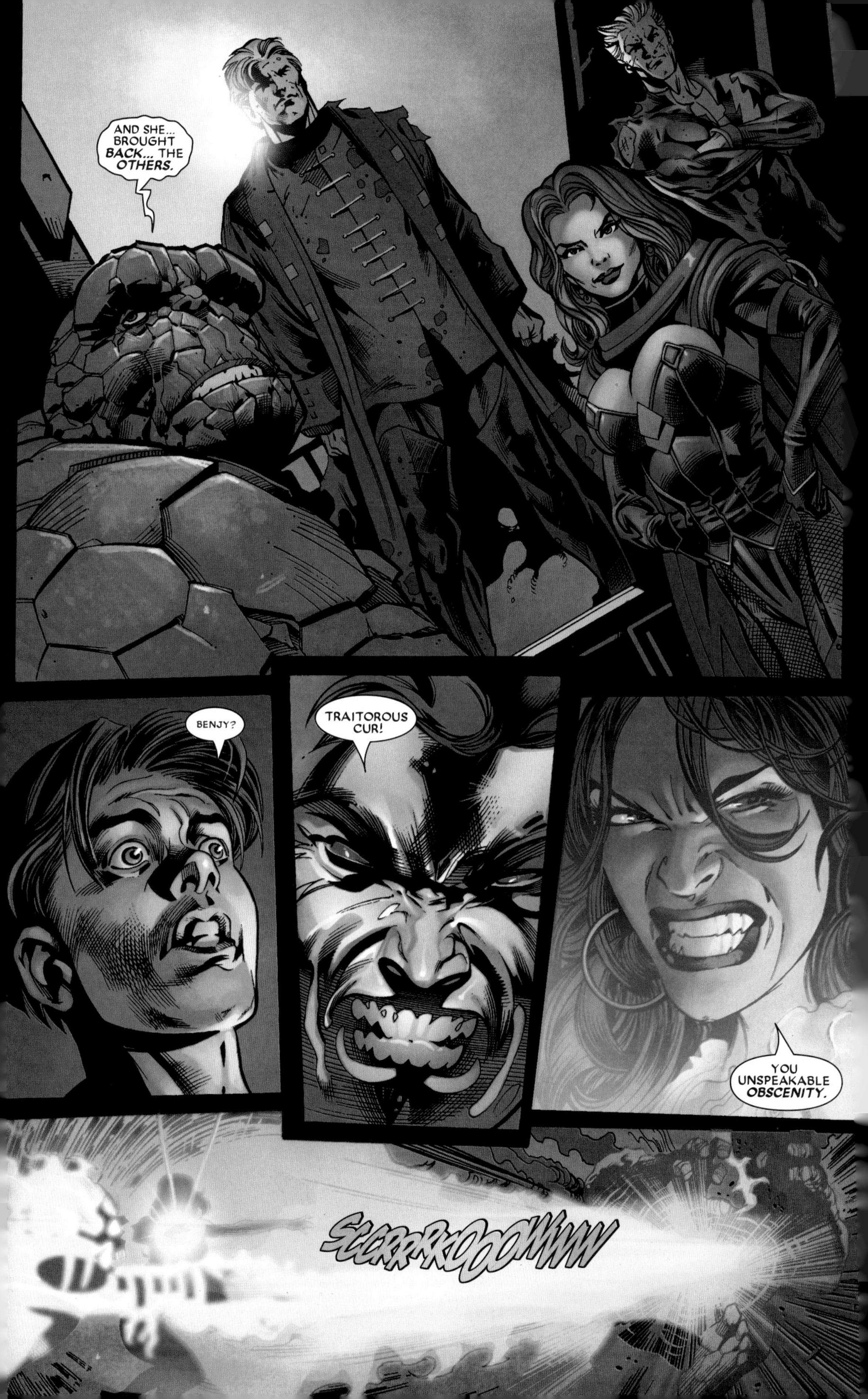
AND SHE... BROUGHT BACK... THE OTHERS.
BENJY?
TRAITOROUS CUR!
YOU UNSPEAKABLE OBSCENITY.
SCRRRKOOOWWWN

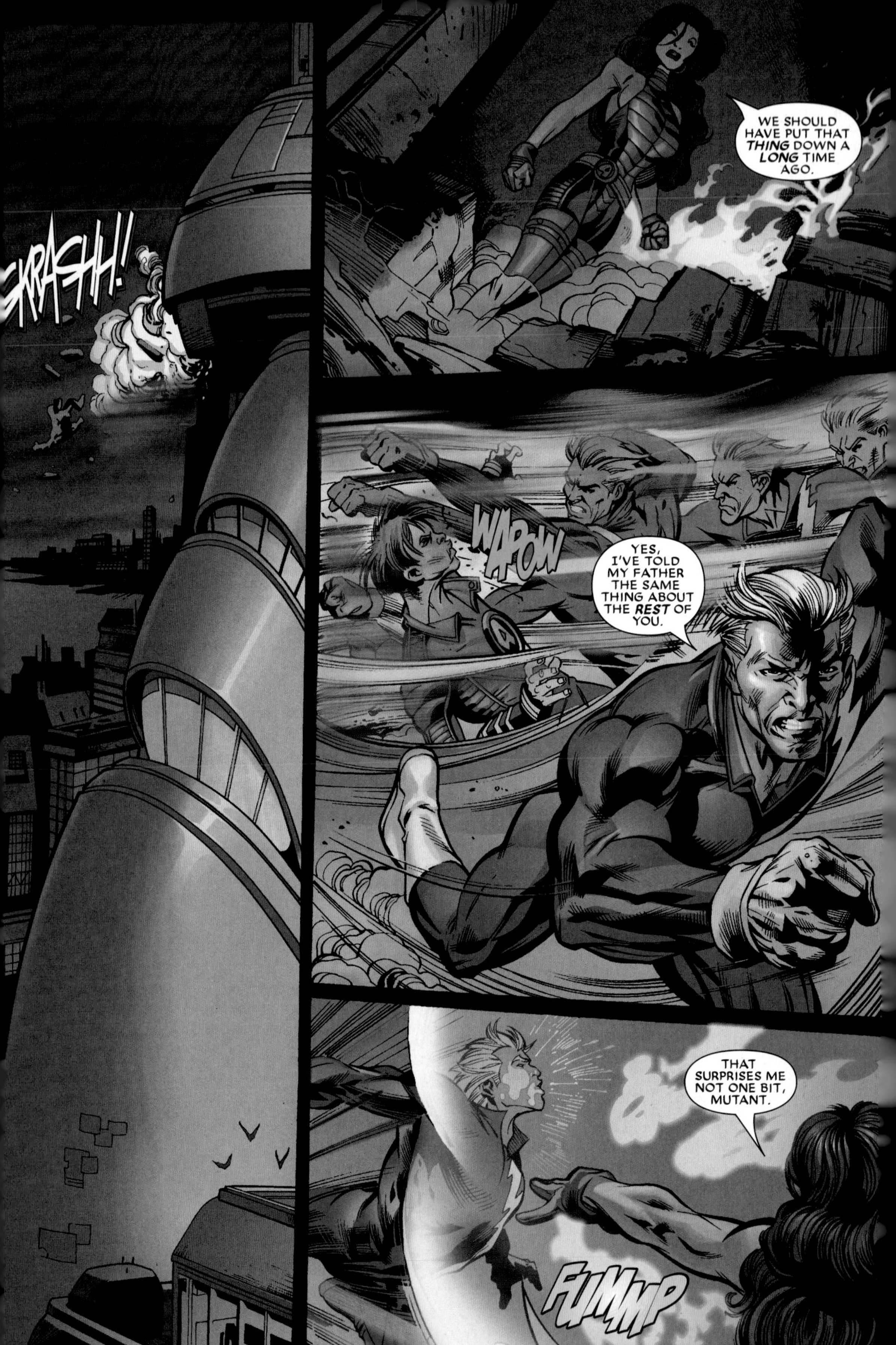
SKRASHH!
WE SHOULD HAVE PUT THAT THING DOWN A LONG TIME AGO.
WAPOW
YES, I'VE TOLD MY FATHER THE SAME THING ABOUT THE REST OF YOU.
THAT SURPRISES ME NOT ONE BIT, MUTANT.
FUMMP

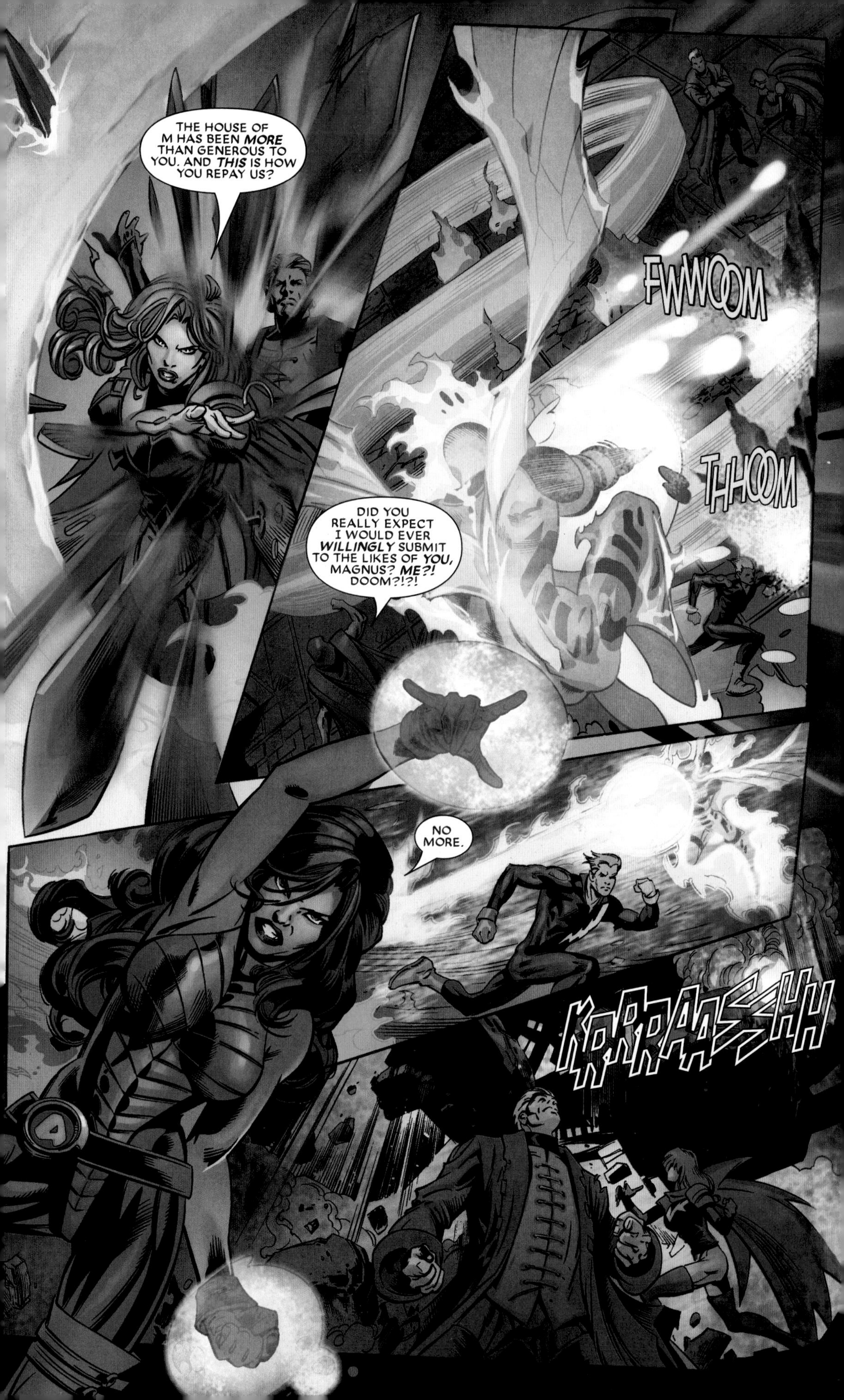
THE HOUSE OF M HAS BEEN MORE THAN GENEROUS TO YOU. AND THIS IS HOW YOU REPAY US?
FWWOOM
THHOOM
DID YOU REALLY EXPECT I WOULD EVER WILLINGLY SUBMIT TO THE LIKES OF YOU, MAGNUS? ME?! DOOM?!?!
NO MORE.
KRRRAASHH

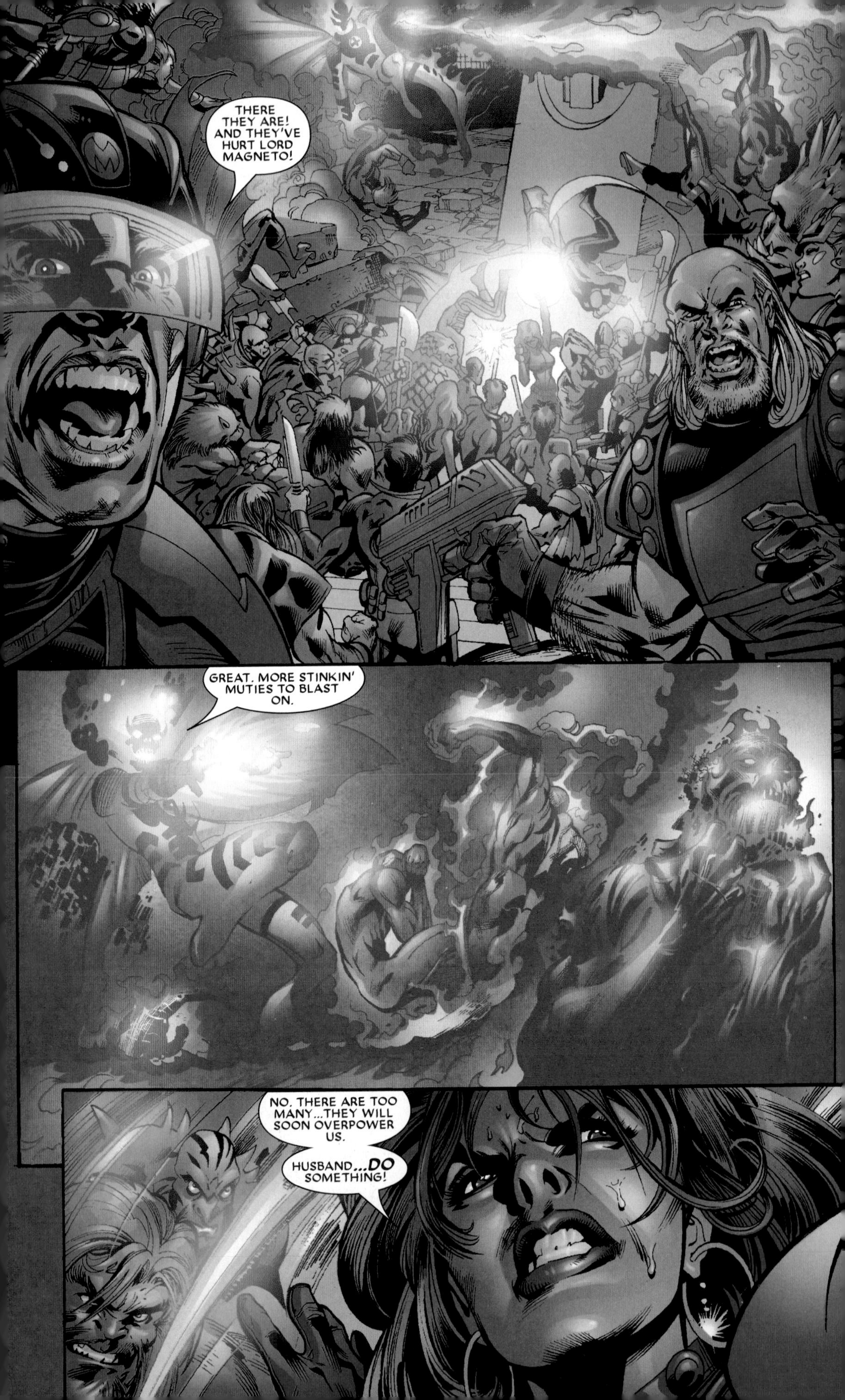
THERE THEY ARE! AND THEY'VE HURT LORD MAGNETO!
GREAT. MORE STINKIN' MUTIES TO BLAST ON.
NO. THERE ARE TOO MANY...THEY WILL SOON OVERPOWER US.
HUSBAND...DO SOMETHING!

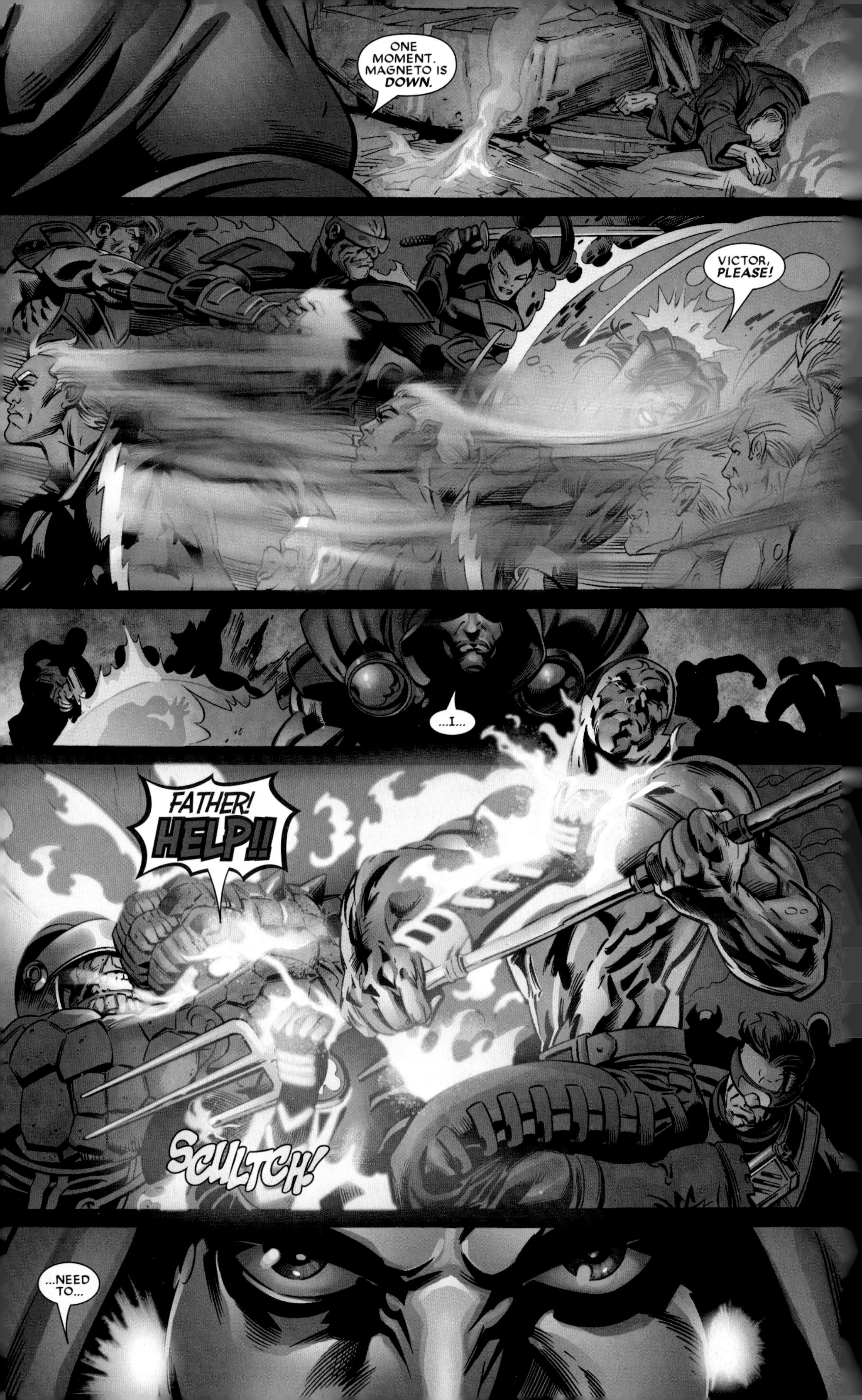
ONE MOMENT. MAGNETO IS DOWN.
VICTOR, PLEASE!
...I...
FATHER! HELP!!
SCULTCH!
...NEED TO...

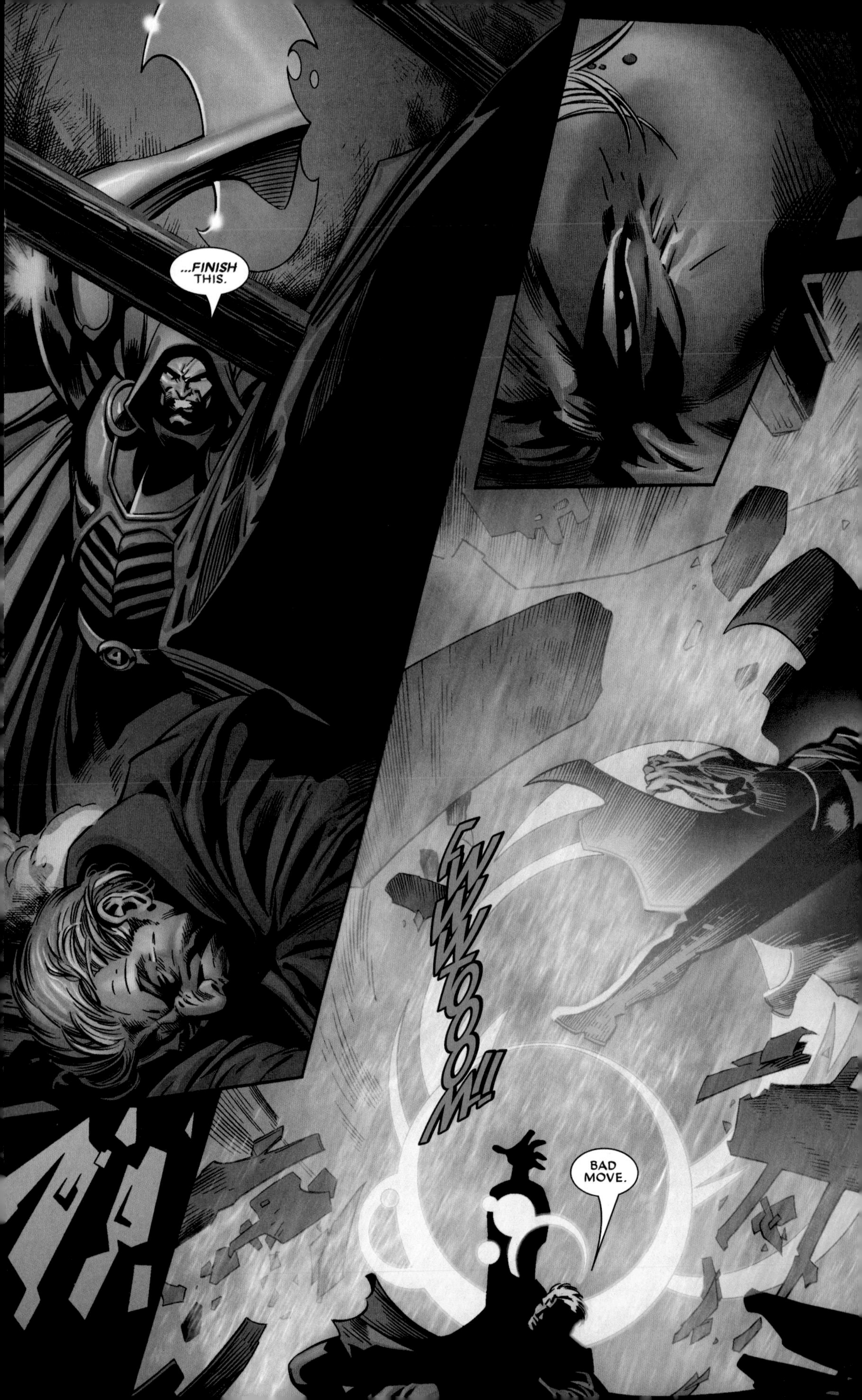
...FINISH THIS.
FWWOOOM!!
BAD MOVE.

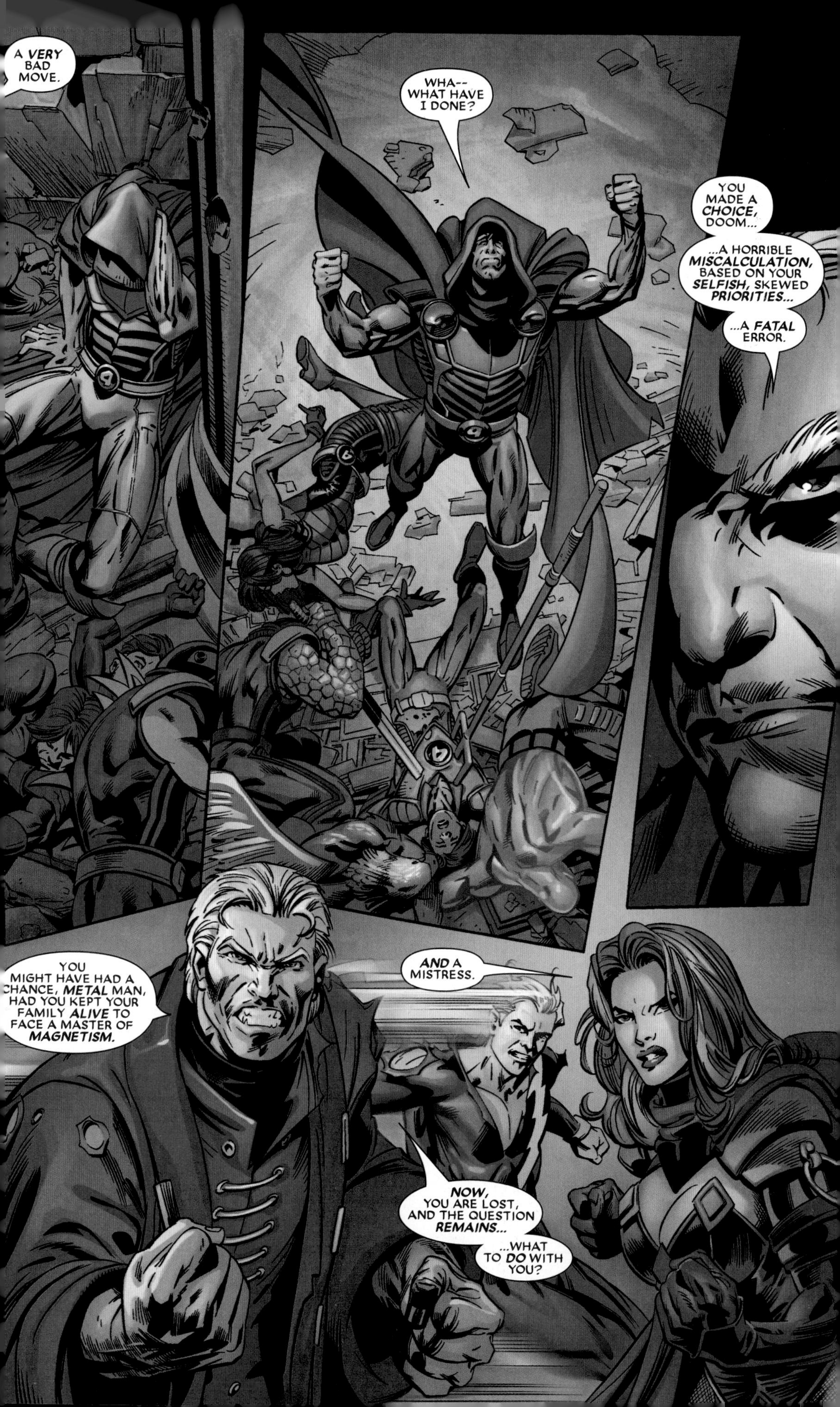

A VERY BAD MOVE.
WHA-- WHAT HAVE I DONE?
YOU MADE A CHOICE, DOOM...
...A HORRIBLE MISCALCULATION, BASED ON YOUR SELFISH, SKEWED PRIORITIES...
...A FATAL ERROR.
YOU MIGHT HAVE HAD A CHANCE, METAL MAN, HAD YOU KEPT YOUR FAMILY ALIVE TO FACE A MASTER OF MAGNETISM.
AND A MISTRESS.
NOW, YOU ARE LOST, AND THE QUESTION REMAINS...
...WHAT TO DO WITH YOU?

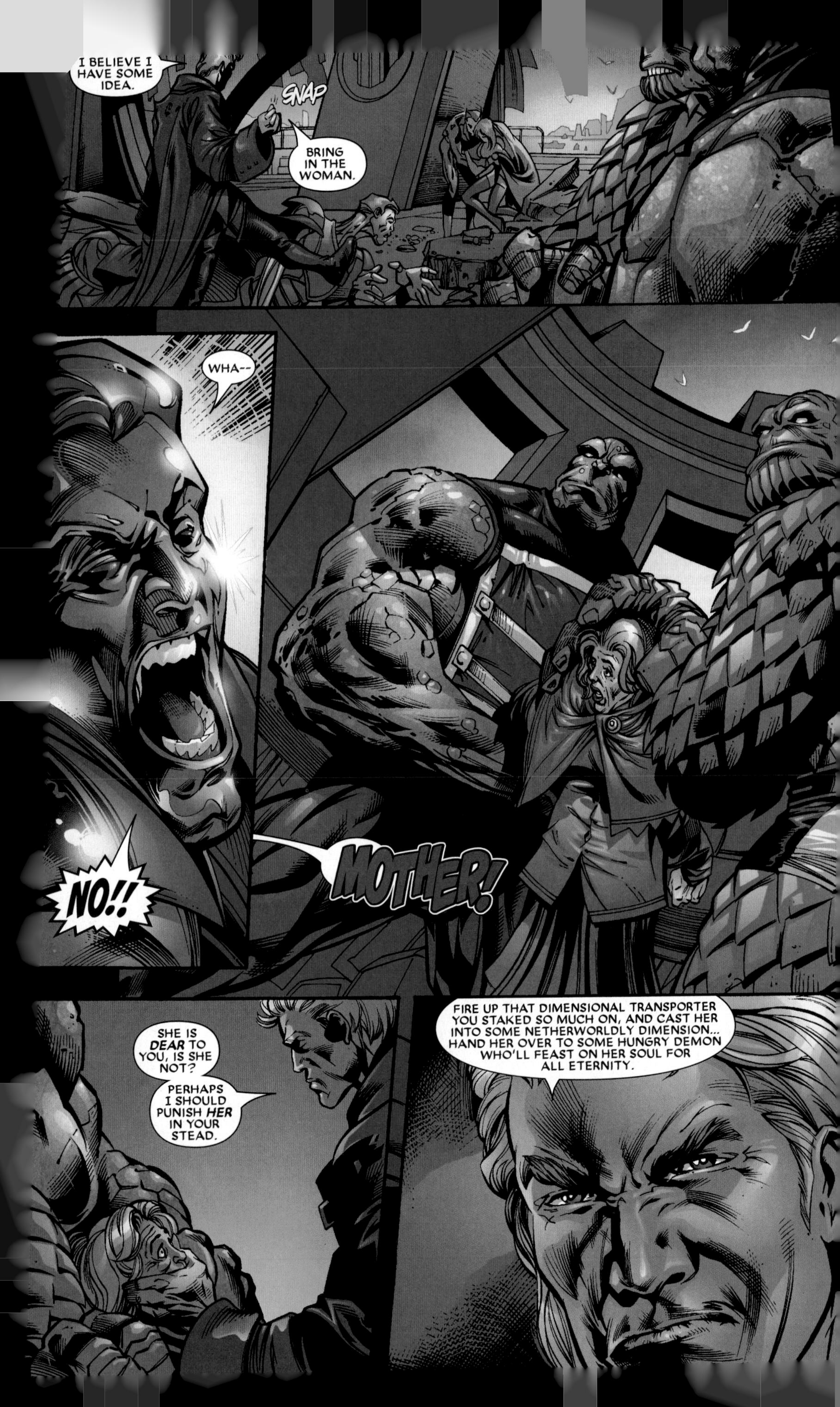
I BELIEVE I HAVE SOME IDEA.
SNAP
BRING IN THE WOMAN.
WHA--
NO!!
MOTHER!
SHE IS DEAR TO YOU, IS SHE NOT?
PERHAPS I SHOULD PUNISH HER IN YOUR STEAD.
FIRE UP THAT DIMENSIONAL TRANSPORTER YOU STAKED SO MUCH ON, AND CAST HER INTO SOME NETHERWORLDLY DIMENSION... HAND HER OVER TO SOME HUNGRY DEMON WHO'LL FEAST ON HER SOUL FOR ALL ETERNITY.

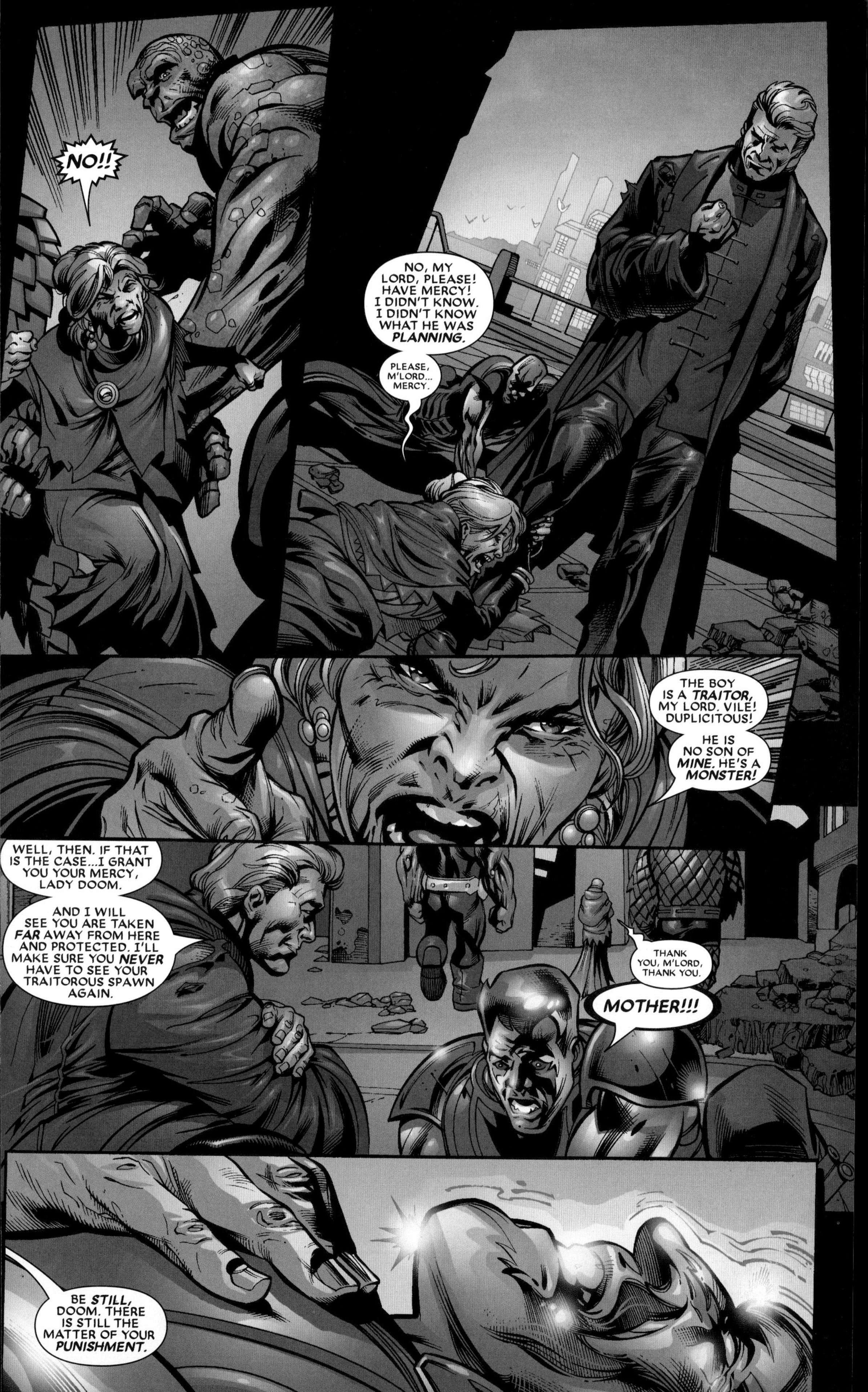
NO!!
NO, MY LORD, PLEASE! HAVE MERCY! I DIDN'T KNOW. I DIDN'T KNOW WHAT HE WAS PLANNING.
PLEASE, M'LORD... MERCY.
THE BOY IS A TRAITOR, MY LORD. VILE! DUPLICITOUS!
HE IS NO SON OF MINE. HE'S A MONSTER!
WELL, THEN. IF THAT IS THE CASE...I GRANT YOU YOUR MERCY, LADY DOOM.
AND I WILL SEE YOU ARE TAKEN FAR AWAY FROM HERE AND PROTECTED. I'LL MAKE SURE YOU NEVER HAVE TO SEE YOUR TRAITOROUS SPAWN AGAIN.
THANK YOU, M'LORD, THANK YOU.
MOTHER!!!
BE STILL, DOOM. THERE IS STILL THE MATTER OF YOUR PUNISHMENT.

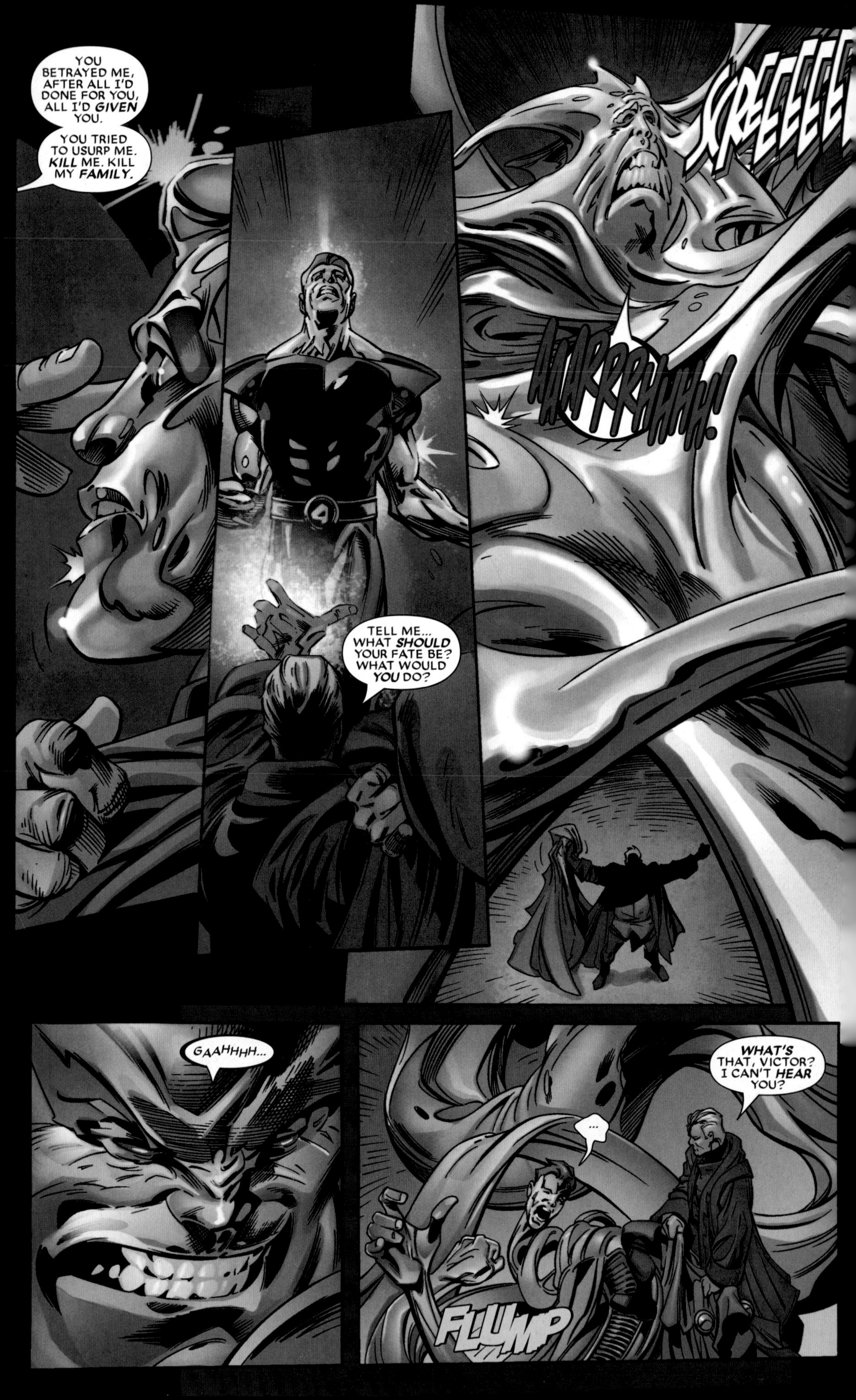
YOU BETRAYED ME, AFTER ALL I'D DONE FOR YOU, ALL I'D GIVEN YOU.
YOU TRIED TO USURP ME. KILL ME. KILL MY FAMILY.
SCREEEEE
AAARRRHHHH!
TELL ME... WHAT SHOULD YOUR FATE BE? WHAT WOULD YOU DO?
GAAHHHH...
WHAT'S THAT, VICTOR? I CAN'T HEAR YOU?
...
FLUMP

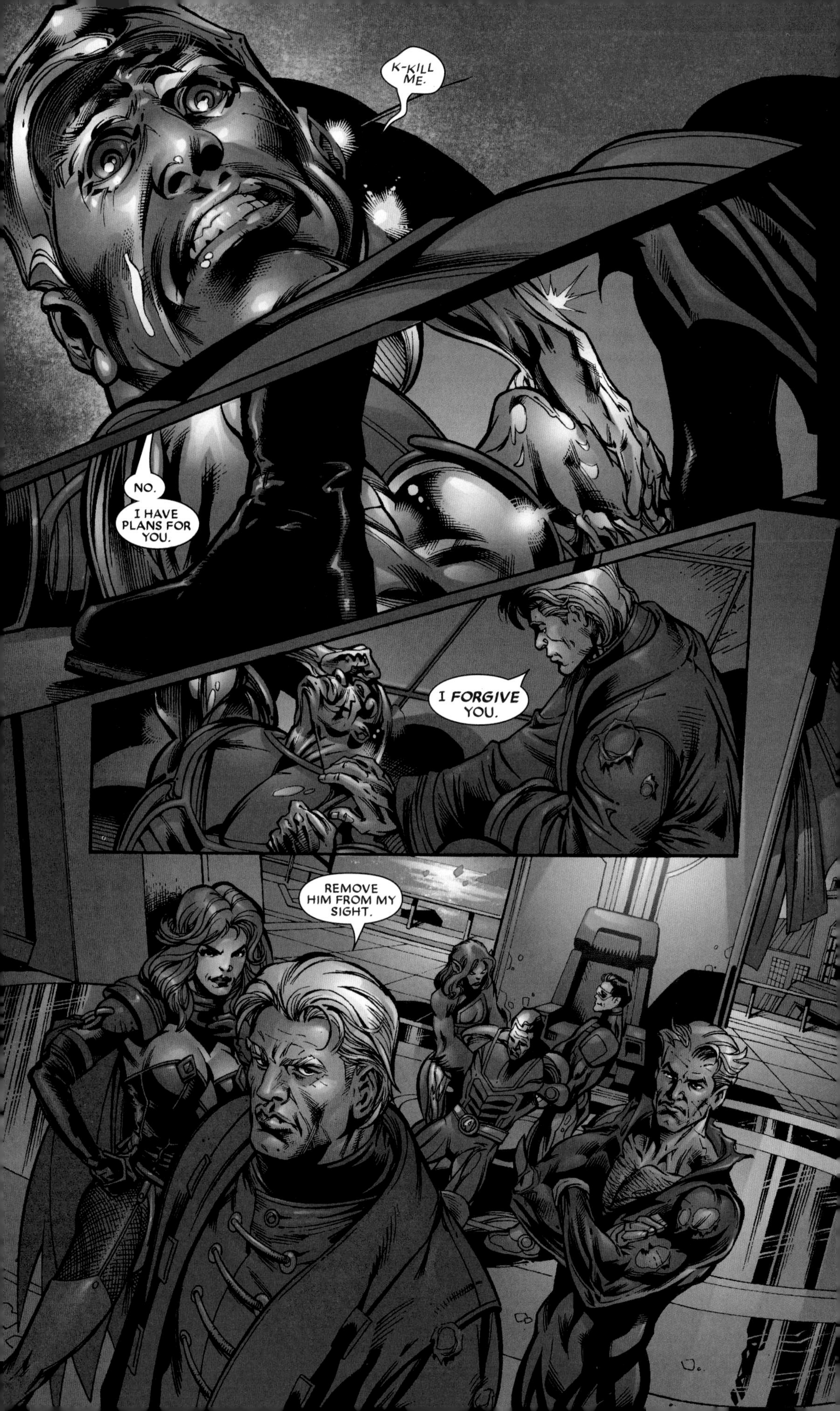
K-KILL ME.
NO.
I HAVE PLANS FOR YOU.
I FORGIVE YOU.
REMOVE HIM FROM MY SIGHT.

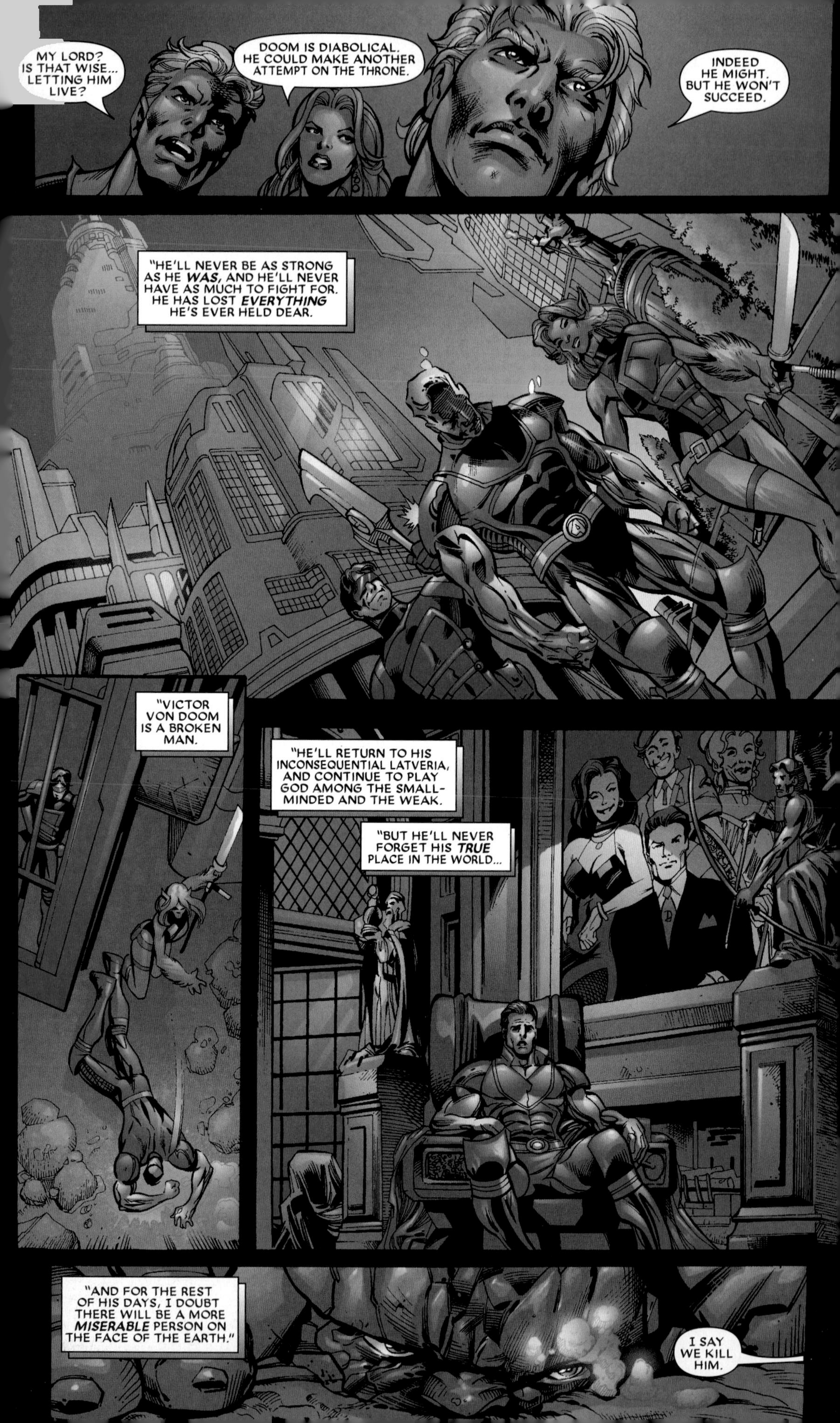
MY LORD? IS THAT WISE... LETTING HIM LIVE?
DOOM IS DIABOLICAL. HE COULD MAKE ANOTHER ATTEMPT ON THE THRONE.
INDEED HE MIGHT. BUT HE WON'T SUCCEED.
"HE'LL NEVER BE AS STRONG AS HE *WAS*, AND HE'LL NEVER HAVE AS MUCH TO FIGHT FOR. HE HAS LOST *EVERYTHING* HE'S EVER HELD DEAR.
"VICTOR VON DOOM IS A BROKEN MAN.
"HE'LL RETURN TO HIS INCONSEQUENTIAL LATVERIA, AND CONTINUE TO PLAY GOD AMONG THE SMALL-MINDED AND THE WEAK.
"BUT HE'LL NEVER FORGET HIS *TRUE* PLACE IN THE WORLD...
"AND FOR THE REST OF HIS DAYS, I DOUBT THERE WILL BE A MORE *MISERABLE* PERSON ON THE FACE OF THE EARTH."
I SAY WE KILL HIM.

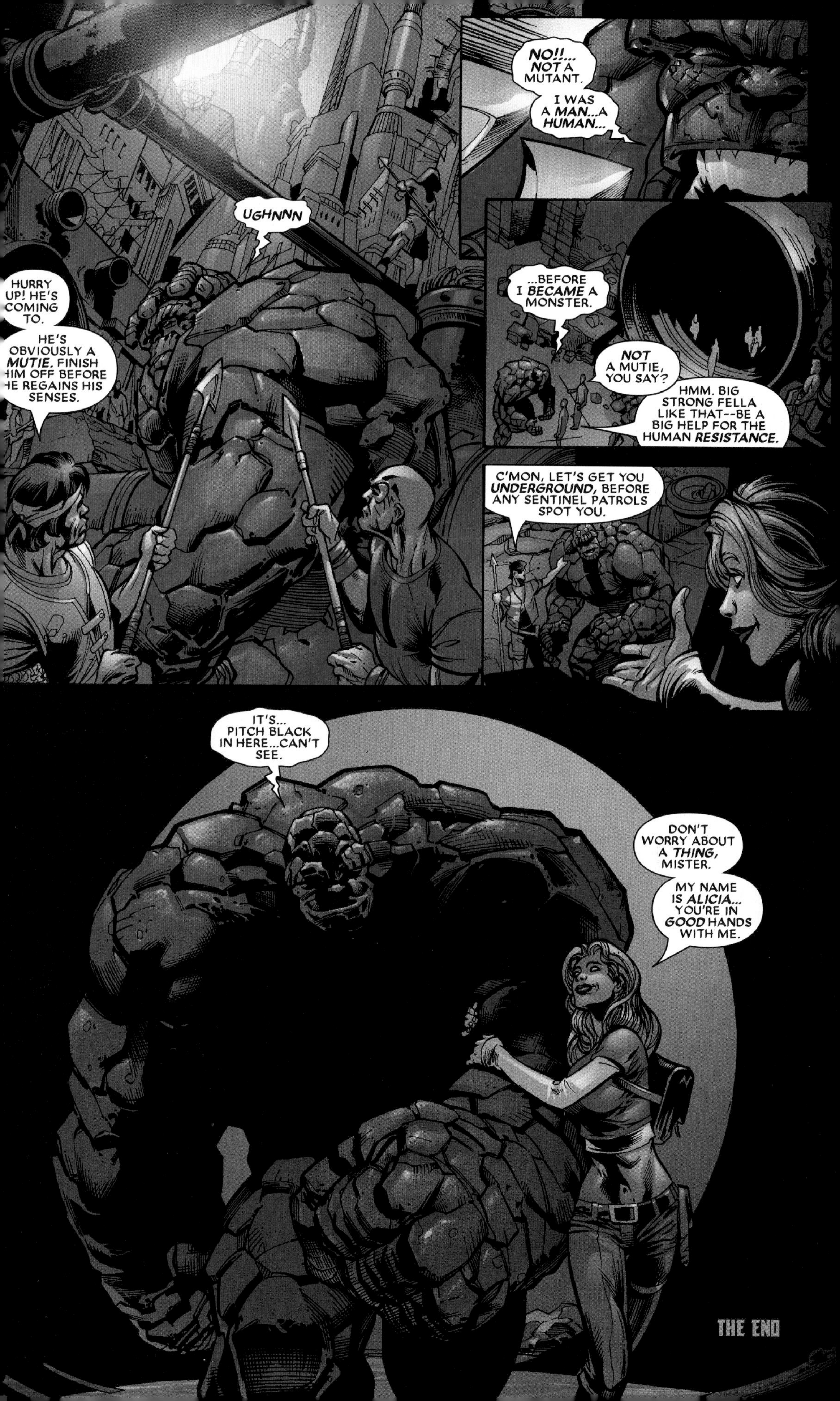

UGHNNN
HURRY UP! HE'S COMING TO.
HE'S OBVIOUSLY A MUTIE. FINISH HIM OFF BEFORE HE REGAINS HIS SENSES.
NO!!... NOT A MUTANT.
I WAS A MAN...A HUMAN...
...BEFORE I BECAME A MONSTER.
NOT A MUTIE, YOU SAY?
HMM. BIG STRONG FELLA LIKE THAT--BE A BIG HELP FOR THE HUMAN RESISTANCE.
C'MON, LET'S GET YOU UNDERGROUND, BEFORE ANY SENTINEL PATROLS SPOT YOU.
IT'S... PITCH BLACK IN HERE...CAN'T SEE.
DON'T WORRY ABOUT A THING, MISTER.
MY NAME IS ALICIA... YOU'RE IN GOOD HANDS WITH ME.
THE END

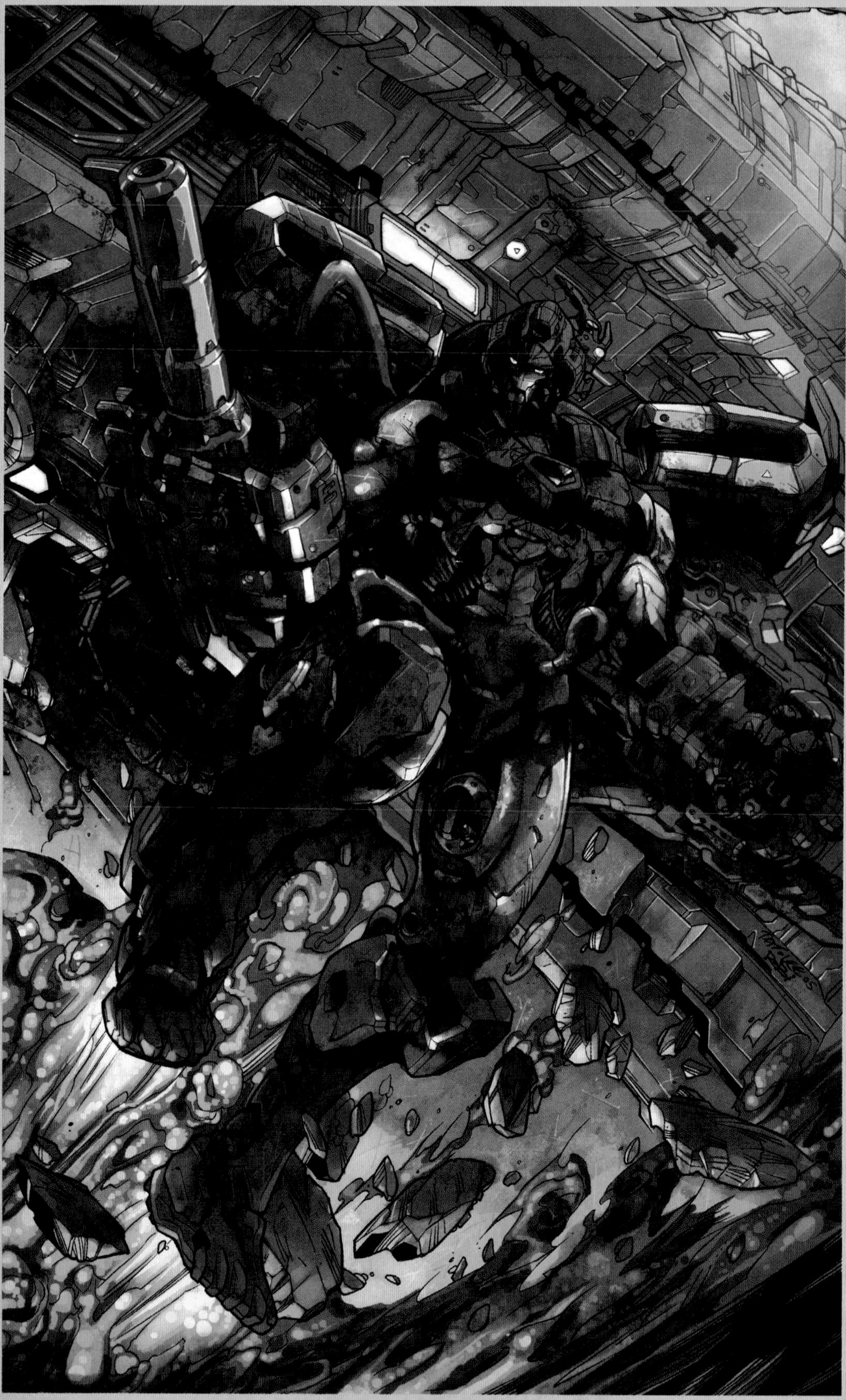

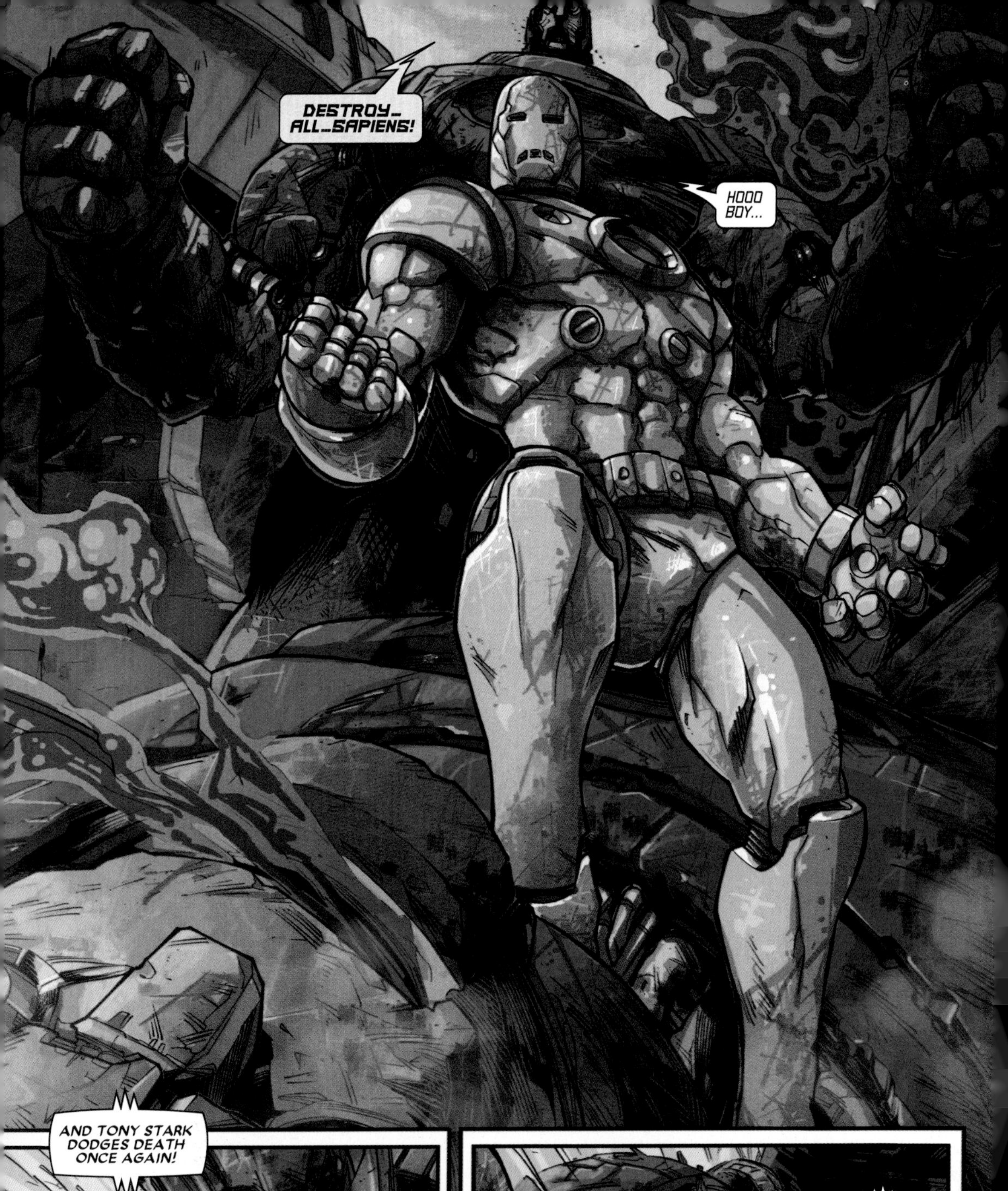
DESTROY_ ALL_SAPIENS!
HOOO BOY...

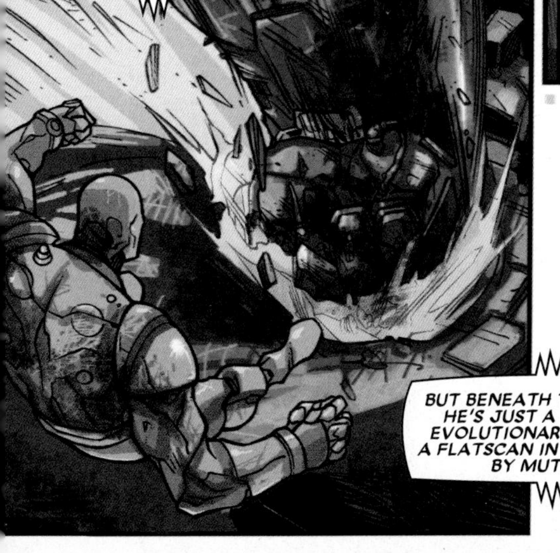
AND TONY STARK DODGES DEATH ONCE AGAIN!
BUT BENEATH THAT ARMOR, HE'S JUST A SAPIEN! AN EVOLUTIONARY DEAD END, A FLATSCAN IN A WORLD RUN BY MUTANTS!

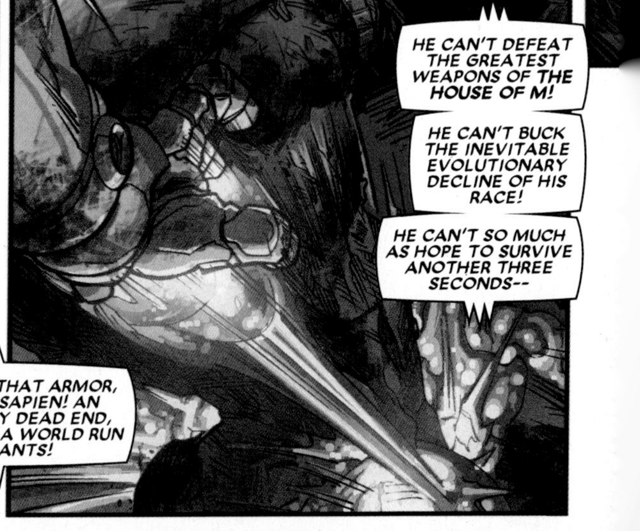
HE CAN'T DEFEAT THE GREATEST WEAPONS OF THE HOUSE OF M!
HE CAN'T BUCK THE INEVITABLE EVOLUTIONARY DECLINE OF HIS RACE!
HE CAN'T SO MUCH AS HOPE TO SURVIVE ANOTHER THREE SECONDS--

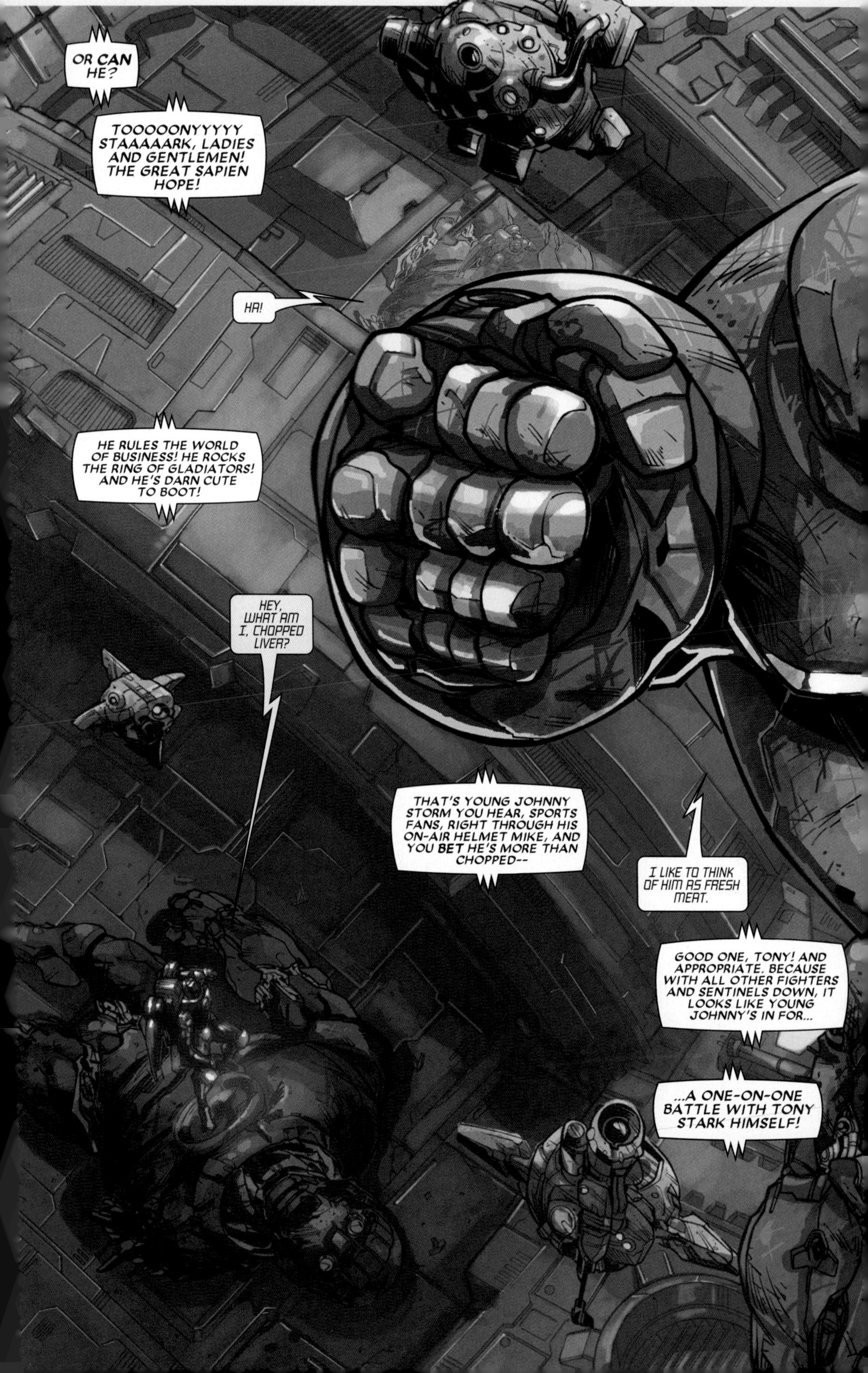
OR CAN HE?
TOOOOONYYYYY STAAAAARK, LADIES AND GENTLEMEN! THE GREAT SAPIEN HOPE!
HA!
HE RULES THE WORLD OF BUSINESS! HE ROCKS THE RING OF GLADIATORS! AND HE'S DARN CUTE TO BOOT!
HEY, WHAT AM I, CHOPPED LIVER?
THAT'S YOUNG JOHNNY STORM YOU HEAR, SPORTS FANS, RIGHT THROUGH HIS ON-AIR HELMET MIKE, AND YOU BET HE'S MORE THAN CHOPPED--
I LIKE TO THINK OF HIM AS FRESH MEAT.
GOOD ONE, TONY! AND APPROPRIATE. BECAUSE WITH ALL OTHER FIGHTERS AND SENTINELS DOWN, IT LOOKS LIKE YOUNG JOHNNY'S IN FOR...
...A ONE-ON-ONE BATTLE WITH TONY STARK HIMSELF!

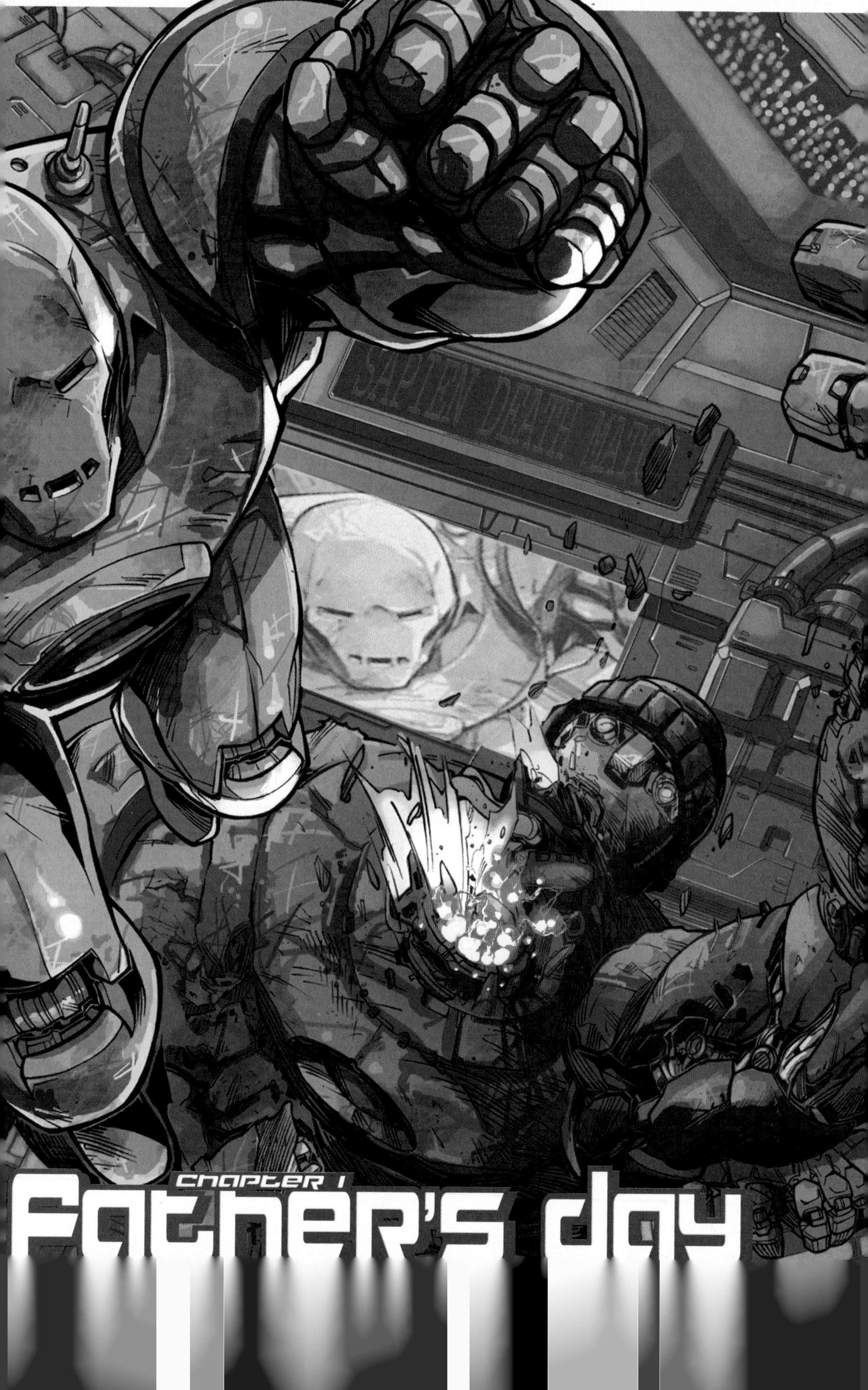
SAPIEN DEATH
CHAPTER 1
Father's day

The New Avengers and the Astonishing X-Men met to discuss the fate of Wanda Maximoff, the Scarlet Witch–the daughter of the powerful mutant terrorist Magneto. After losing control of her reality-altering powers and suffering a total nervous breakdown, Wanda unleashed chaos upon the Avengers, killing and injuring many of their number. Magneto intervened and took his daughter to the devastated island-nation of Genosha, where Charles Xavier—Professor X, the founder of the X-Men—was to help her recover. Xavier failed, and now it is up to Wanda's friends and teammates to decide whether she will live or die. But Magneto, Wanda, and her brother Pietro disappear...

Then the world burns to white. Reality as we knew it is gone...

...to be replaced by a society in which humans are the oppressed minority and mutants run the culture, ruling over all existing countries, religions, and politics. A kingdom united under the House of M.

HOUSE OF M

Mutants rule the world. Homo sapiens, few in number, cling to the margins, warming themselves on the last faint flickers of life before extinction.

The new masters won by changing the past. Those who would fight to restore the human order have been given impossible new lives, impossible new histories to keep them occupied.

Tony Stark's genius and business savvy have made Stark Enterprises one of the biggest corporations on the planet, making Tony the world's most successful Sapien. But he's just that...a Sapien. And in a world run by mutants, a Sapien can only go so high.

Tony also owes much of his success to his father, Howard Stark, who continues to aid and advise him in the running of Stark Enterprises. For all his success, Tony has never really stepped out of his father's long shadow...

SURE YOU'RE UP FOR THIS, HOTSHOT?

BRING IT ON, PLAYBOY.

'CAUSE WE CAN ALWAYS JUST SHAKE HANDS AND--

FLAME ON!

WELL, THAT'S--

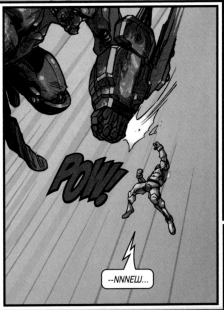

POW!

--NNNEW...

UNBELIEVABLE! TONY STARK, SURPRISED BY A BLAST OF FIRE AND KNOCKED INTO A PILE OF DEBRIS BY JOHNNY STORM?

WHAT'S SO UNBELIEVABLE ABOUT--

RRRRUUUMMMBLE

UH-OH.

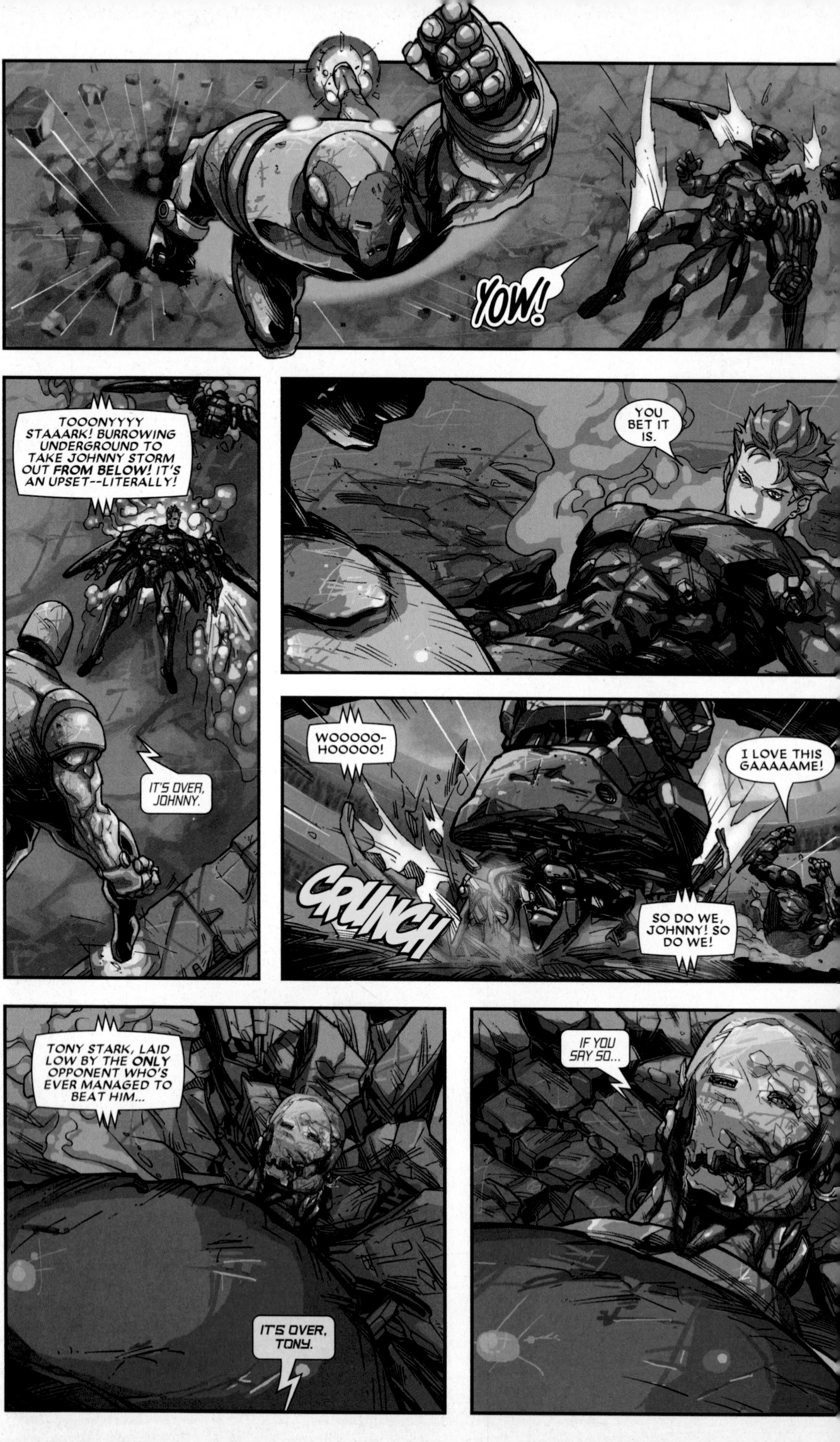
YOW!
TOOONYYYY STAAARK! BURROWING UNDERGROUND TO TAKE JOHNNY STORM OUT FROM BELOW! IT'S AN UPSET--LITERALLY!
IT'S OVER, JOHNNY.
YOU BET IT IS.
WOOOOO-HOOOOO!
I LOVE THIS GAAAAAME!
CRUNCH
SO DO WE, JOHNNY! SO DO WE!
TONY STARK, LAID LOW BY THE ONLY OPPONENT WHO'S EVER MANAGED TO BEAT HIM...
IT'S OVER, TONY.
IF YOU SAY SO...

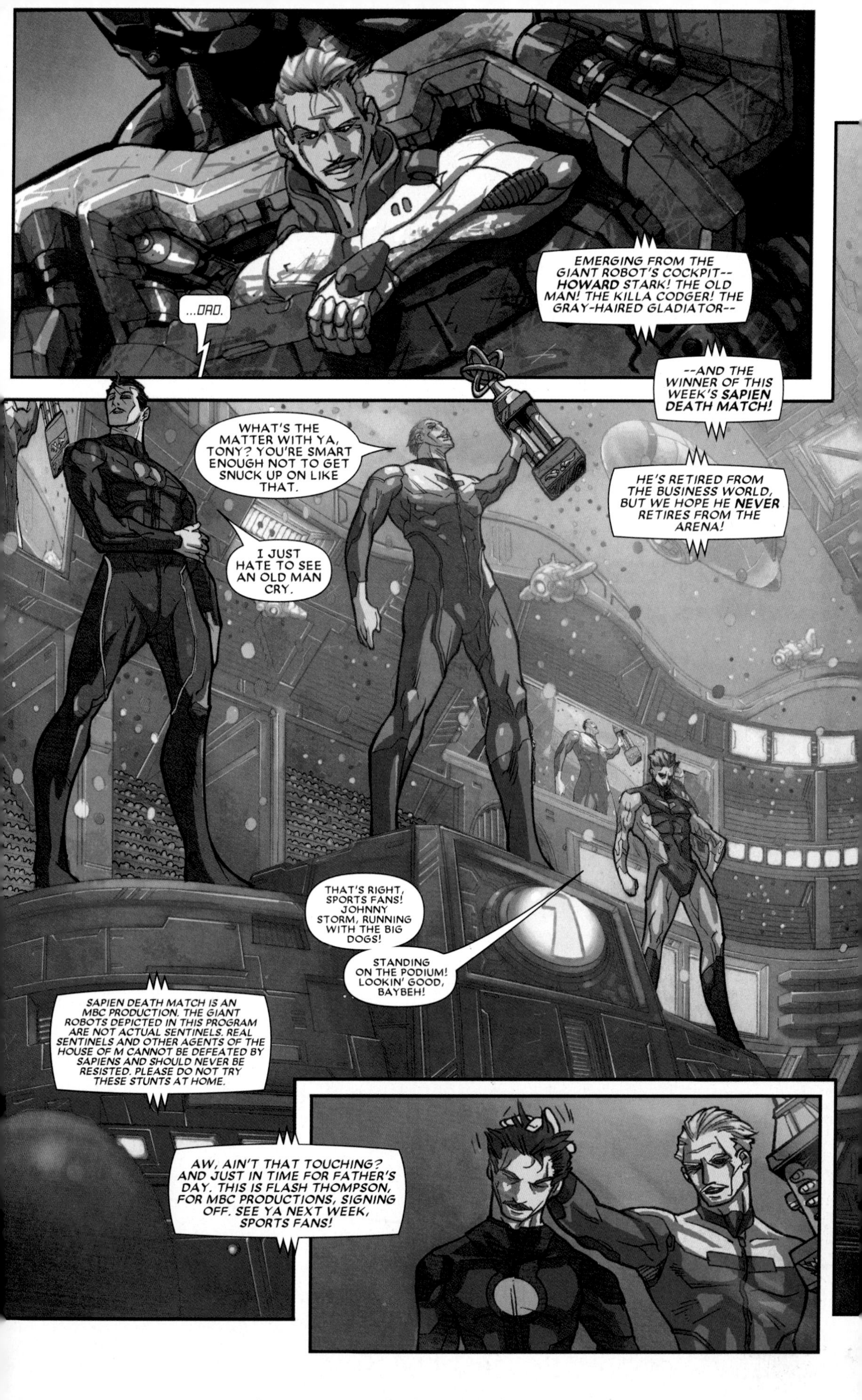
EMERGING FROM THE GIANT ROBOT'S COCKPIT-- HOWARD STARK! THE OLD MAN! THE KILLA CODGER! THE GRAY-HAIRED GLADIATOR--
...DAD.
--AND THE WINNER OF THIS WEEK'S SAPIEN DEATH MATCH!
WHAT'S THE MATTER WITH YA, TONY? YOU'RE SMART ENOUGH NOT TO GET SNUCK UP ON LIKE THAT.
I JUST HATE TO SEE AN OLD MAN CRY.
HE'S RETIRED FROM THE BUSINESS WORLD, BUT WE HOPE HE NEVER RETIRES FROM THE ARENA!
THAT'S RIGHT, SPORTS FANS! JOHNNY STORM, RUNNING WITH THE BIG DOGS!
STANDING ON THE PODIUM! LOOKIN' GOOD, BAYBEH!
SAPIEN DEATH MATCH IS AN MBC PRODUCTION. THE GIANT ROBOTS DEPICTED IN THIS PROGRAM ARE NOT ACTUAL SENTINELS. REAL SENTINELS AND OTHER AGENTS OF THE HOUSE OF M CANNOT BE DEFEATED BY SAPIENS AND SHOULD NEVER BE RESISTED. PLEASE DO NOT TRY THESE STUNTS AT HOME.
AW, AIN'T THAT TOUCHING? AND JUST IN TIME FOR FATHER'S DAY. THIS IS FLASH THOMPSON, FOR MBC PRODUCTIONS, SIGNING OFF. SEE YA NEXT WEEK, SPORTS FANS!

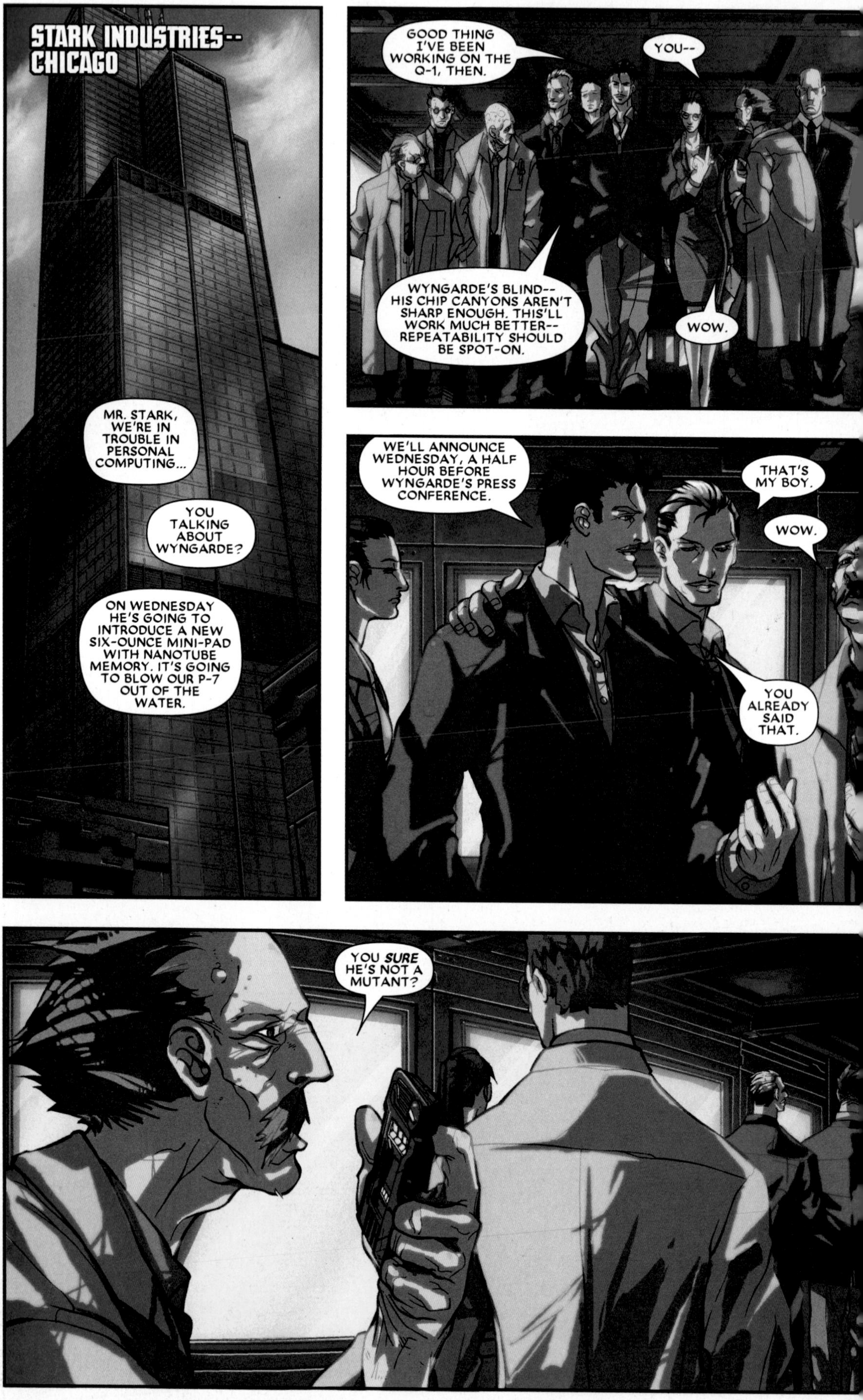
STARK INDUSTRIES-- CHICAGO
MR. STARK, WE'RE IN TROUBLE IN PERSONAL COMPUTING...
YOU TALKING ABOUT WYNGARDE?
ON WEDNESDAY HE'S GOING TO INTRODUCE A NEW SIX-OUNCE MINI-PAD WITH NANOTUBE MEMORY. IT'S GOING TO BLOW OUR P-7 OUT OF THE WATER.
GOOD THING I'VE BEEN WORKING ON THE Q-1, THEN.
YOU--
WYNGARDE'S BLIND-- HIS CHIP CANYONS AREN'T SHARP ENOUGH. THIS'LL WORK MUCH BETTER-- REPEATABILITY SHOULD BE SPOT-ON.
WOW.
WE'LL ANNOUNCE WEDNESDAY, A HALF HOUR BEFORE WYNGARDE'S PRESS CONFERENCE.
THAT'S MY BOY.
WOW.
YOU ALREADY SAID THAT.
YOU *SURE* HE'S NOT A MUTANT?

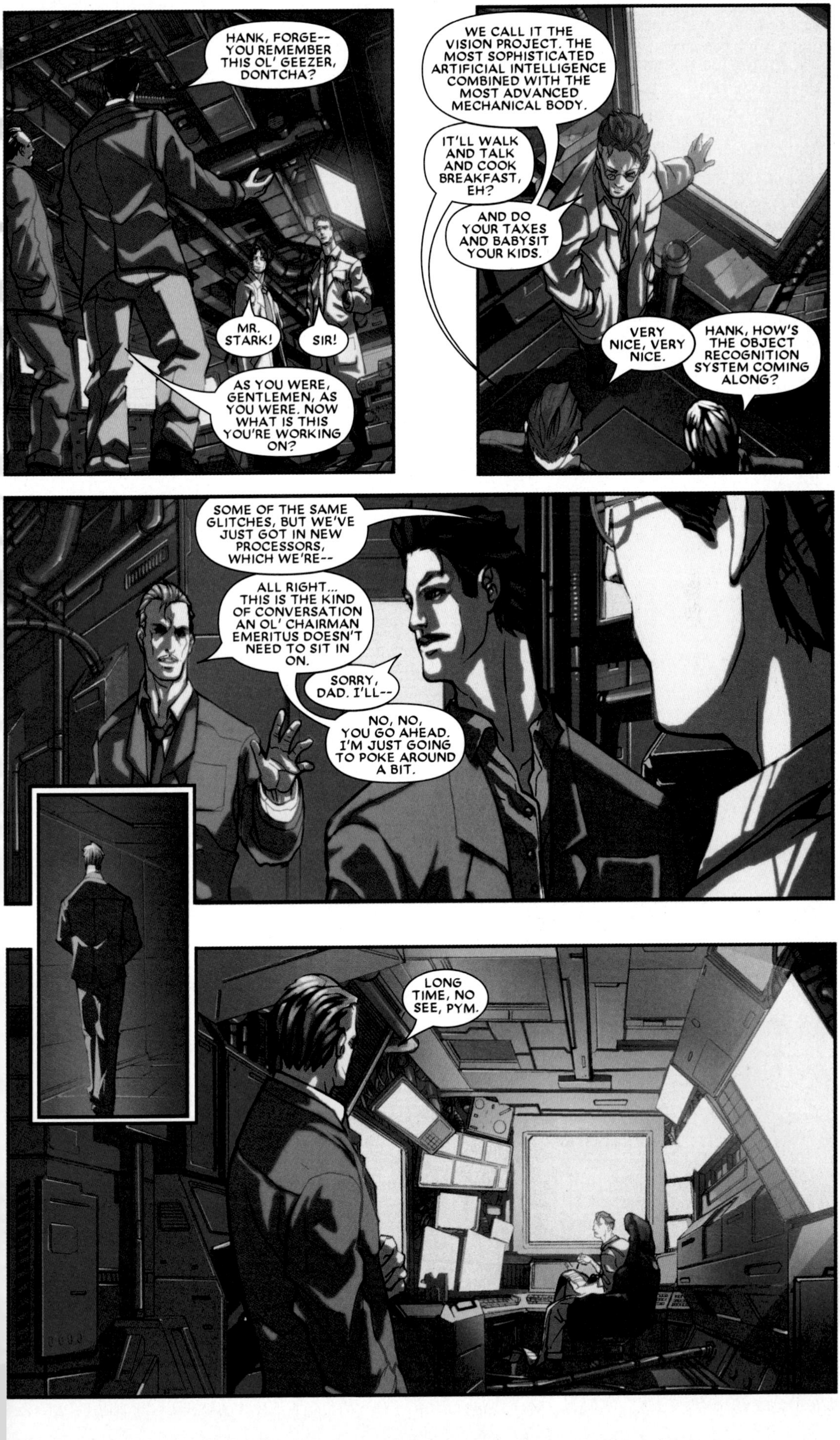
HANK, FORGE-- YOU REMEMBER THIS OL' GEEZER, DONTCHA?
MR. STARK!
SIR!
AS YOU WERE, GENTLEMEN, AS YOU WERE. NOW WHAT IS THIS YOU'RE WORKING ON?
WE CALL IT THE VISION PROJECT. THE MOST SOPHISTICATED ARTIFICIAL INTELLIGENCE COMBINED WITH THE MOST ADVANCED MECHANICAL BODY.
IT'LL WALK AND TALK AND COOK BREAKFAST, EH?
AND DO YOUR TAXES AND BABYSIT YOUR KIDS.
VERY NICE, VERY NICE.
HANK, HOW'S THE OBJECT RECOGNITION SYSTEM COMING ALONG?
SOME OF THE SAME GLITCHES, BUT WE'VE JUST GOT IN NEW PROCESSORS, WHICH WE'RE--
ALL RIGHT... THIS IS THE KIND OF CONVERSATION AN OL' CHAIRMAN EMERITUS DOESN'T NEED TO SIT IN ON.
SORRY, DAD. I'LL--
NO, NO, YOU GO AHEAD. I'M JUST GOING TO POKE AROUND A BIT.
LONG TIME, NO SEE, PYM.

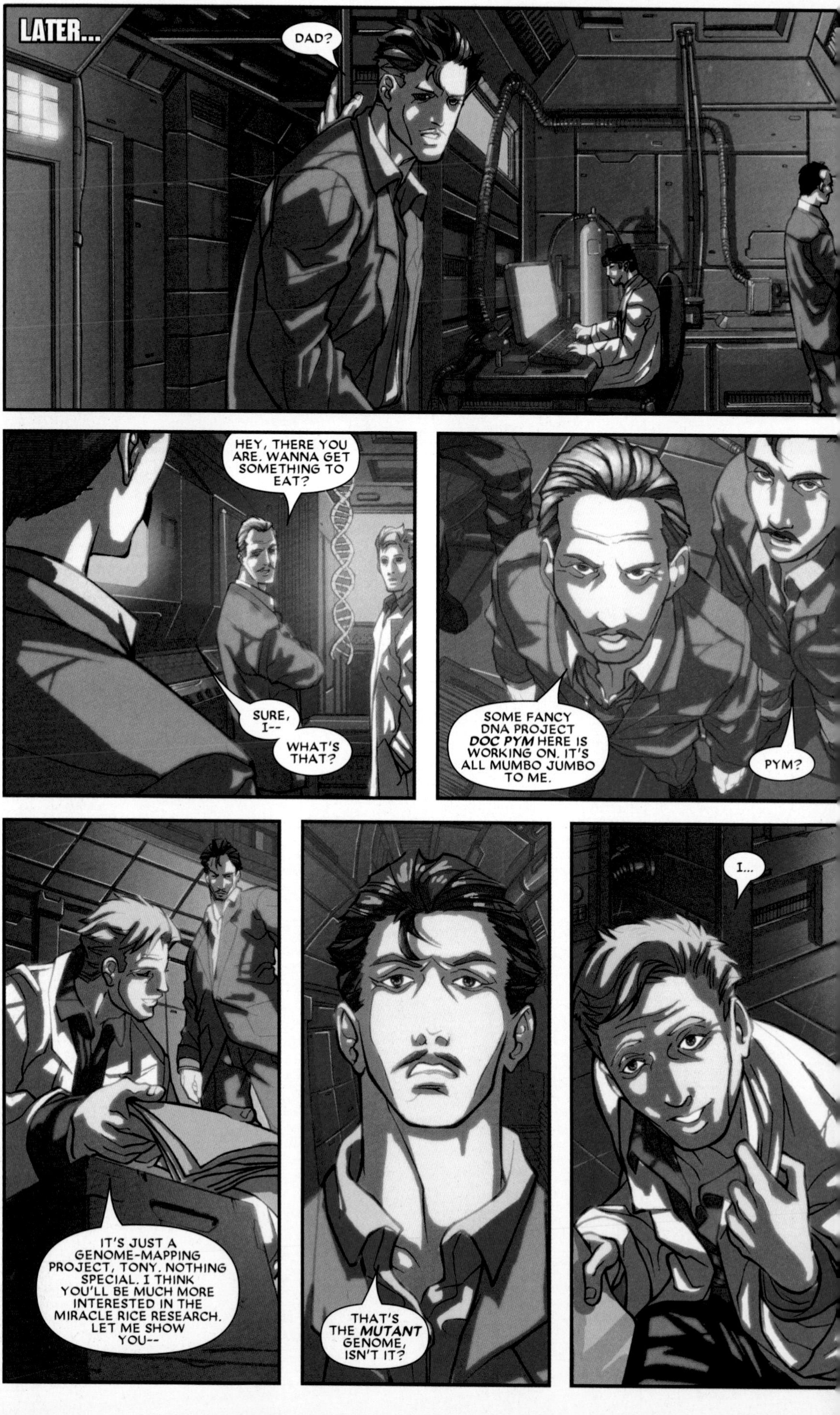

LATER...
DAD?
HEY, THERE YOU ARE. WANNA GET SOMETHING TO EAT?
SURE, I--
WHAT'S THAT?
SOME FANCY DNA PROJECT *DOC PYM* HERE IS WORKING ON. IT'S ALL MUMBO JUMBO TO ME.
PYM?
IT'S JUST A GENOME-MAPPING PROJECT, TONY. NOTHING SPECIAL. I THINK YOU'LL BE MUCH MORE INTERESTED IN THE MIRACLE RICE RESEARCH. LET ME SHOW YOU--
THAT'S THE *MUTANT* GENOME, ISN'T IT?
I...

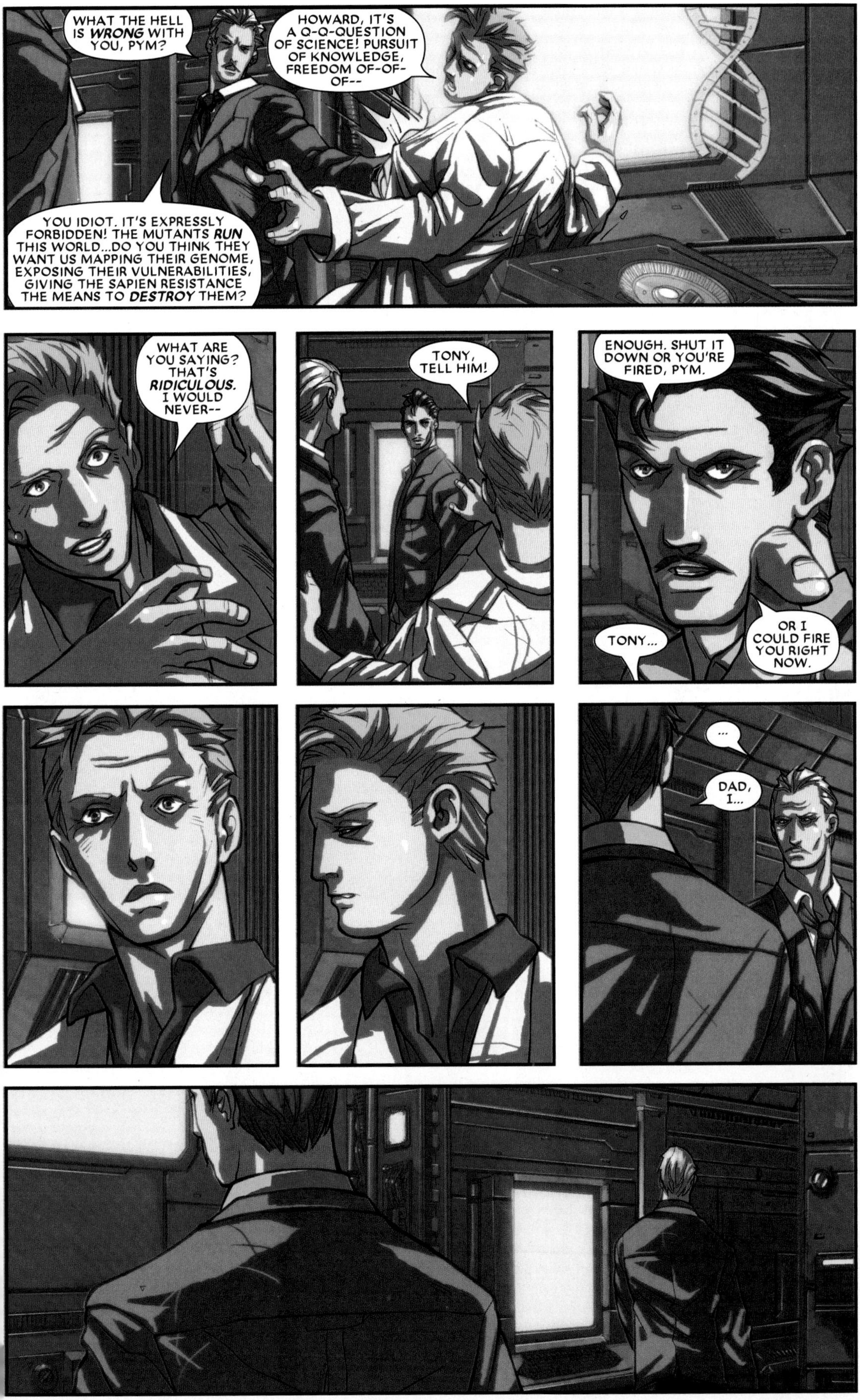

WHAT THE HELL IS *WRONG* WITH YOU, PYM?
HOWARD, IT'S A Q-Q-QUESTION OF SCIENCE! PURSUIT OF KNOWLEDGE, FREEDOM OF-OF-OF--
YOU IDIOT. IT'S EXPRESSLY FORBIDDEN! THE MUTANTS *RUN* THIS WORLD...DO YOU THINK THEY WANT US MAPPING THEIR GENOME, EXPOSING THEIR VULNERABILITIES, GIVING THE SAPIEN RESISTANCE THE MEANS TO *DESTROY* THEM?
WHAT ARE YOU SAYING? THAT'S *RIDICULOUS.* I WOULD NEVER--
TONY, TELL HIM!
ENOUGH. SHUT IT DOWN OR YOU'RE FIRED, PYM.
TONY...
OR I COULD FIRE YOU RIGHT NOW.
...
DAD, I...

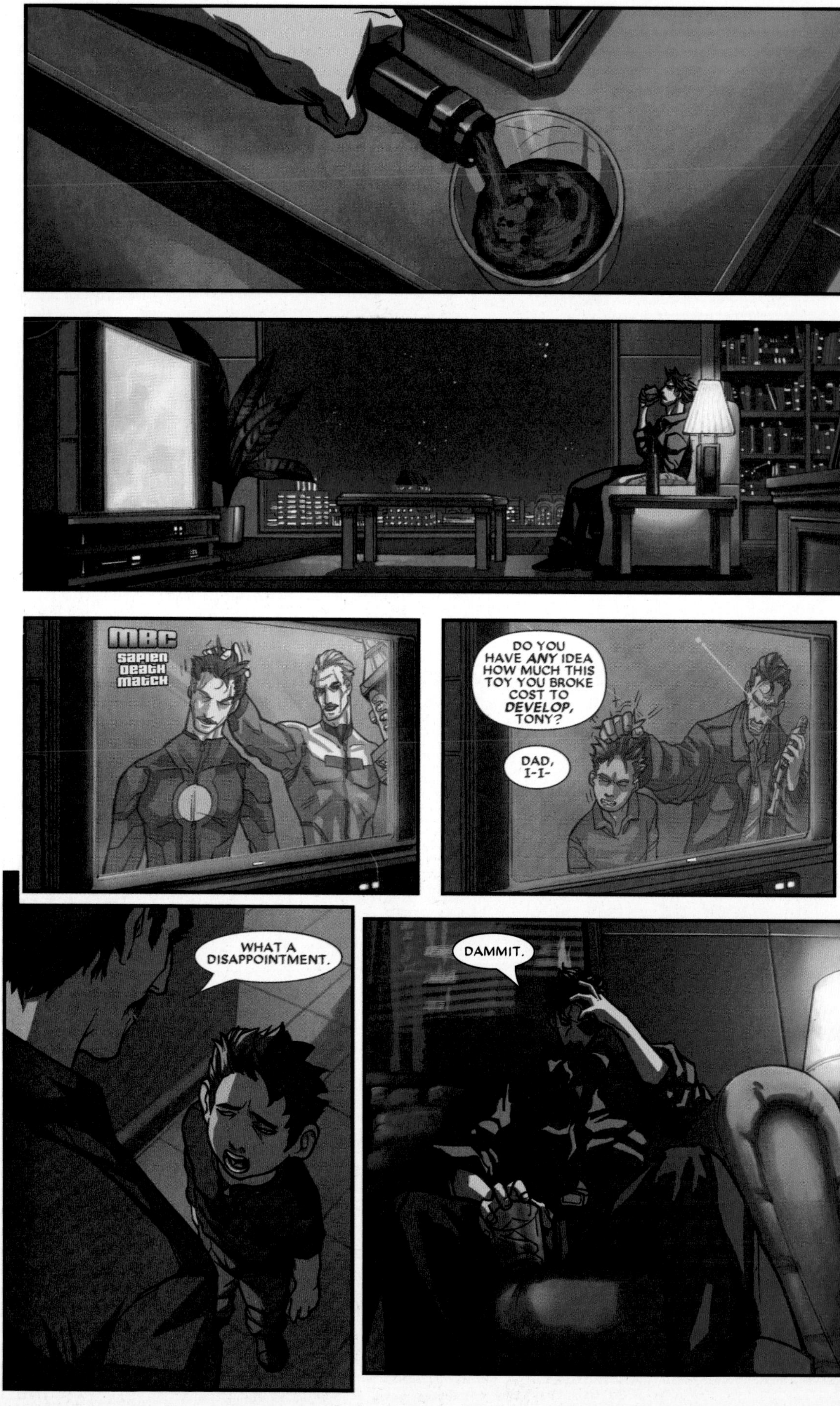

MBC
SAPIEN DEATH MATCH
DO YOU HAVE ANY IDEA HOW MUCH THIS TOY YOU BROKE COST TO DEVELOP, TONY?
DAD, I-I-
WHAT A DISAPPOINTMENT.
DAMMIT.

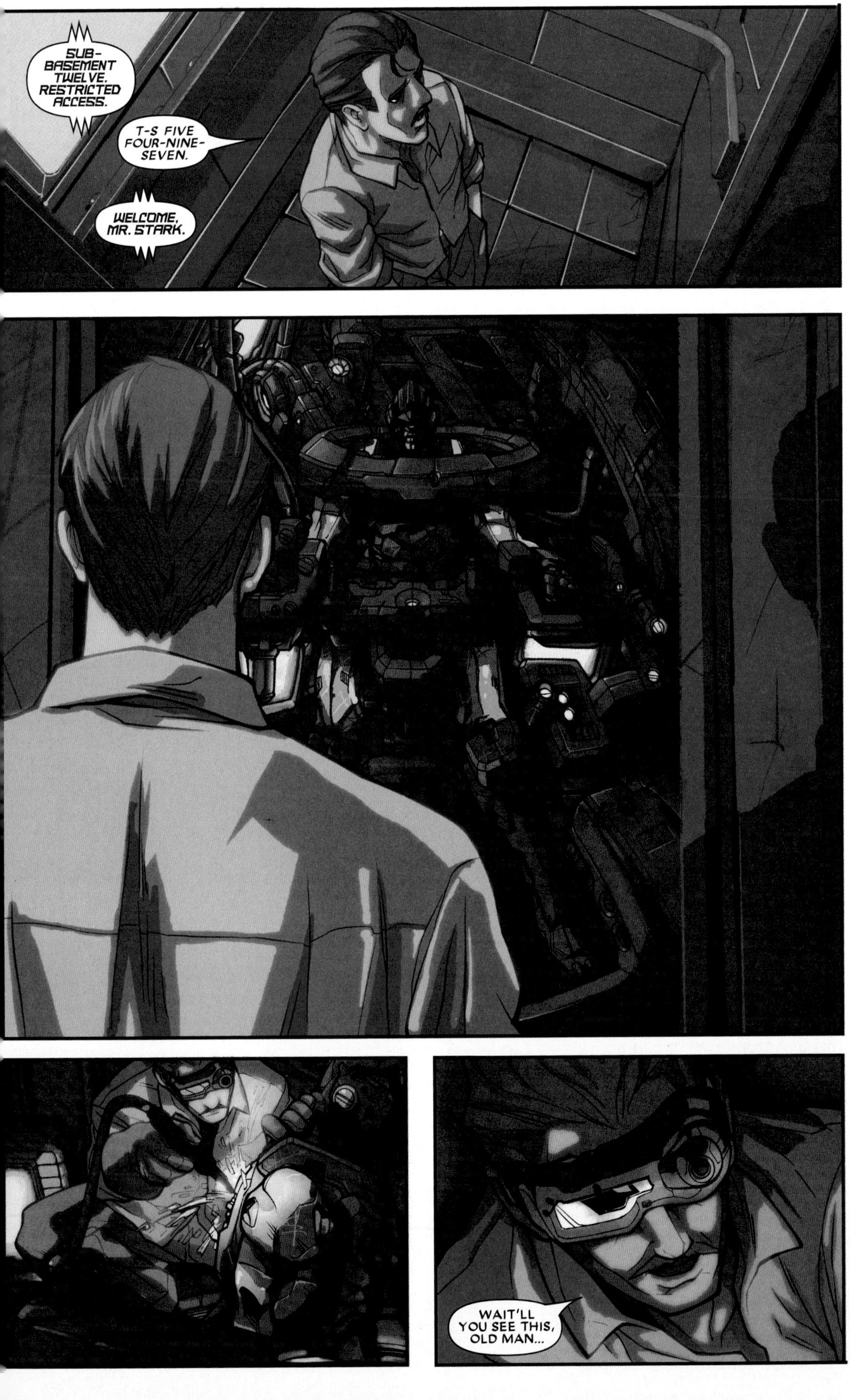
SUB-BASEMENT TWELVE. RESTRICTED ACCESS.
T-S FIVE FOUR-NINE-SEVEN.
WELCOME, MR. STARK.
WAIT'LL YOU SEE THIS, OLD MAN...

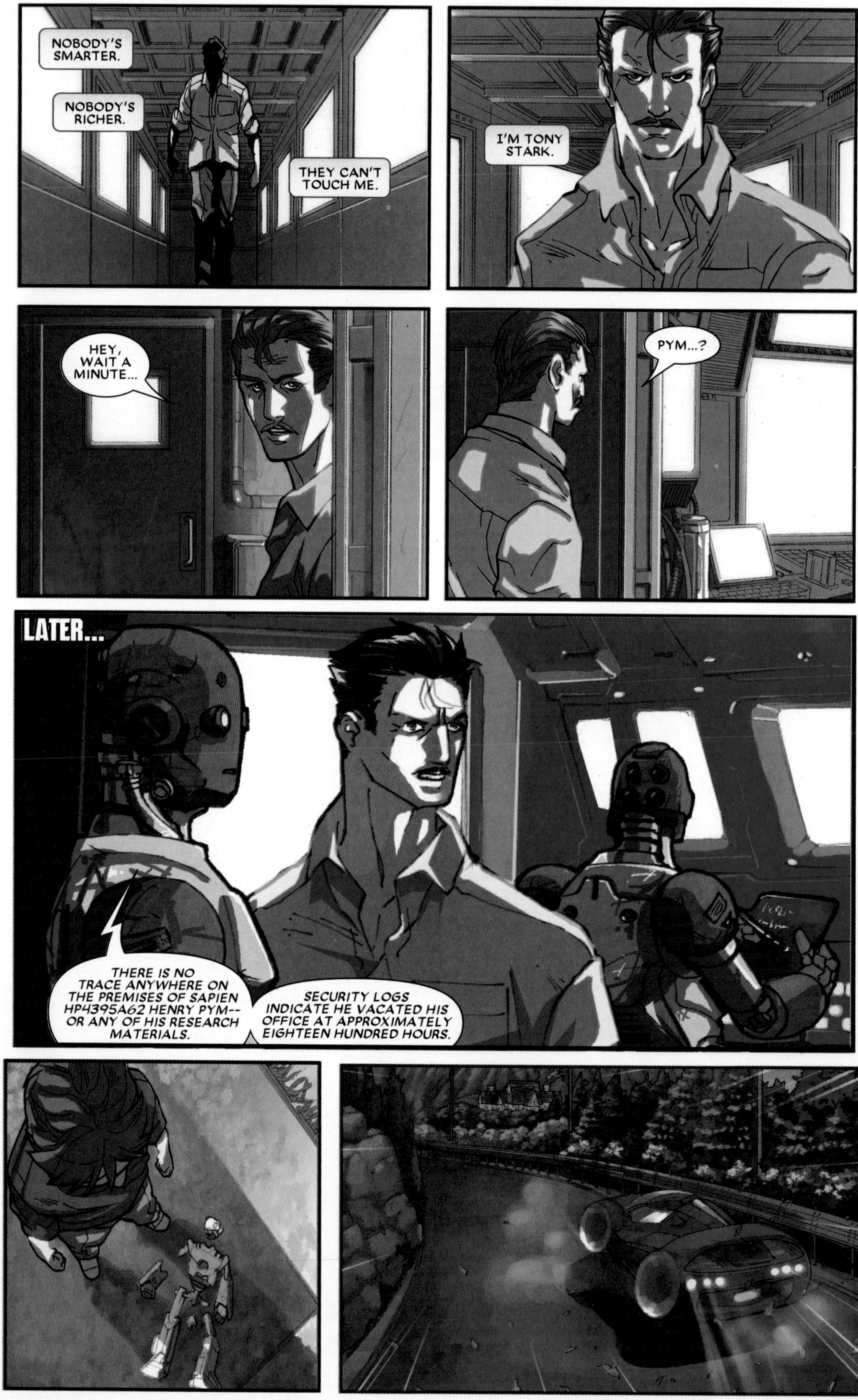
NOBODY'S SMARTER.
NOBODY'S RICHER.
THEY CAN'T TOUCH ME.
I'M TONY STARK.
HEY, WAIT A MINUTE...
PYM...?
LATER...
THERE IS NO TRACE ANYWHERE ON THE PREMISES OF SAPIEN HP4395A62 HENRY PYM-- OR ANY OF HIS RESEARCH MATERIALS.
SECURITY LOGS INDICATE HE VACATED HIS OFFICE AT APPROXIMATELY EIGHTEEN HUNDRED HOURS.

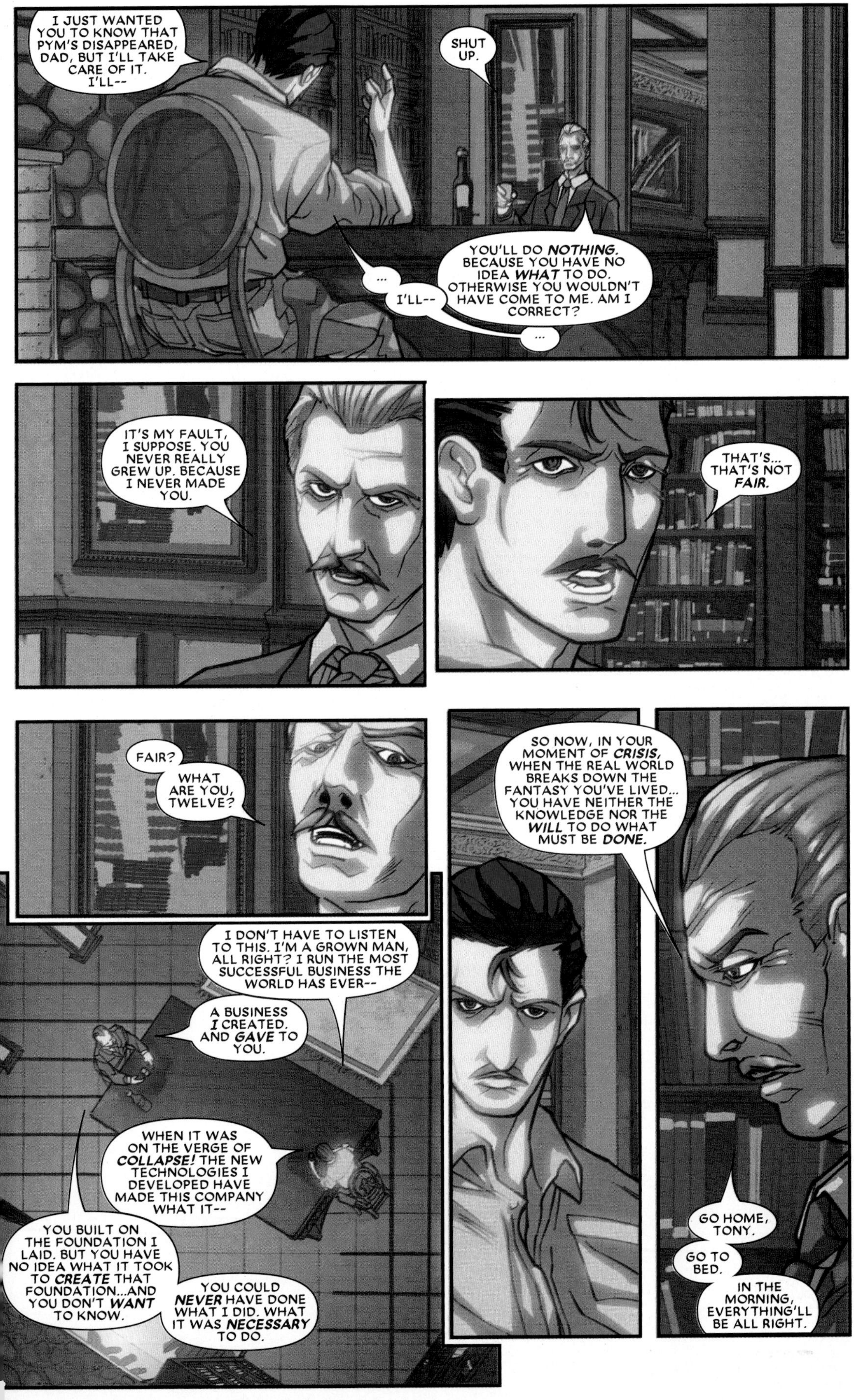

I JUST WANTED YOU TO KNOW THAT PYM'S DISAPPEARED, DAD, BUT I'LL TAKE CARE OF IT. I'LL--
SHUT UP.
...
YOU'LL DO ***NOTHING.*** BECAUSE YOU HAVE NO IDEA ***WHAT*** TO DO. OTHERWISE YOU WOULDN'T HAVE COME TO ME. AM I CORRECT?
I'LL--
...
IT'S MY FAULT, I SUPPOSE. YOU NEVER REALLY GREW UP. BECAUSE I NEVER MADE YOU.
THAT'S... THAT'S NOT ***FAIR.***
FAIR?
WHAT ARE YOU, TWELVE?
I DON'T HAVE TO LISTEN TO THIS. I'M A GROWN MAN, ALL RIGHT? I RUN THE MOST SUCCESSFUL BUSINESS THE WORLD HAS EVER--
A BUSINESS ***I*** CREATED. AND ***GAVE*** TO YOU.
WHEN IT WAS ON THE VERGE OF ***COLLAPSE!*** THE NEW TECHNOLOGIES I DEVELOPED HAVE MADE THIS COMPANY WHAT IT--
YOU BUILT ON THE FOUNDATION I LAID. BUT YOU HAVE NO IDEA WHAT IT TOOK TO ***CREATE*** THAT FOUNDATION...AND YOU DON'T ***WANT*** TO KNOW.
YOU COULD ***NEVER*** HAVE DONE WHAT I DID. WHAT IT WAS ***NECESSARY*** TO DO.
SO NOW, IN YOUR MOMENT OF ***CRISIS,*** WHEN THE REAL WORLD BREAKS DOWN THE FANTASY YOU'VE LIVED... YOU HAVE NEITHER THE KNOWLEDGE NOR THE ***WILL*** TO DO WHAT MUST BE ***DONE.***
GO HOME, TONY.
GO TO BED.
IN THE MORNING, EVERYTHING'LL BE ALL RIGHT.

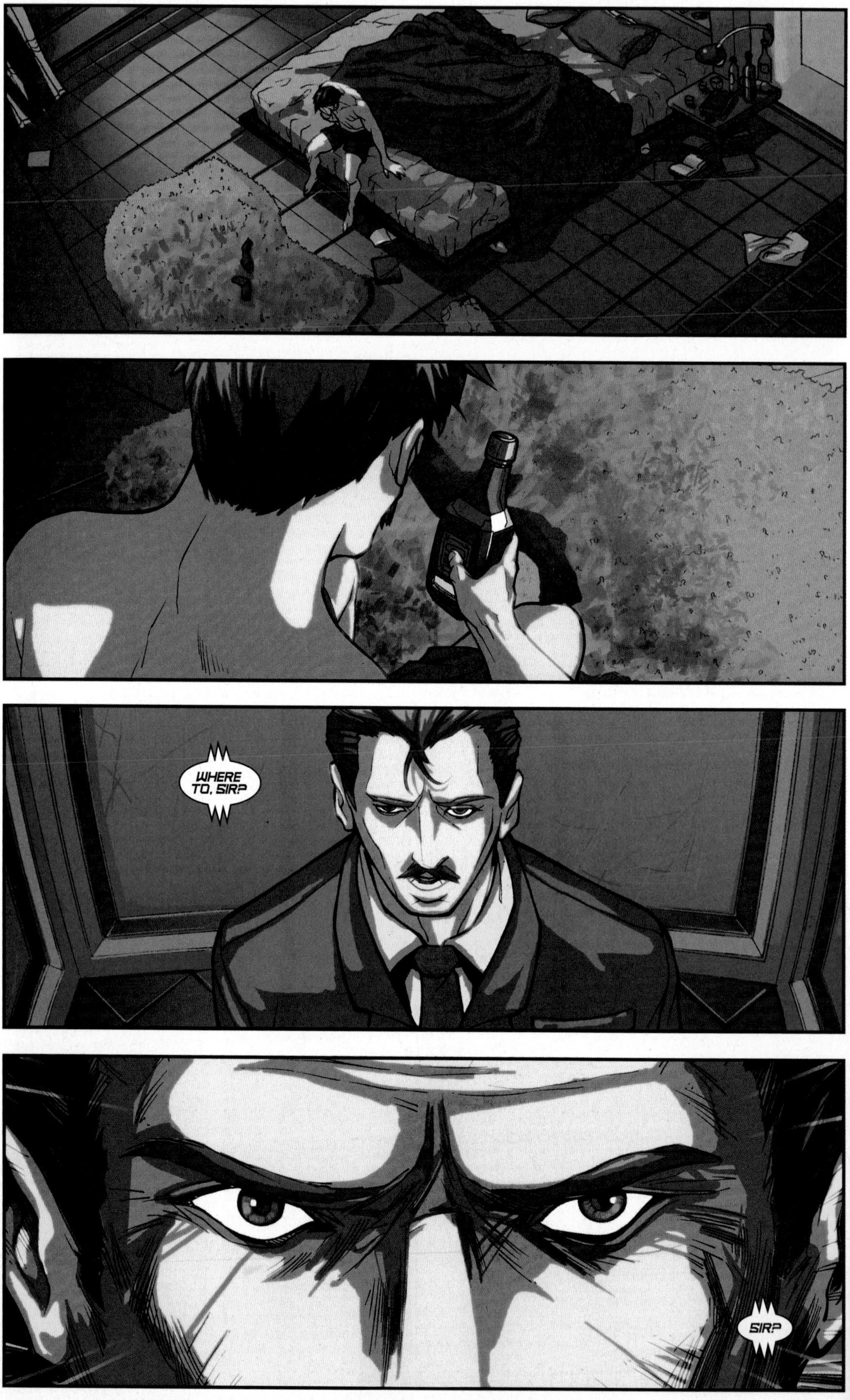
WHERE TO, SIR?
SIR?

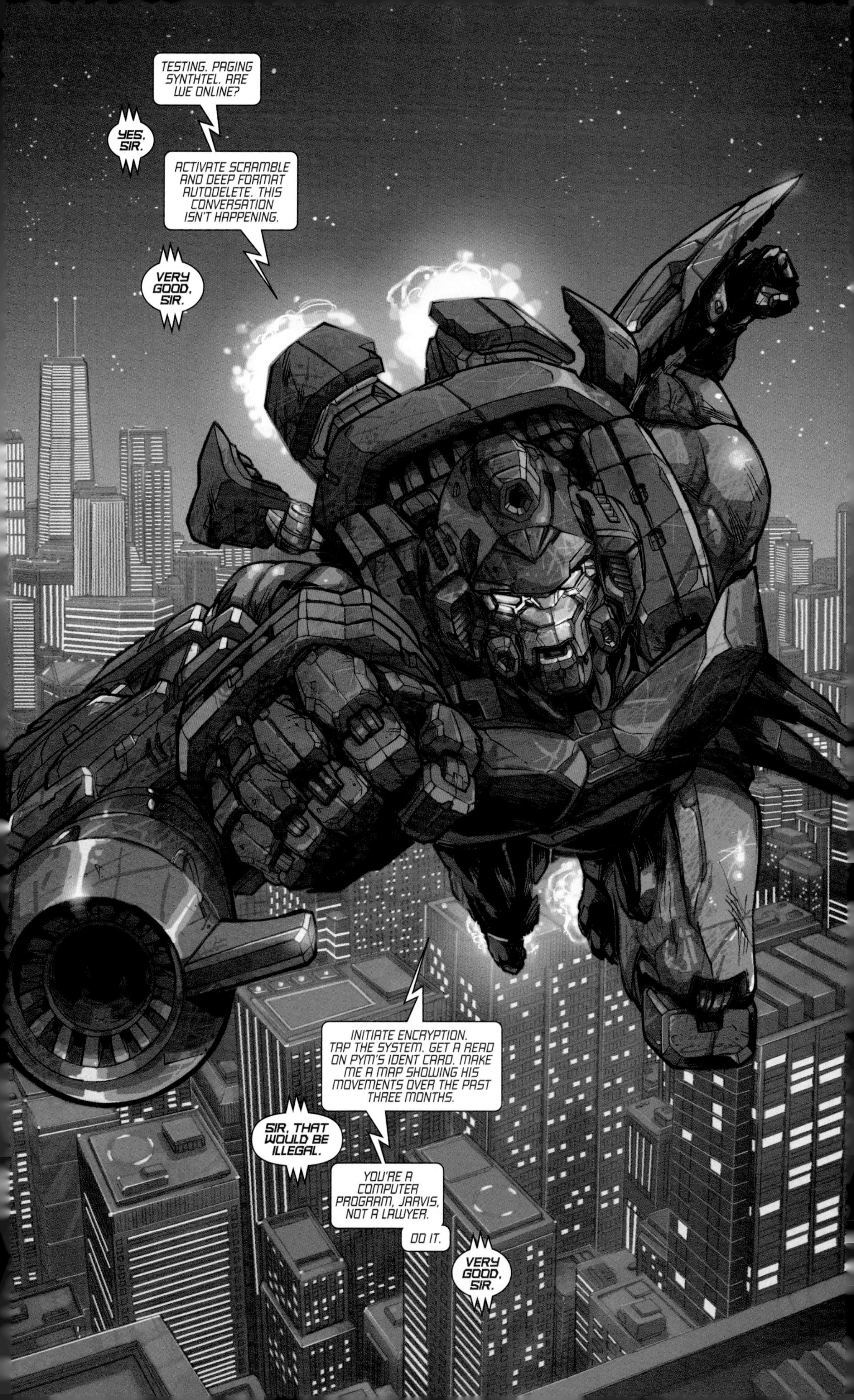
TESTING. PAGING SYNTHTEL. ARE WE ONLINE?
YES, SIR.
ACTIVATE SCRAMBLE AND DEEP FORMAT AUTODELETE. THIS CONVERSATION ISN'T HAPPENING.
VERY GOOD, SIR.
INITIATE ENCRYPTION. TAP THE SYSTEM. GET A READ ON PYM'S IDENT CARD. MAKE ME A MAP SHOWING HIS MOVEMENTS OVER THE PAST THREE MONTHS.
SIR, THAT WOULD BE ILLEGAL.
YOU'RE A COMPUTER PROGRAM, JARVIS, NOT A LAWYER.
DO IT.
VERY GOOD, SIR.

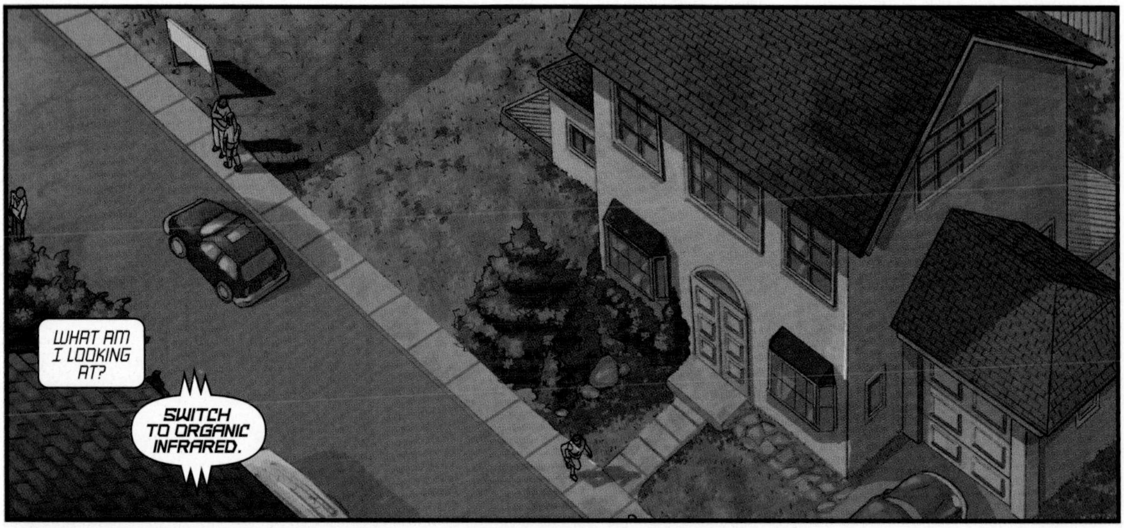
WHAT AM I LOOKING AT?
SWITCH TO ORGANIC INFRARED.

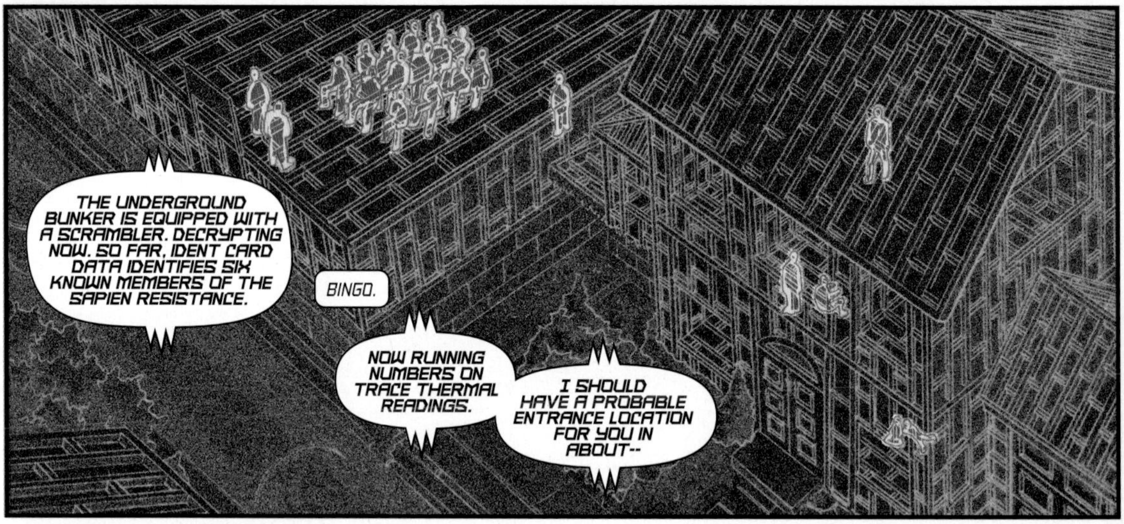
THE UNDERGROUND BUNKER IS EQUIPPED WITH A SCRAMBLER. DECRYPTING NOW. SO FAR, IDENT CARD DATA IDENTIFIES SIX KNOWN MEMBERS OF THE SAPIEN RESISTANCE.
BINGO.
NOW RUNNING NUMBERS ON TRACE THERMAL READINGS.
I SHOULD HAVE A PROBABLE ENTRANCE LOCATION FOR YOU IN ABOUT--

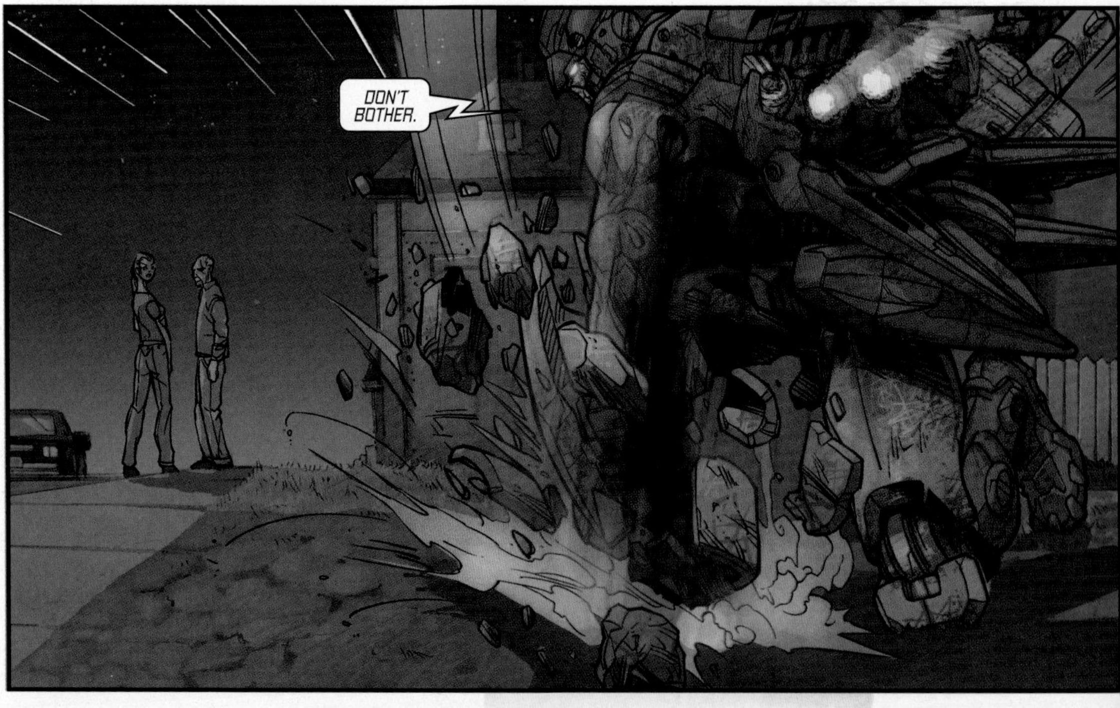
DON'T BOTHER.

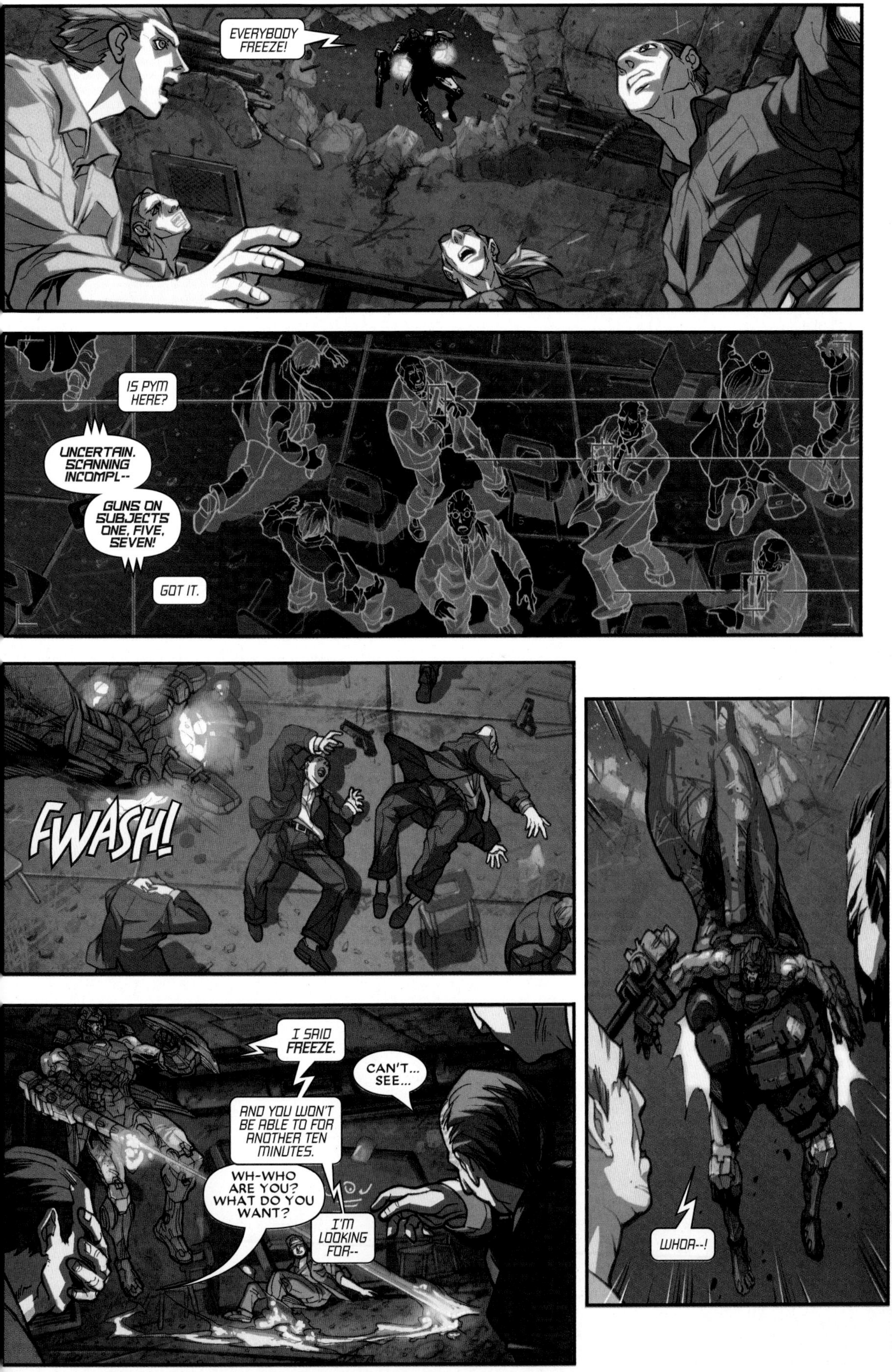
EVERYBODY FREEZE!
IS PYM HERE?
UNCERTAIN. SCANNING INCOMPL--
GUNS ON SUBJECTS ONE, FIVE, SEVEN!
GOT IT.
FWASH!
WHOA--!
I SAID FREEZE.
CAN'T... SEE...
AND YOU WON'T BE ABLE TO FOR ANOTHER TEN MINUTES.
WH-WHO ARE YOU? WHAT DO YOU WANT?
I'M LOOKING FOR--

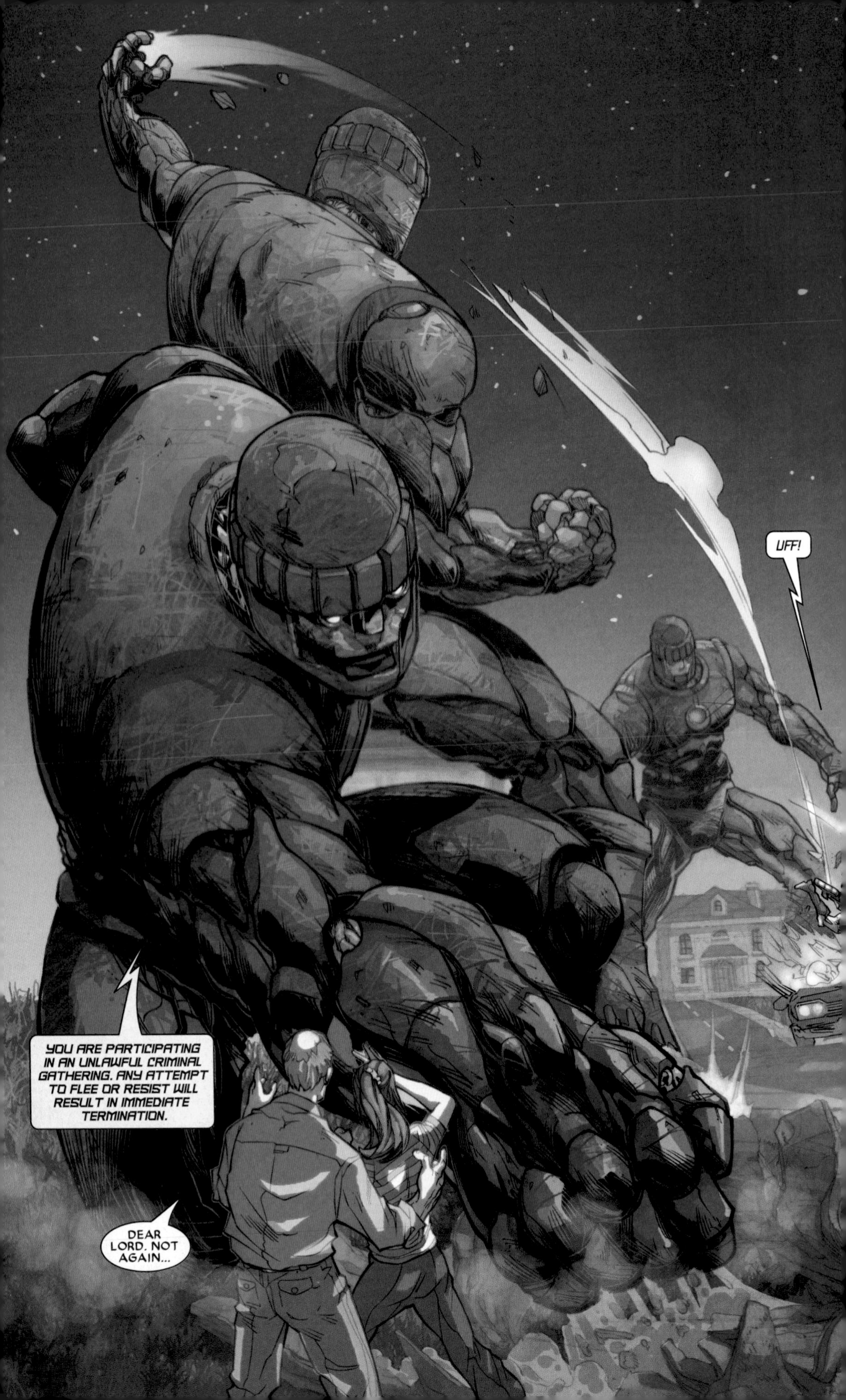
UFF!
YOU ARE PARTICIPATING IN AN UNLAWFUL CRIMINAL GATHERING. ANY ATTEMPT TO FLEE OR RESIST WILL RESULT IN IMMEDIATE TERMINATION.
DEAR LORD, NOT AGAIN...

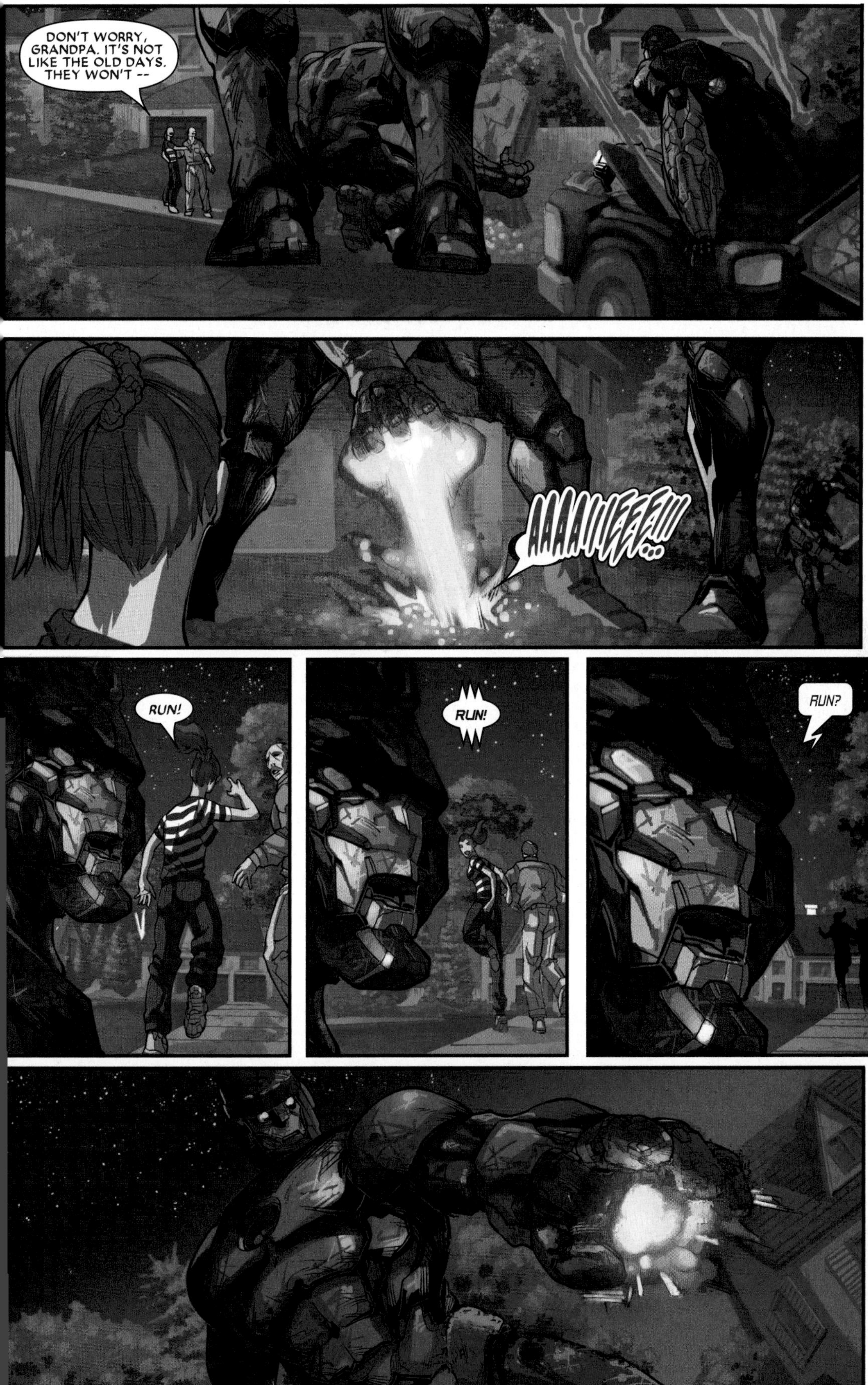
DON'T WORRY, GRANDPA. IT'S NOT LIKE THE OLD DAYS. THEY WON'T --
AAAAIIIEEE!!!
RUN!
RUN!
RUN?

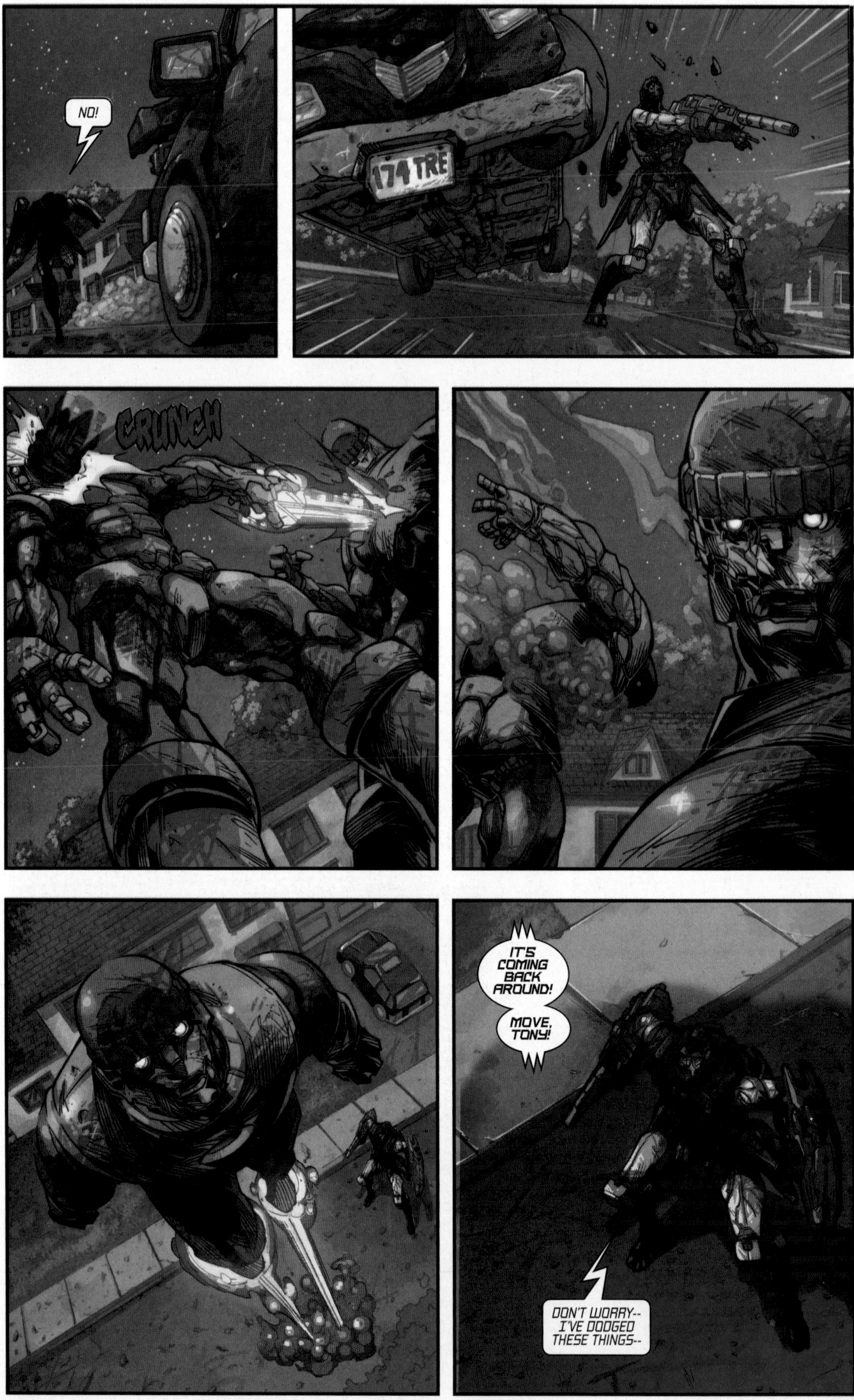
NO!
174 TRE
CRUNCH
IT'S COMING BACK AROUND!
MOVE, TONY!
DON'T WORRY-- I'VE DODGED THESE THINGS--

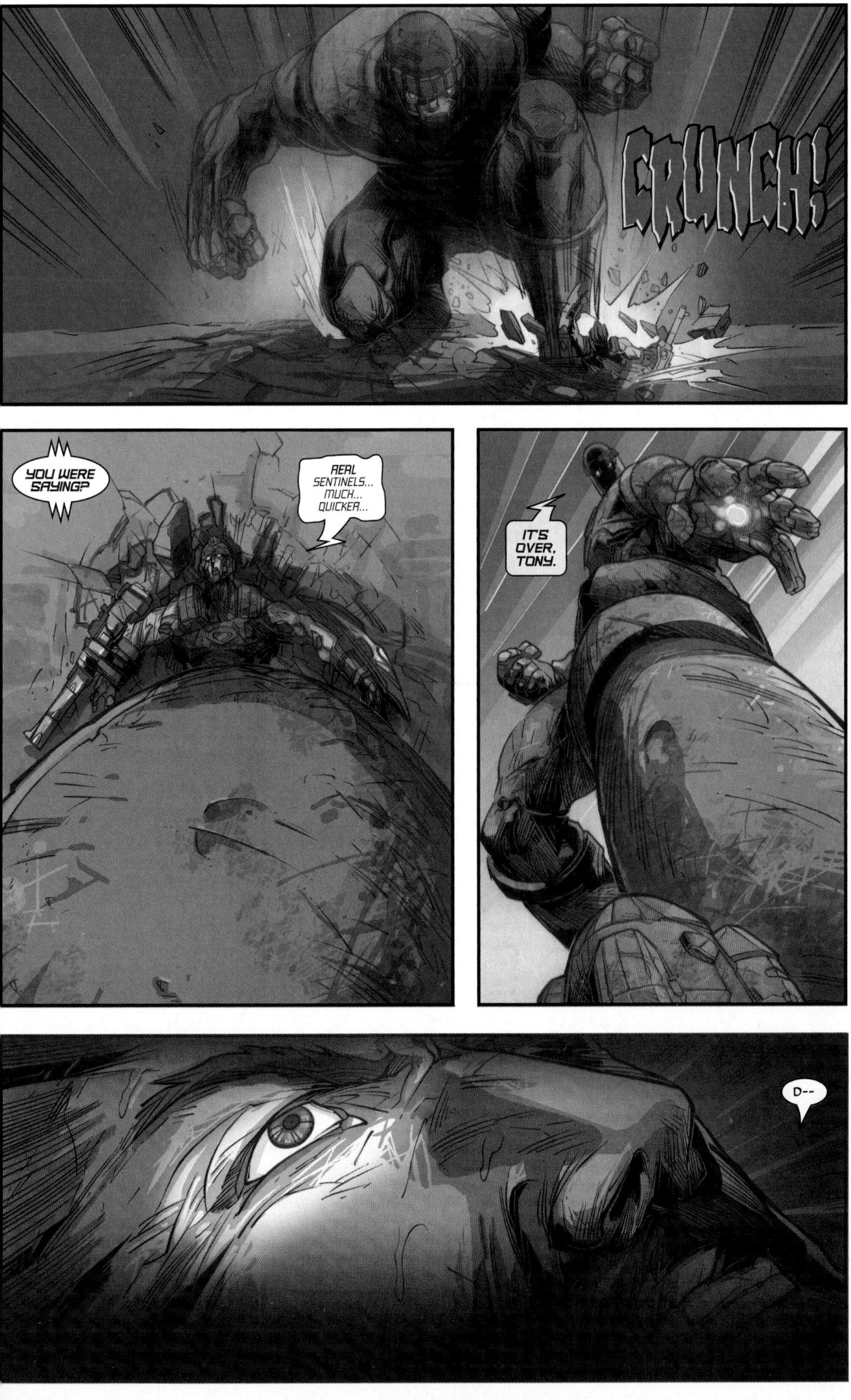
CRUNCH!
YOU WERE SAYING?
REAL SENTINELS... MUCH... QUICKER...
IT'S OVER, TONY.
D--

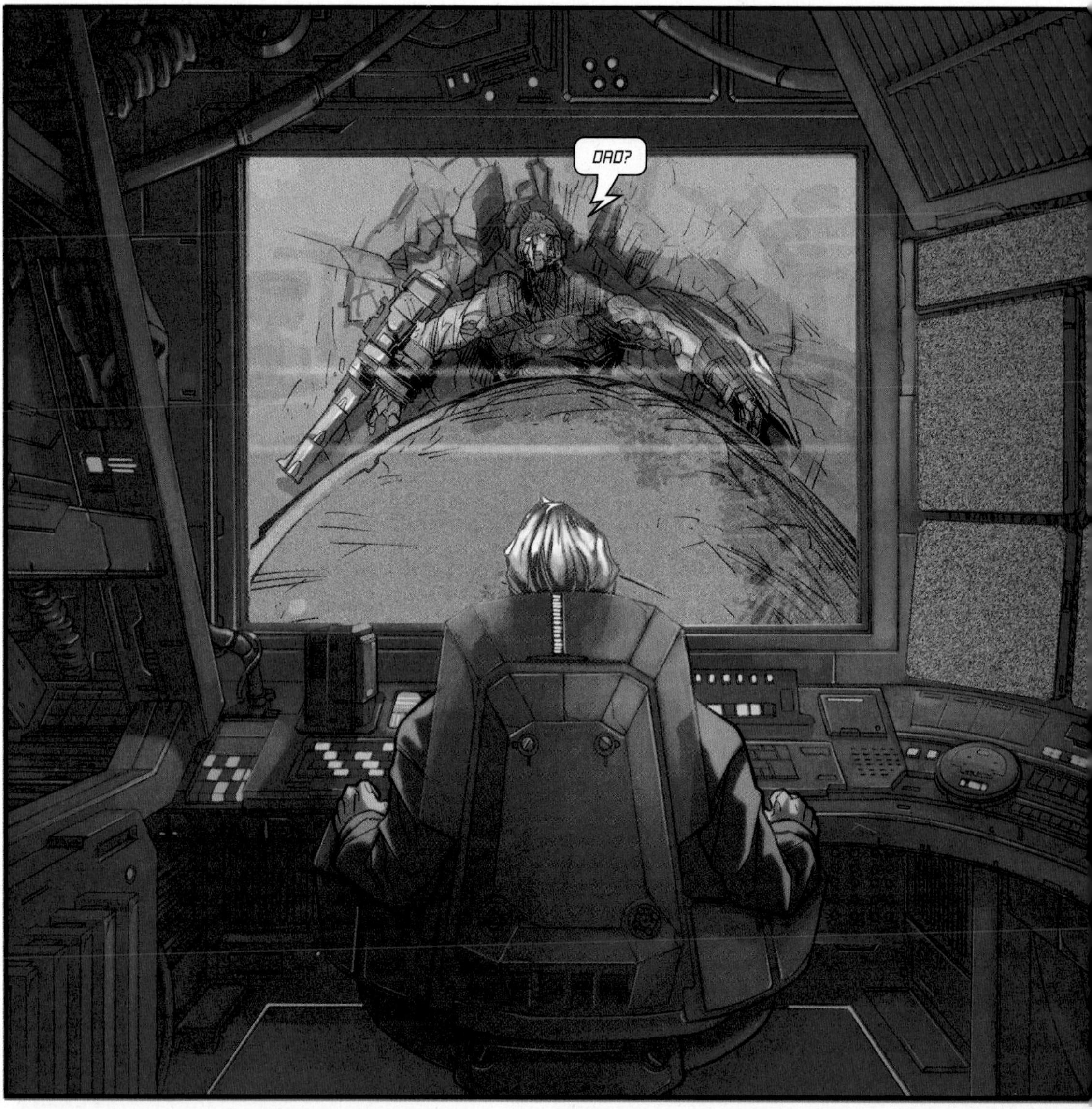
DAD?

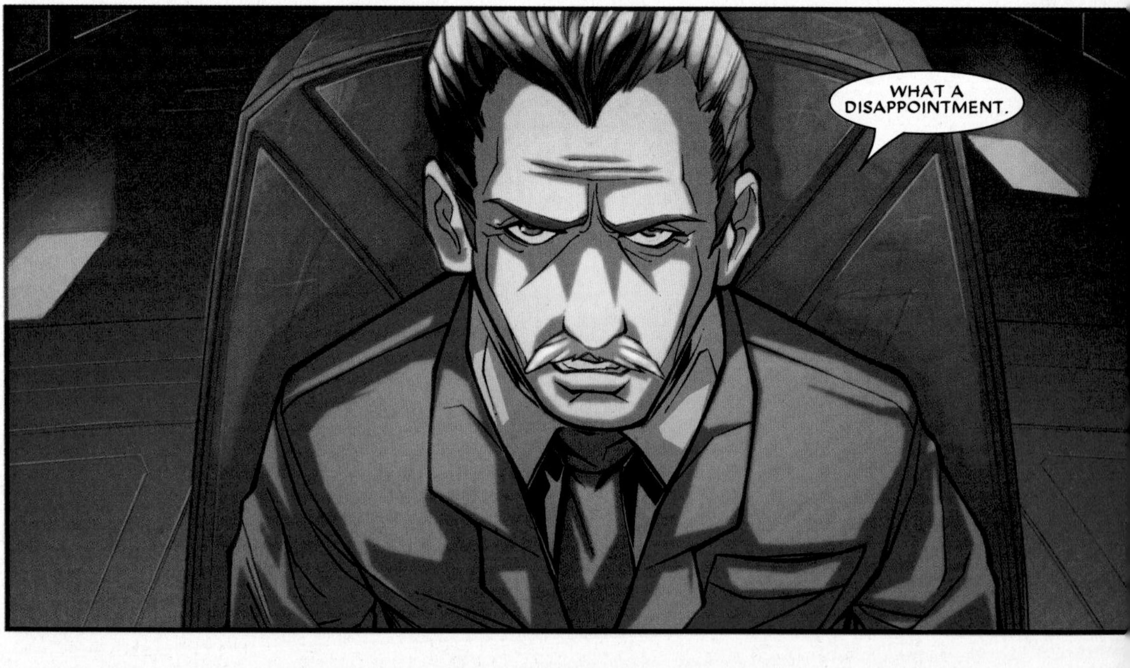
WHAT A DISAPPOINTMENT.

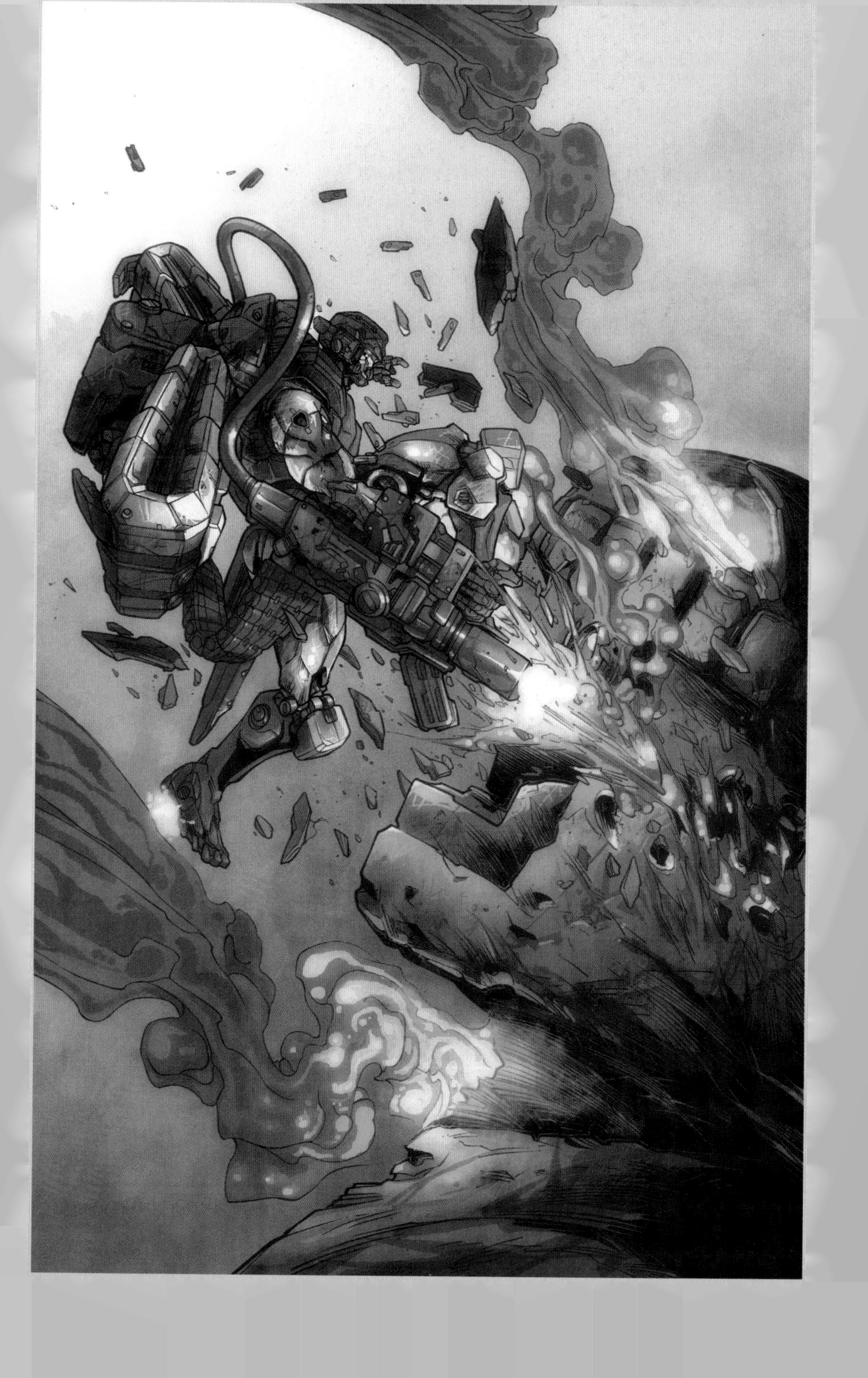

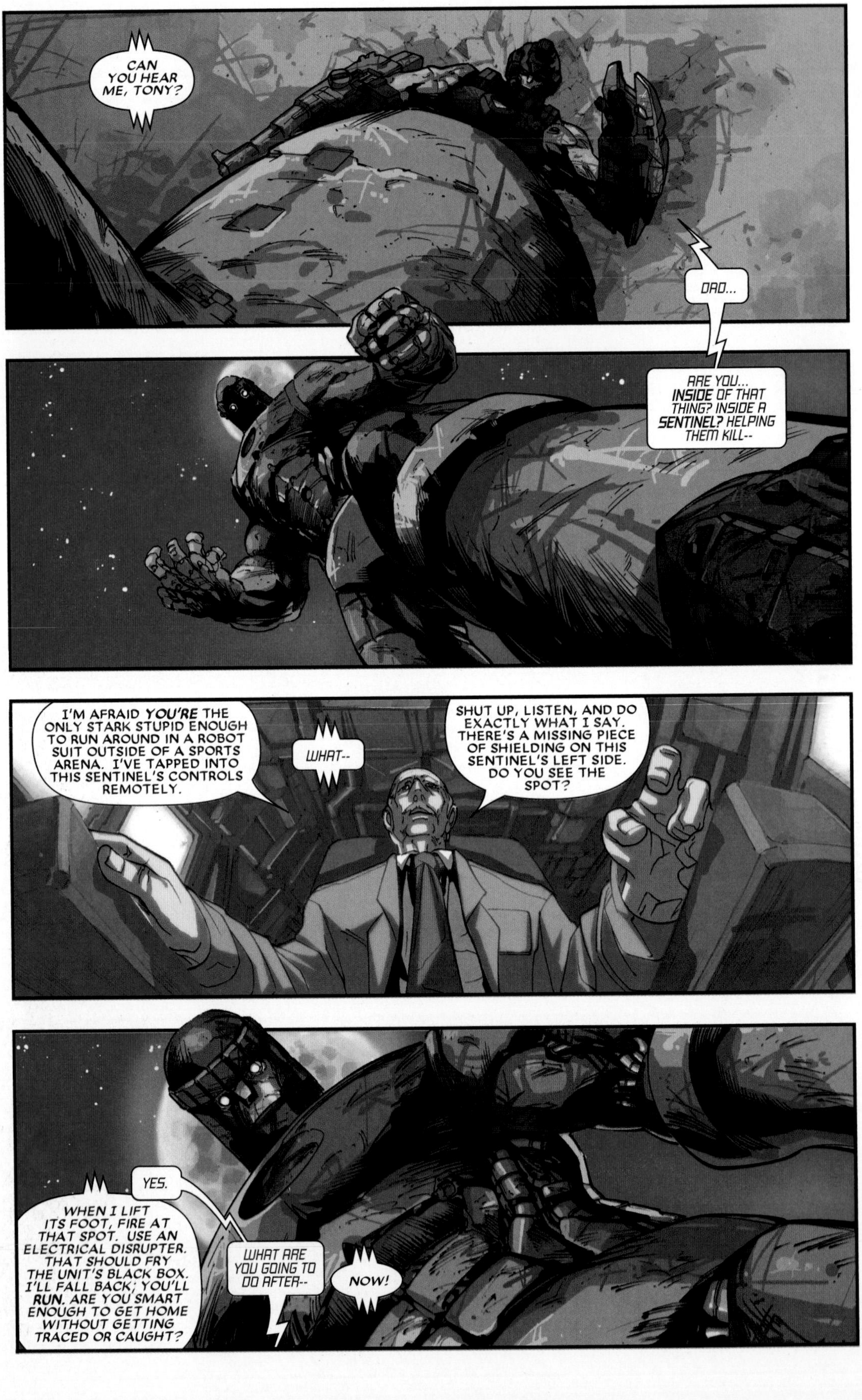
CAN YOU HEAR ME, TONY?
DAD...
ARE YOU... INSIDE OF THAT THING? INSIDE HELPING A SENTINEL? HELPING THEM KILL--
I'M AFRAID YOU'RE THE ONLY STARK STUPID ENOUGH TO RUN AROUND IN A ROBOT SUIT OUTSIDE OF A SPORTS ARENA. I'VE TAPPED INTO THIS SENTINEL'S CONTROLS REMOTELY.
WHAT--
SHUT UP, LISTEN, AND DO EXACTLY WHAT I SAY. THERE'S A MISSING PIECE OF SHIELDING ON THIS SENTINEL'S LEFT SIDE. DO YOU SEE THE SPOT?
YES.
WHEN I LIFT ITS FOOT, FIRE AT THAT SPOT. USE AN ELECTRICAL DISRUPTER. THAT SHOULD FRY THE UNIT'S BLACK BOX. I'LL FALL BACK; YOU'LL RUN. ARE YOU SMART ENOUGH TO GET HOME WITHOUT GETTING TRACED OR CAUGHT?
WHAT ARE YOU GOING TO DO AFTER--
NOW!

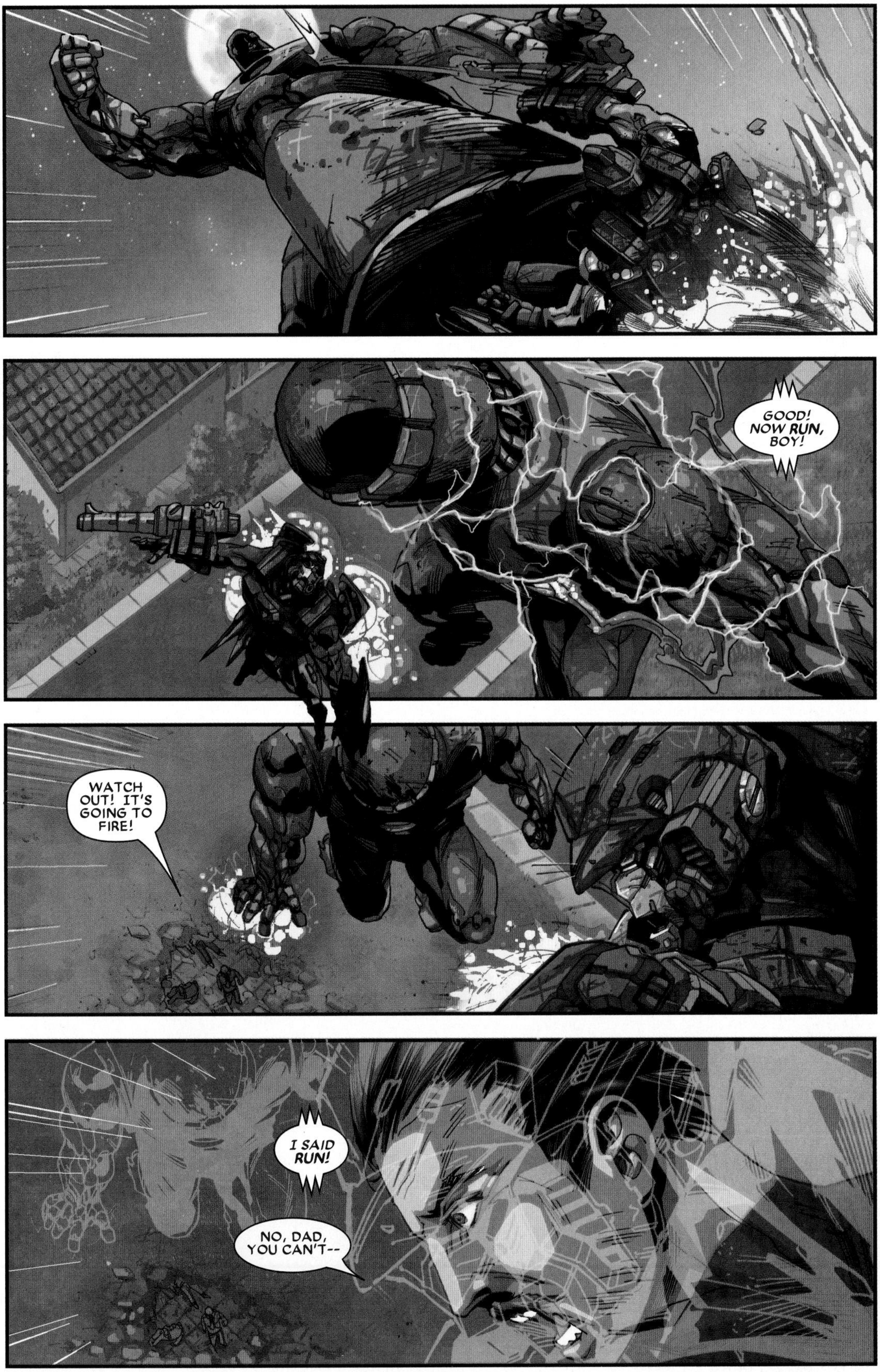
GOOD! NOW RUN, BOY!
WATCH OUT! IT'S GOING TO FIRE!
I SAID RUN!
NO, DAD, YOU CAN'T--

TONY! WHAT ARE YOU DOING!

YOU THINK I'M JUST GOING TO FLY AWAY WHILE YOU KILL THOSE PEOPLE?

YOU'RE INSANE.

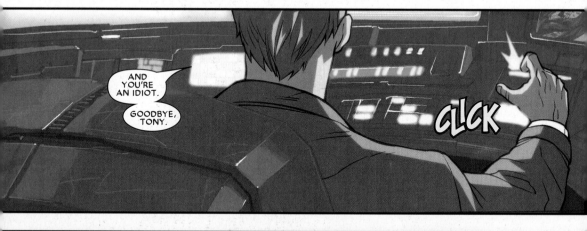

AND YOU'RE AN IDIOT.

GOODBYE, TONY.

CLICK

HEY, YOU!

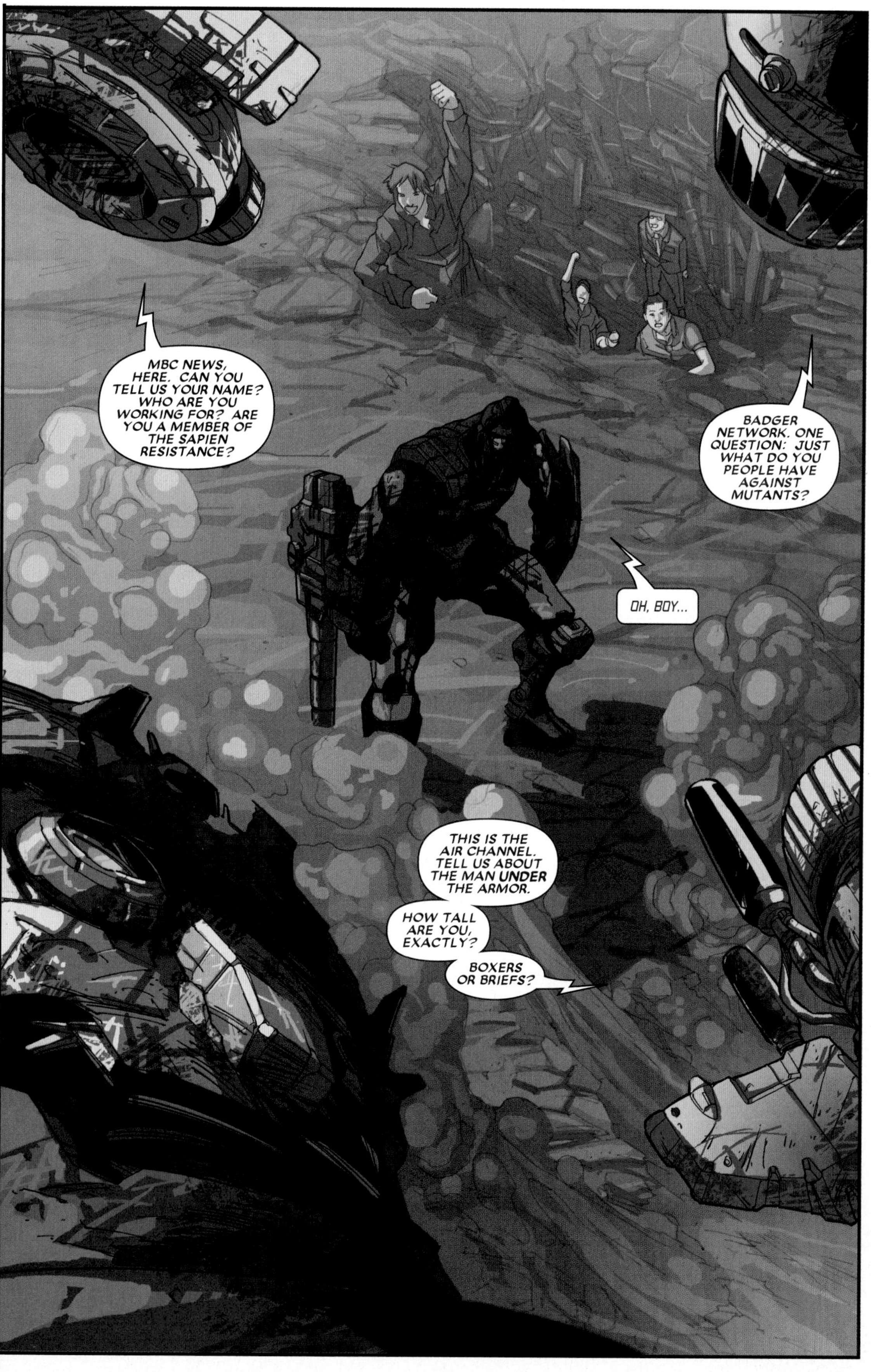
MBC NEWS, HERE. CAN YOU TELL US YOUR NAME? WHO ARE YOU WORKING FOR? ARE YOU A MEMBER OF THE SAPIEN RESISTANCE?
BADGER NETWORK. ONE QUESTION: JUST WHAT DO YOU PEOPLE HAVE AGAINST MUTANTS?
OH, BOY...
THIS IS THE AIR CHANNEL. TELL US ABOUT THE MAN UNDER THE ARMOR.
HOW TALL ARE YOU, EXACTLY?
BOXERS OR BRIEFS?

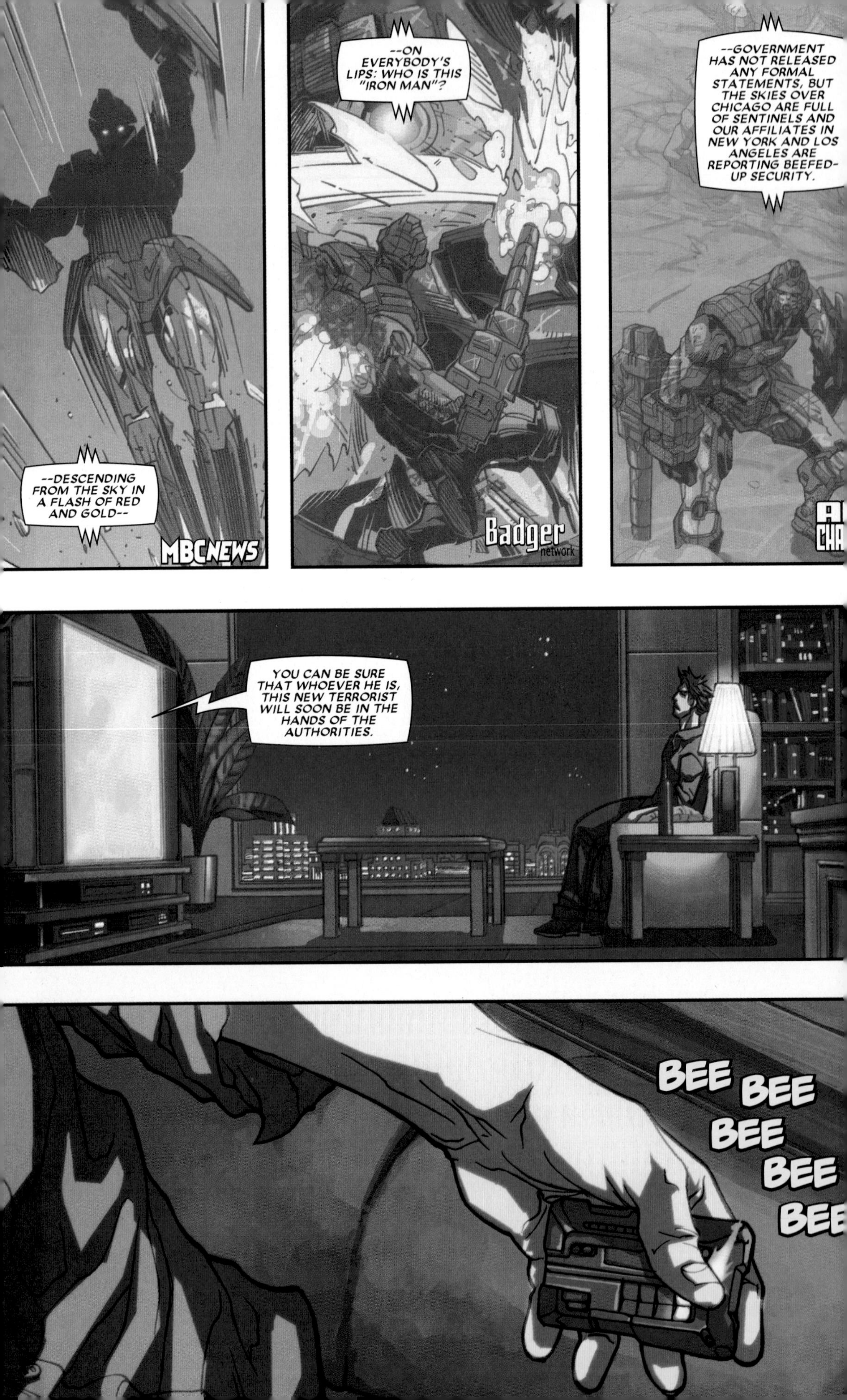
--DESCENDING FROM THE SKY IN A FLASH OF RED AND GOLD--
MBC NEWS
--ON EVERYBODY'S LIPS: WHO IS THIS "IRON MAN"?
Badger network
--GOVERNMENT HAS NOT RELEASED ANY FORMAL STATEMENTS, BUT THE SKIES OVER CHICAGO ARE FULL OF SENTINELS AND OUR AFFILIATES IN NEW YORK AND LOS ANGELES ARE REPORTING BEEFED-UP SECURITY.
YOU CAN BE SURE THAT WHOEVER HE IS, THIS NEW TERRORIST WILL SOON BE IN THE HANDS OF THE AUTHORITIES.
BEE BEE BEE BEE BEE

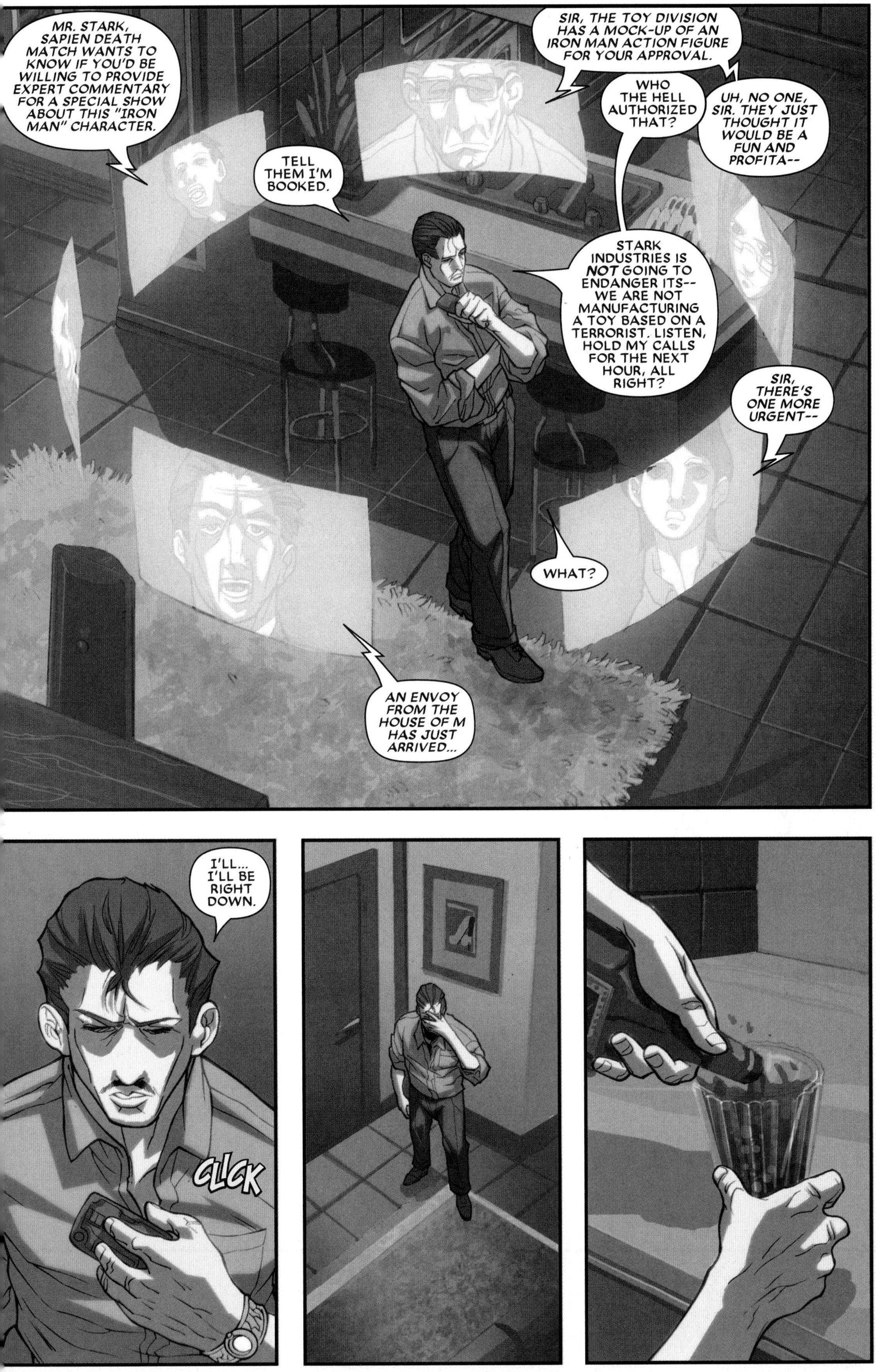
MR. STARK, SAPIEN DEATH MATCH WANTS TO KNOW IF YOU'D BE WILLING TO PROVIDE EXPERT COMMENTARY FOR A SPECIAL SHOW ABOUT THIS "IRON MAN" CHARACTER.
TELL THEM I'M BOOKED.
SIR, THE TOY DIVISION HAS A MOCK-UP OF AN IRON MAN ACTION FIGURE FOR YOUR APPROVAL.
WHO THE HELL AUTHORIZED THAT?
UH, NO ONE, SIR. THEY JUST THOUGHT IT WOULD BE A FUN AND PROFITA--
STARK INDUSTRIES IS NOT GOING TO ENDANGER ITS-- WE ARE NOT MANUFACTURING A TOY BASED ON A TERRORIST. LISTEN, HOLD MY CALLS FOR THE NEXT HOUR, ALL RIGHT?
SIR, THERE'S ONE MORE URGENT--
WHAT?
AN ENVOY FROM THE HOUSE OF M HAS JUST ARRIVED...
I'LL... I'LL BE RIGHT DOWN.
CLICK

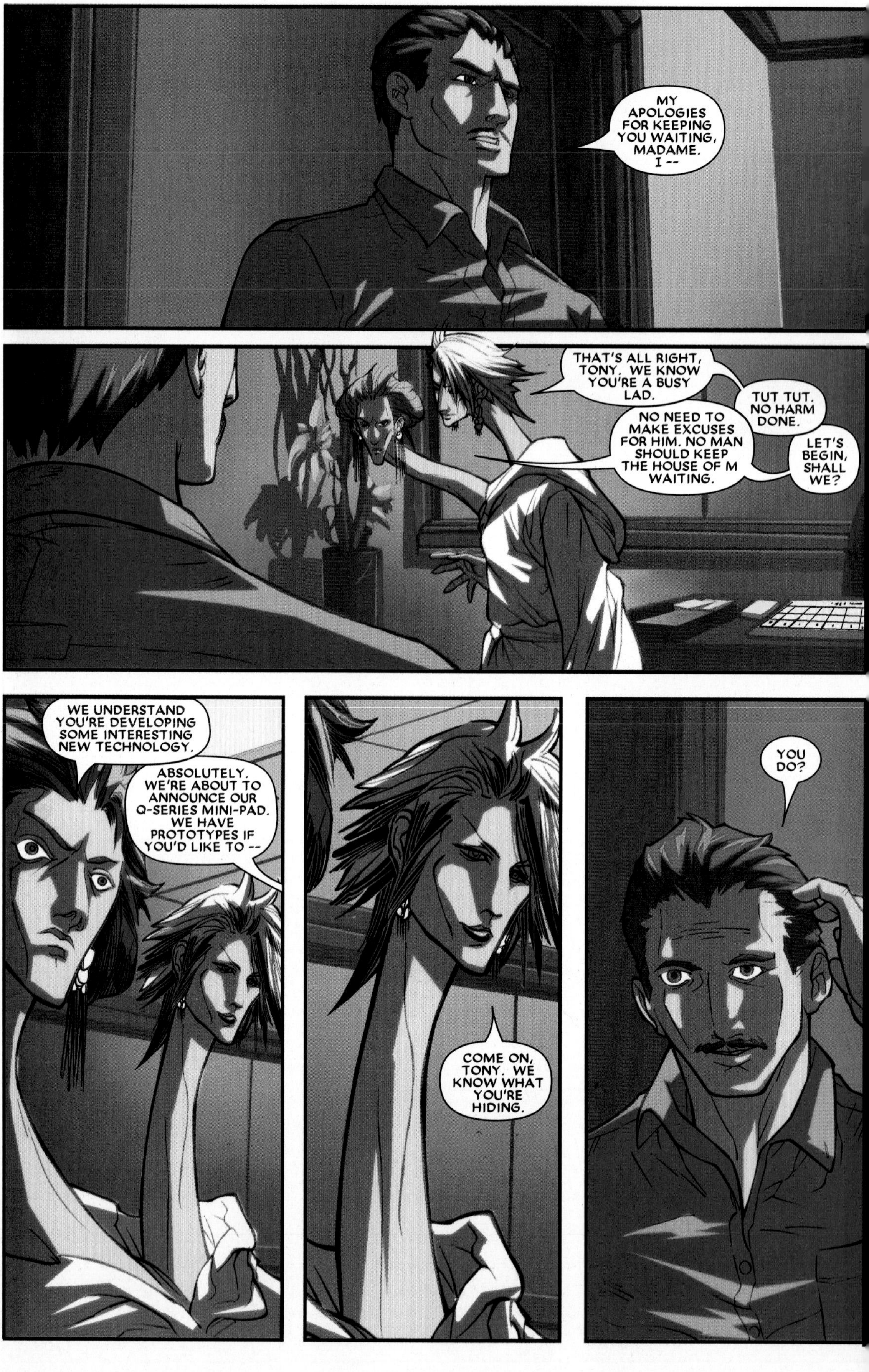
MY APOLOGIES FOR KEEPING YOU WAITING, MADAME. I --
THAT'S ALL RIGHT, TONY. WE KNOW YOU'RE A BUSY LAD.
TUT TUT. NO HARM DONE.
NO NEED TO MAKE EXCUSES FOR HIM. NO MAN SHOULD KEEP THE HOUSE OF M WAITING.
LET'S BEGIN, SHALL WE?
WE UNDERSTAND YOU'RE DEVELOPING SOME INTERESTING NEW TECHNOLOGY.
ABSOLUTELY. WE'RE ABOUT TO ANNOUNCE OUR Q-SERIES MINI-PAD. WE HAVE PROTOTYPES IF YOU'D LIKE TO --
COME ON, TONY. WE KNOW WHAT YOU'RE HIDING.
YOU DO?

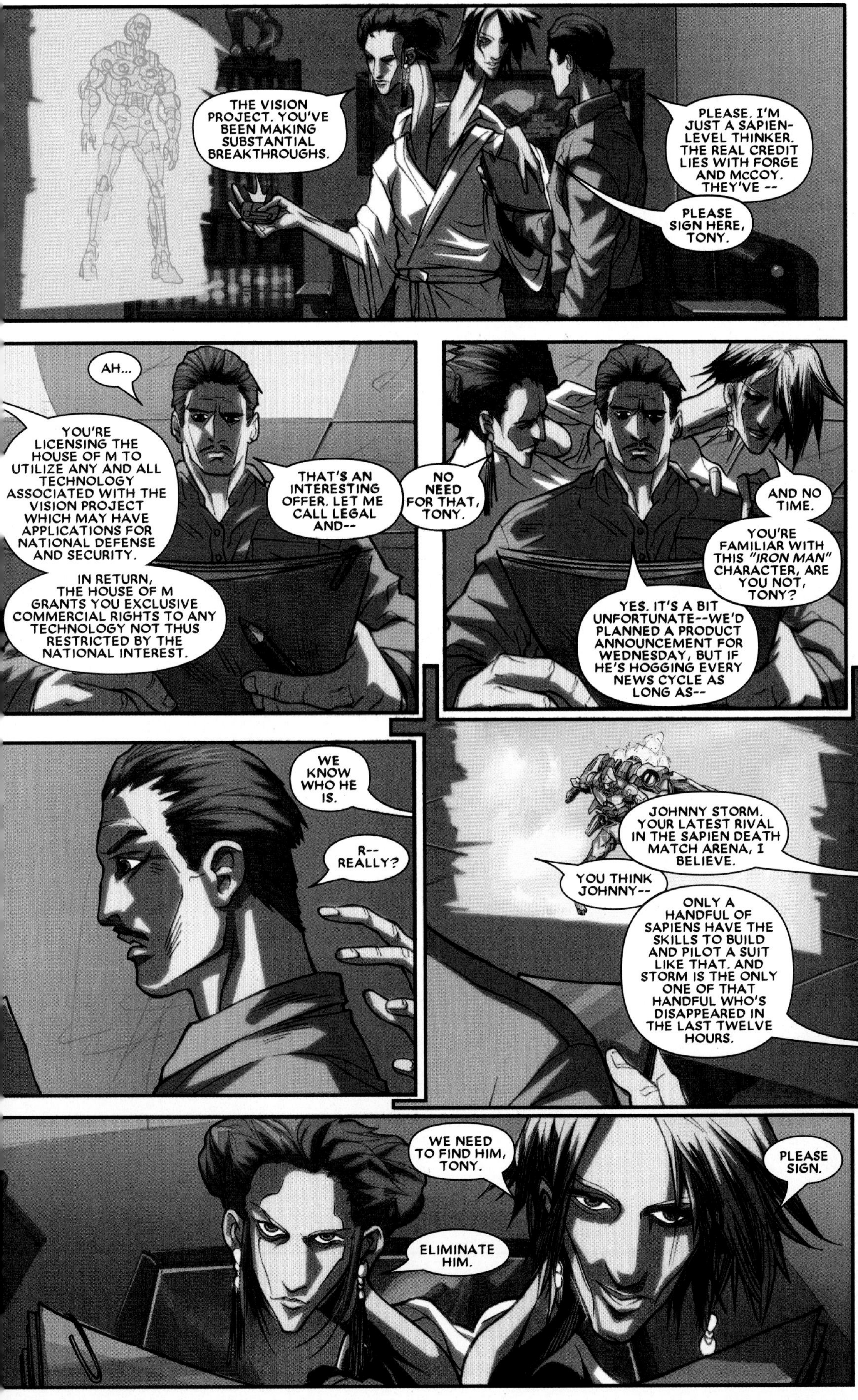
THE VISION PROJECT. YOU'VE BEEN MAKING SUBSTANTIAL BREAKTHROUGHS.
PLEASE. I'M JUST A SAPIEN-LEVEL THINKER. THE REAL CREDIT LIES WITH FORGE AND McCOY. THEY'VE --
PLEASE SIGN HERE, TONY.
AH...
YOU'RE LICENSING THE HOUSE OF M TO UTILIZE ANY AND ALL TECHNOLOGY ASSOCIATED WITH THE VISION PROJECT WHICH MAY HAVE APPLICATIONS FOR NATIONAL DEFENSE AND SECURITY.
IN RETURN, THE HOUSE OF M GRANTS YOU EXCLUSIVE COMMERCIAL RIGHTS TO ANY TECHNOLOGY NOT THUS RESTRICTED BY THE NATIONAL INTEREST.
THAT'S AN INTERESTING OFFER. LET ME CALL LEGAL AND--
NO NEED FOR THAT, TONY.
AND NO TIME.
YOU'RE FAMILIAR WITH THIS "IRON MAN" CHARACTER, ARE YOU NOT, TONY?
YES. IT'S A BIT UNFORTUNATE--WE'D PLANNED A PRODUCT ANNOUNCEMENT FOR WEDNESDAY, BUT IF HE'S HOGGING EVERY NEWS CYCLE AS LONG AS--
WE KNOW WHO HE IS.
R-- REALLY?
JOHNNY STORM. YOUR LATEST RIVAL IN THE SAPIEN DEATH MATCH ARENA, I BELIEVE.
YOU THINK JOHNNY--
ONLY A HANDFUL OF SAPIENS HAVE THE SKILLS TO BUILD AND PILOT A SUIT LIKE THAT. AND STORM IS THE ONLY ONE OF THAT HANDFUL WHO'S DISAPPEARED IN THE LAST TWELVE HOURS.
WE NEED TO FIND HIM, TONY.
ELIMINATE HIM.
PLEASE SIGN.

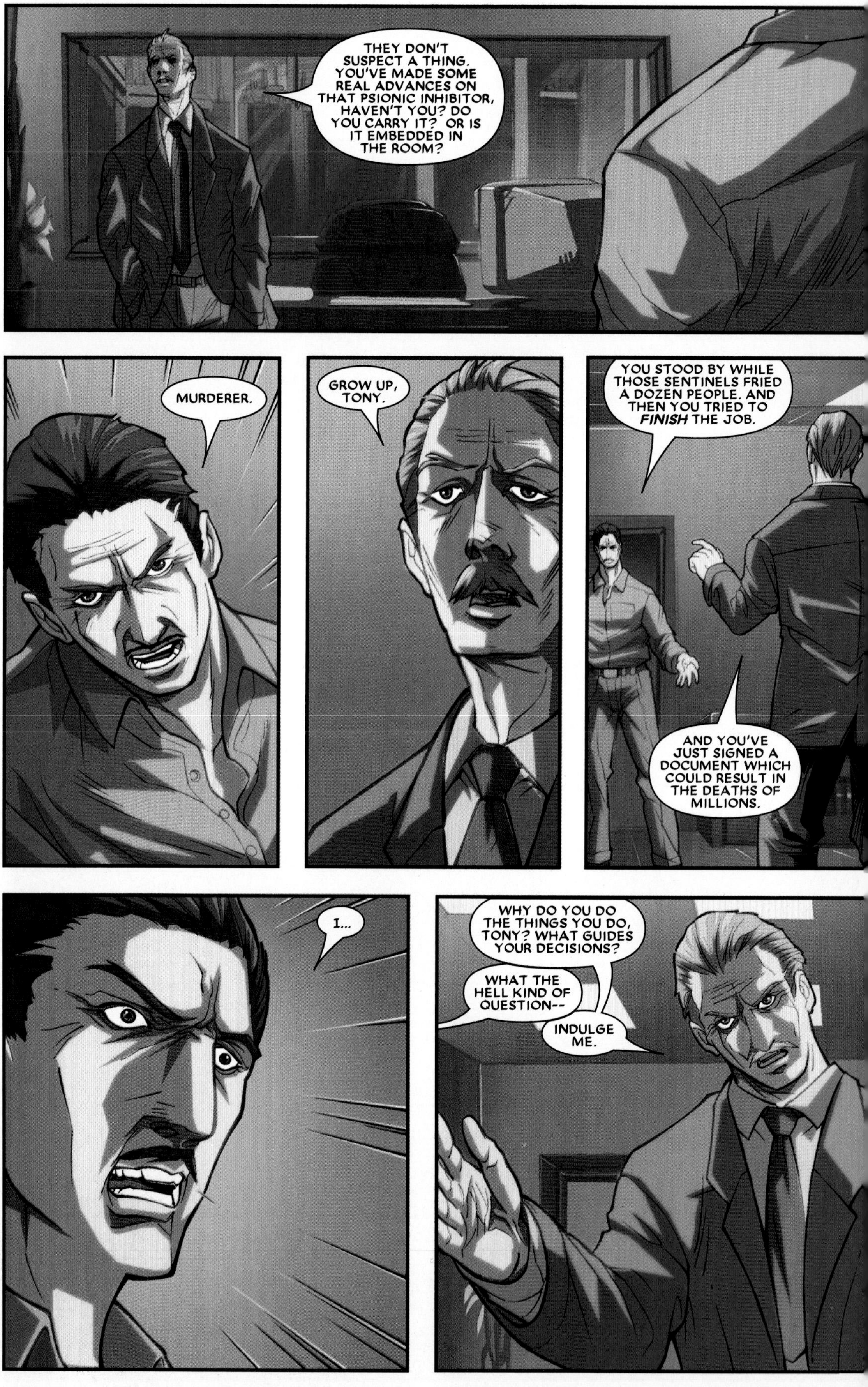
THEY DON'T SUSPECT A THING. YOU'VE MADE SOME REAL ADVANCES ON THAT PSIONIC INHIBITOR, HAVEN'T YOU? DO YOU CARRY IT? OR IS IT EMBEDDED IN THE ROOM?
MURDERER.
GROW UP, TONY.
YOU STOOD BY WHILE THOSE SENTINELS FRIED A DOZEN PEOPLE. AND THEN YOU TRIED TO FINISH THE JOB.
AND YOU'VE JUST SIGNED A DOCUMENT WHICH COULD RESULT IN THE DEATHS OF MILLIONS.
I...
WHY DO YOU DO THE THINGS YOU DO, TONY? WHAT GUIDES YOUR DECISIONS?
WHAT THE HELL KIND OF QUESTION--
INDULGE ME.

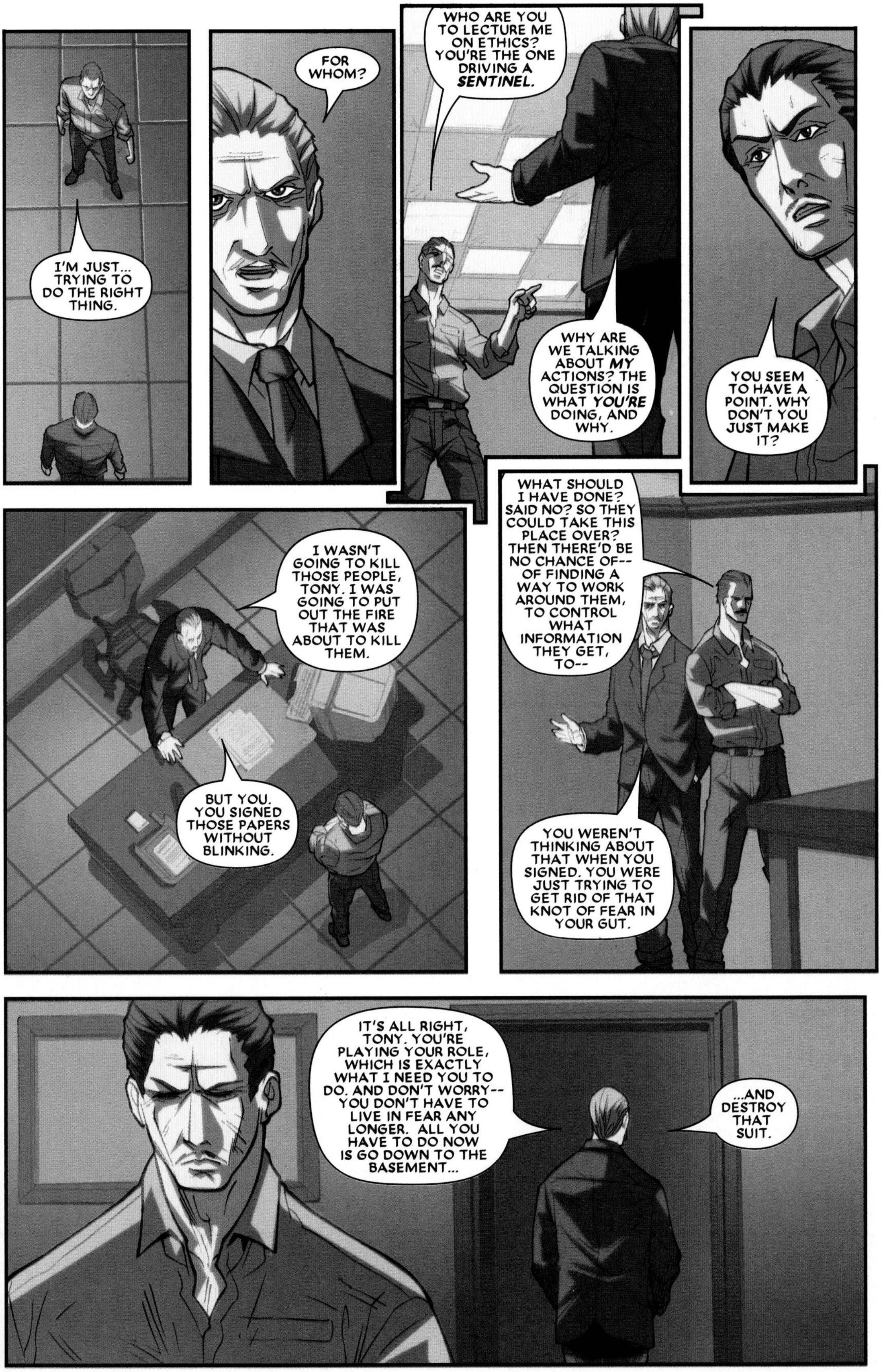
I'M JUST... TRYING TO DO THE RIGHT THING.
FOR WHOM?
WHO ARE YOU TO LECTURE ME ON ETHICS? YOU'RE THE ONE DRIVING A SENTINEL.
WHY ARE WE TALKING ABOUT MY ACTIONS? THE QUESTION IS WHAT YOU'RE DOING, AND WHY.
YOU SEEM TO HAVE A POINT. WHY DON'T YOU JUST MAKE IT?
I WASN'T GOING TO KILL THOSE PEOPLE, TONY. I WAS GOING TO PUT OUT THE FIRE THAT WAS ABOUT TO KILL THEM.
BUT YOU. YOU SIGNED THOSE PAPERS WITHOUT BLINKING.
WHAT SHOULD I HAVE DONE? SAID NO? SO THEY COULD TAKE THIS PLACE OVER? THEN THERE'D BE NO CHANCE OF-- OF FINDING A WAY TO WORK AROUND THEM, TO CONTROL WHAT INFORMATION THEY GET, TO--
YOU WEREN'T THINKING ABOUT THAT WHEN YOU SIGNED. YOU WERE JUST TRYING TO GET RID OF THAT KNOT OF FEAR IN YOUR GUT.
IT'S ALL RIGHT, TONY. YOU'RE PLAYING YOUR ROLE, WHICH IS EXACTLY WHAT I NEED YOU TO DO. AND DON'T WORRY-- YOU DON'T HAVE TO LIVE IN FEAR ANY LONGER. ALL YOU HAVE TO DO NOW IS GO DOWN TO THE BASEMENT...
...AND DESTROY THAT SUIT.

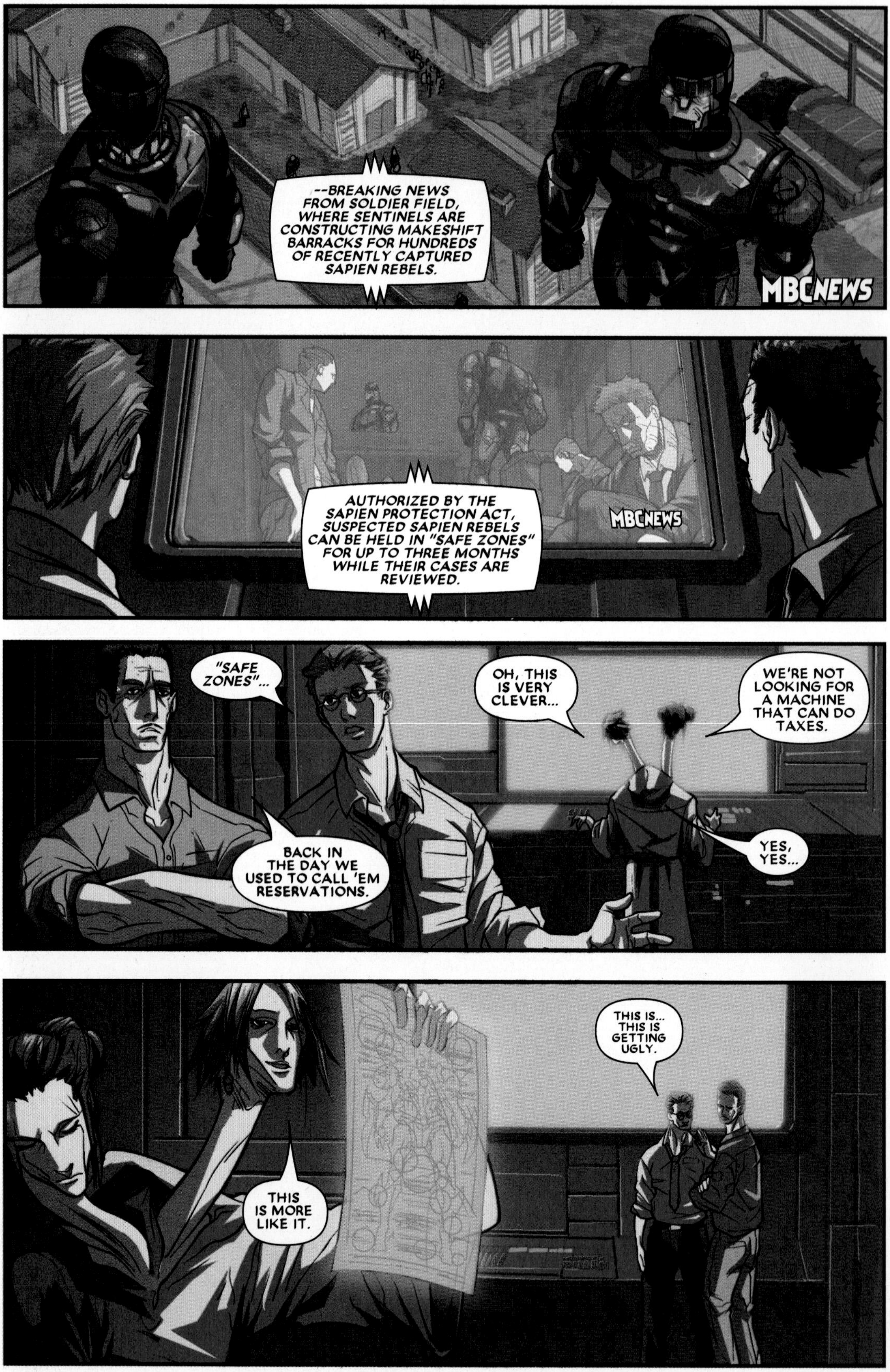
--BREAKING NEWS FROM SOLDIER FIELD, WHERE SENTINELS ARE CONSTRUCTING MAKESHIFT BARRACKS FOR HUNDREDS OF RECENTLY CAPTURED SAPIEN REBELS.
MBC NEWS
MBC NEWS
AUTHORIZED BY THE SAPIEN PROTECTION ACT, SUSPECTED SAPIEN REBELS CAN BE HELD IN "SAFE ZONES" FOR UP TO THREE MONTHS WHILE THEIR CASES ARE REVIEWED.
"SAFE ZONES"...
BACK IN THE DAY WE USED TO CALL 'EM RESERVATIONS.
OH, THIS IS VERY CLEVER...
WE'RE NOT LOOKING FOR A MACHINE THAT CAN DO TAXES.
YES, YES...
THIS IS MORE LIKE IT.
THIS IS... THIS IS GETTING UGLY.

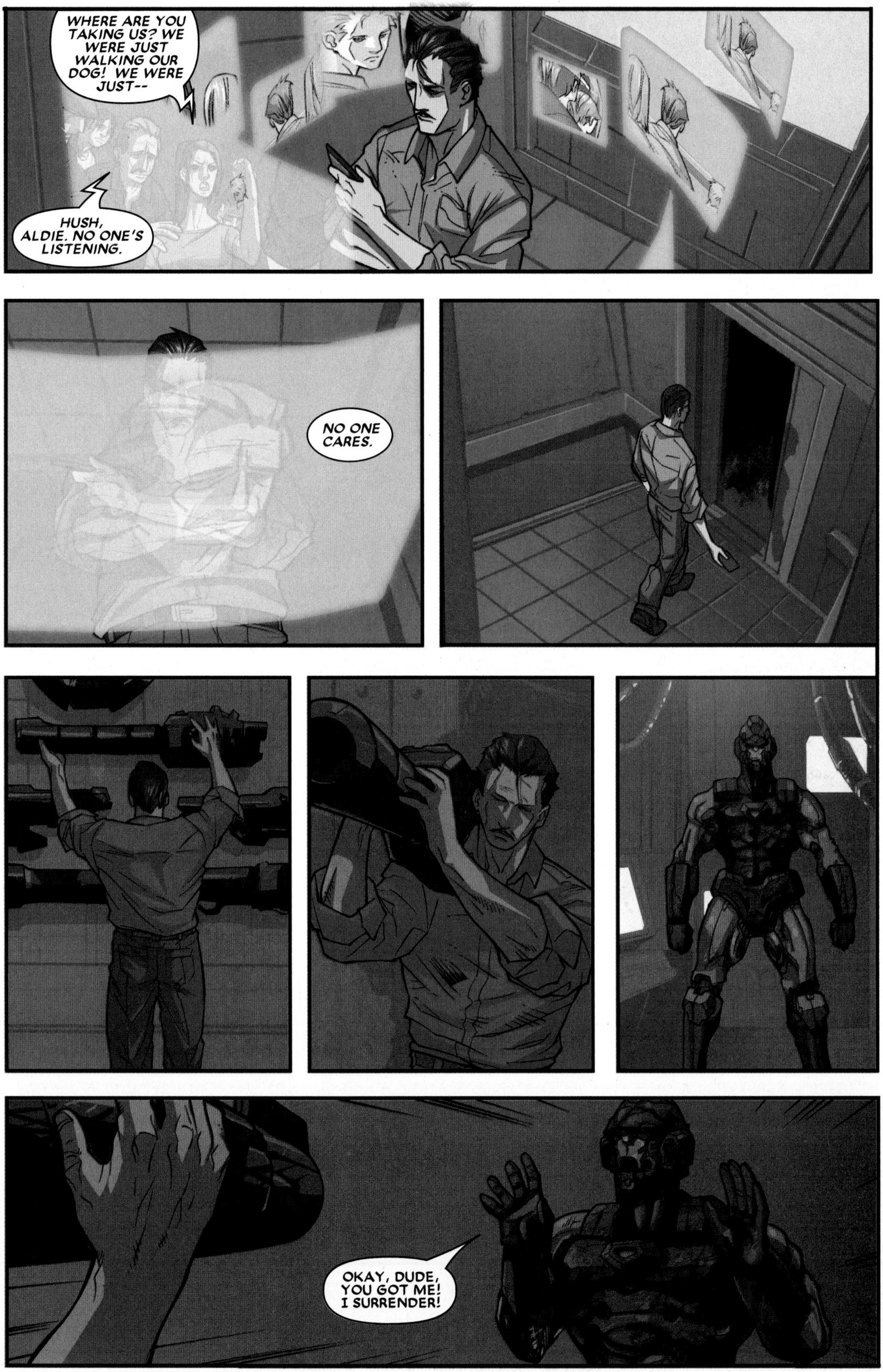
WHERE ARE YOU TAKING US? WE WERE JUST WALKING OUR DOG! WE WERE JUST--
HUSH, ALDIE. NO ONE'S LISTENING.
NO ONE CARES.
OKAY, DUDE, YOU GOT ME! I SURRENDER!

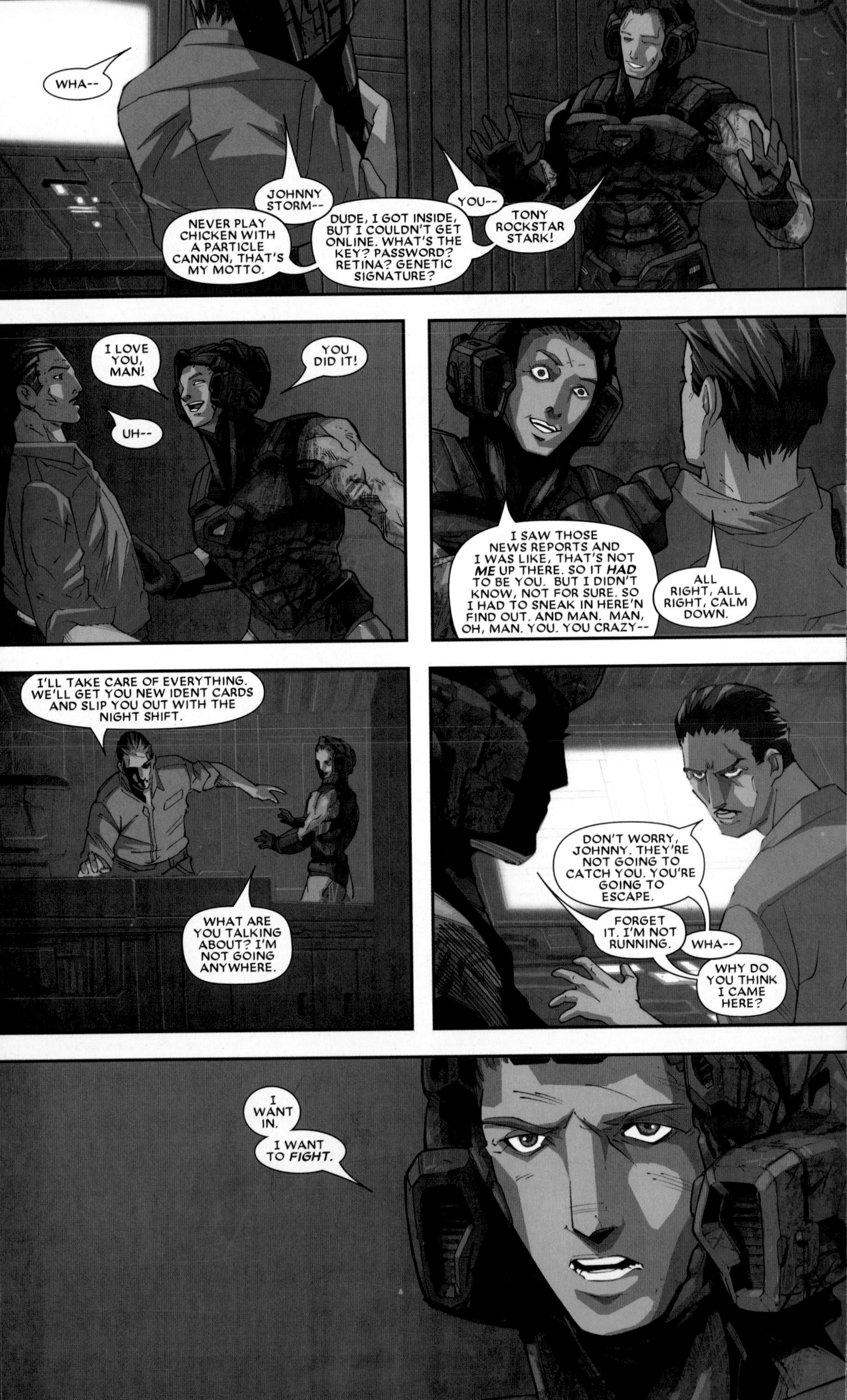
WHA--
JOHNNY STORM--
NEVER PLAY CHICKEN WITH A PARTICLE CANNON, THAT'S MY MOTTO.
YOU--
TONY ROCKSTAR STARK!
DUDE, I GOT INSIDE, BUT I COULDN'T GET ONLINE. WHAT'S THE KEY? PASSWORD? RETINA? GENETIC SIGNATURE?
I LOVE YOU, MAN!
YOU DID IT!
UH--
I SAW THOSE NEWS REPORTS AND I WAS LIKE, THAT'S NOT ME UP THERE. SO IT HAD TO BE YOU. BUT I DIDN'T KNOW, NOT FOR SURE. SO I HAD TO SNEAK IN HERE'N FIND OUT. AND MAN. MAN, OH, MAN. YOU. YOU CRAZY--
ALL RIGHT, ALL RIGHT, CALM DOWN.
I'LL TAKE CARE OF EVERYTHING. WE'LL GET YOU NEW IDENT CARDS AND SLIP YOU OUT WITH THE NIGHT SHIFT.
WHAT ARE YOU TALKING ABOUT? I'M NOT GOING ANYWHERE.
DON'T WORRY, JOHNNY. THEY'RE NOT GOING TO CATCH YOU. YOU'RE GOING TO ESCAPE.
FORGET IT. I'M NOT RUNNING.
WHA--
WHY DO YOU THINK I CAME HERE?
I WANT IN.
I WANT TO FIGHT.

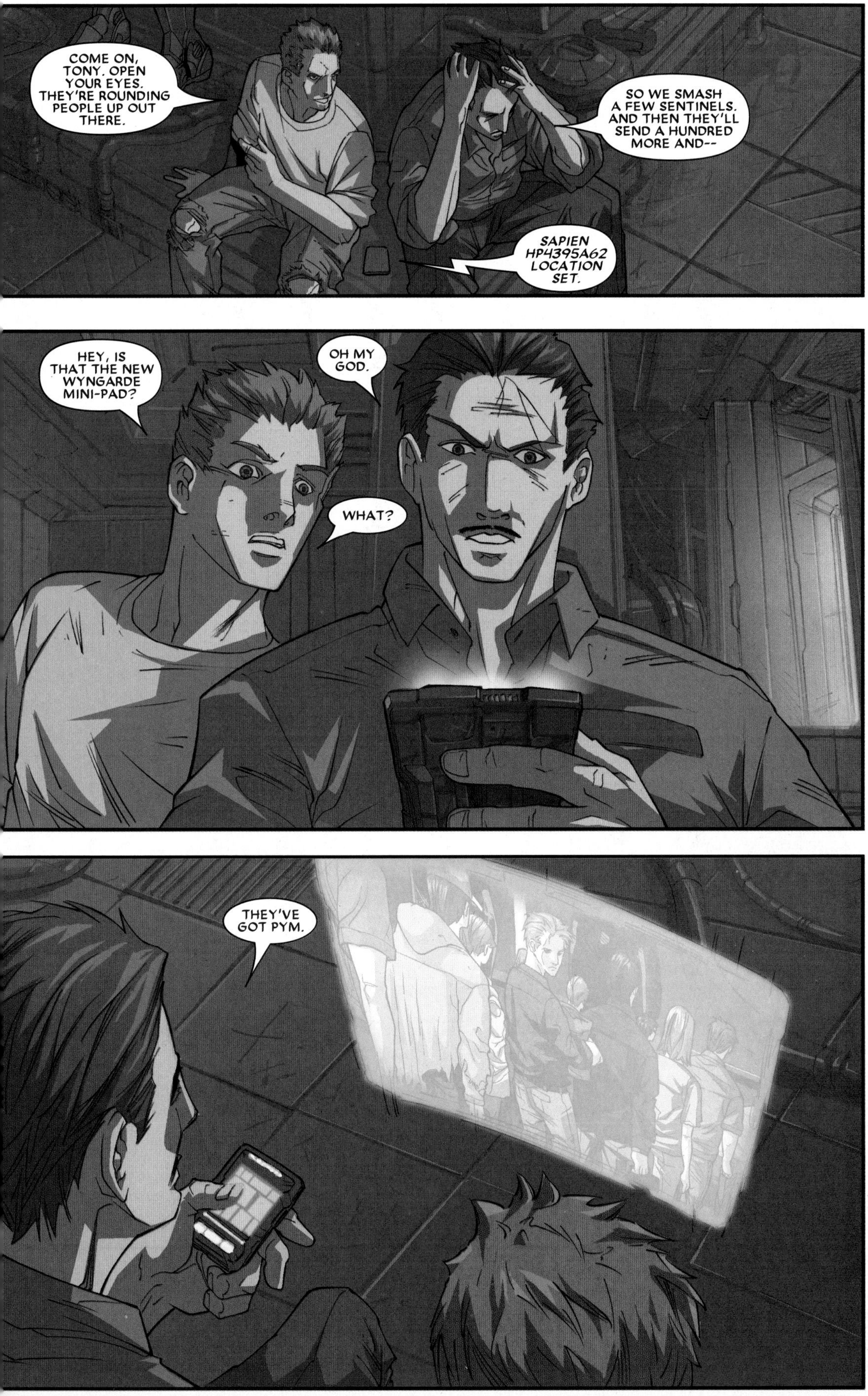
COME ON, TONY. OPEN YOUR EYES. THEY'RE ROUNDING PEOPLE UP OUT THERE.
SO WE SMASH A FEW SENTINELS. AND THEN THEY'LL SEND A HUNDRED MORE AND--
SAPIEN HP4395A62 LOCATION SET.
HEY, IS THAT THE NEW WYNGARDE MINI-PAD?
OH MY GOD.
WHAT?
THEY'VE GOT PYM.

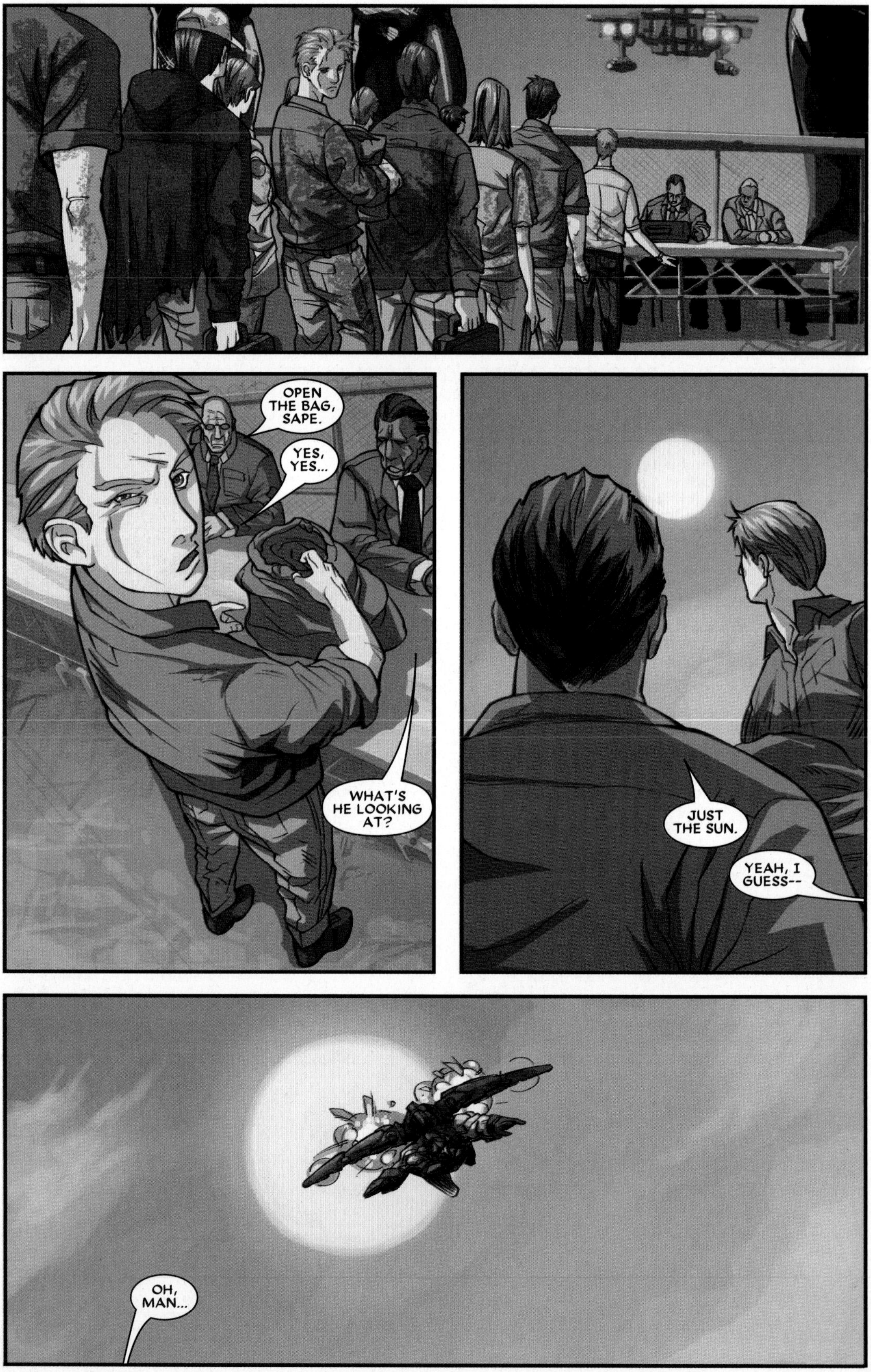
OPEN THE BAG, SAPE.
YES, YES...
WHAT'S HE LOOKING AT?
JUST THE SUN.
YEAH, I GUESS--
OH, MAN...

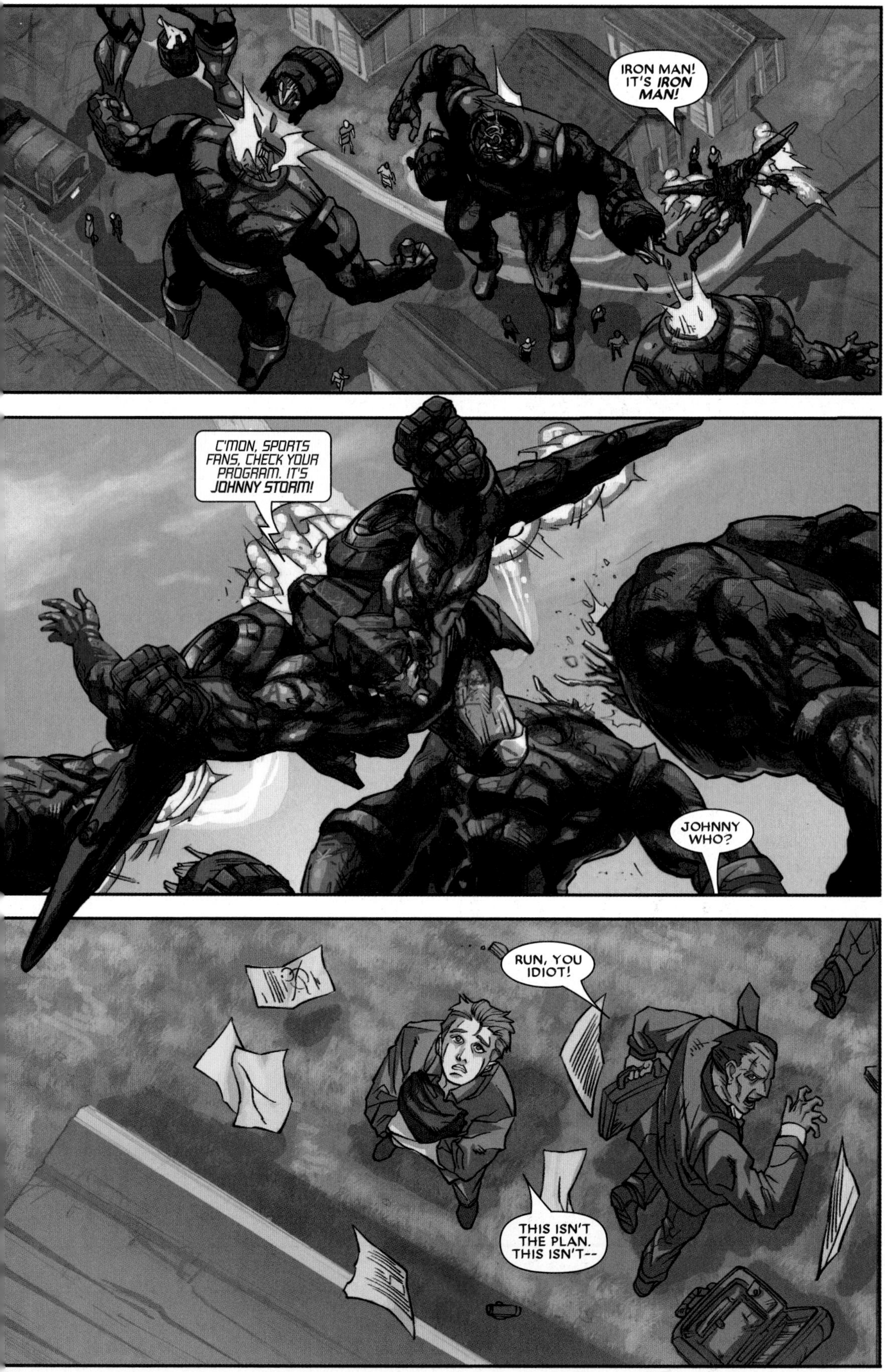
IRON MAN! IT'S *IRON MAN!*
C'MON, SPORTS FANS, CHECK YOUR PROGRAM. IT'S *JOHNNY STORM!*
JOHNNY WHO?
RUN, YOU IDIOT!
THIS ISN'T THE PLAN. THIS ISN'T--

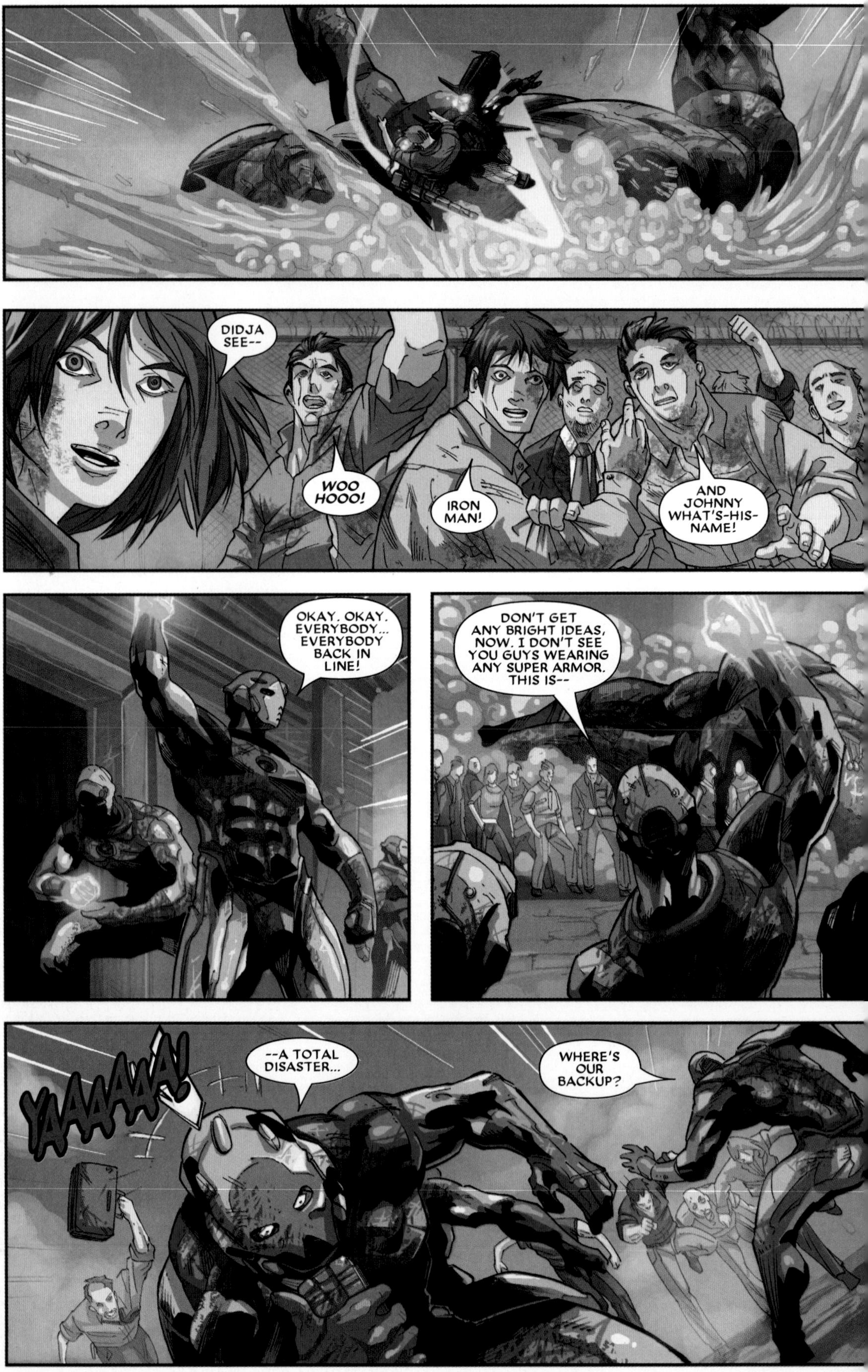
DIDJA SEE--
WOO HOOO!
IRON MAN!
AND JOHNNY WHAT'S-HIS-NAME!
OKAY. OKAY. EVERYBODY... EVERYBODY BACK IN LINE!
DON'T GET ANY BRIGHT IDEAS, NOW. I DON'T SEE YOU GUYS WEARING ANY SUPER ARMOR. THIS IS--
YAAAAAA!
--A TOTAL DISASTER...
WHERE'S OUR BACKUP?

PURSUING TARGET ONE.

MUTANT GUARDS. THEY'RE ON US, TONY.

IT'S ME THEY WANT.

TAKE PYM.

TONY, WAIT!

DO IT!

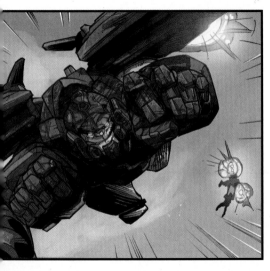

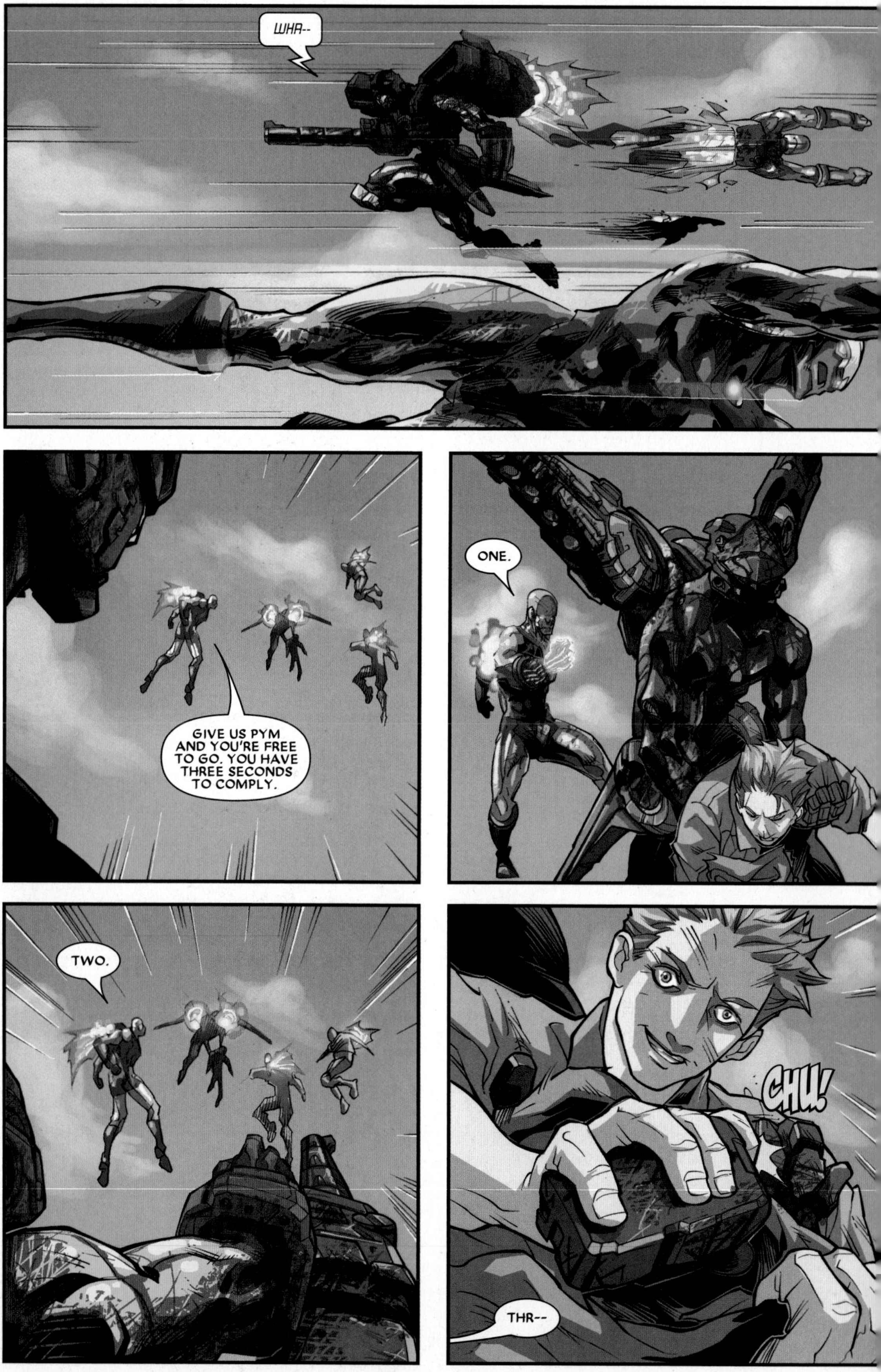
WHA--
GIVE US PYM AND YOU'RE FREE TO GO. YOU HAVE THREE SECONDS TO COMPLY.
ONE.
TWO.
CHU!
THR--

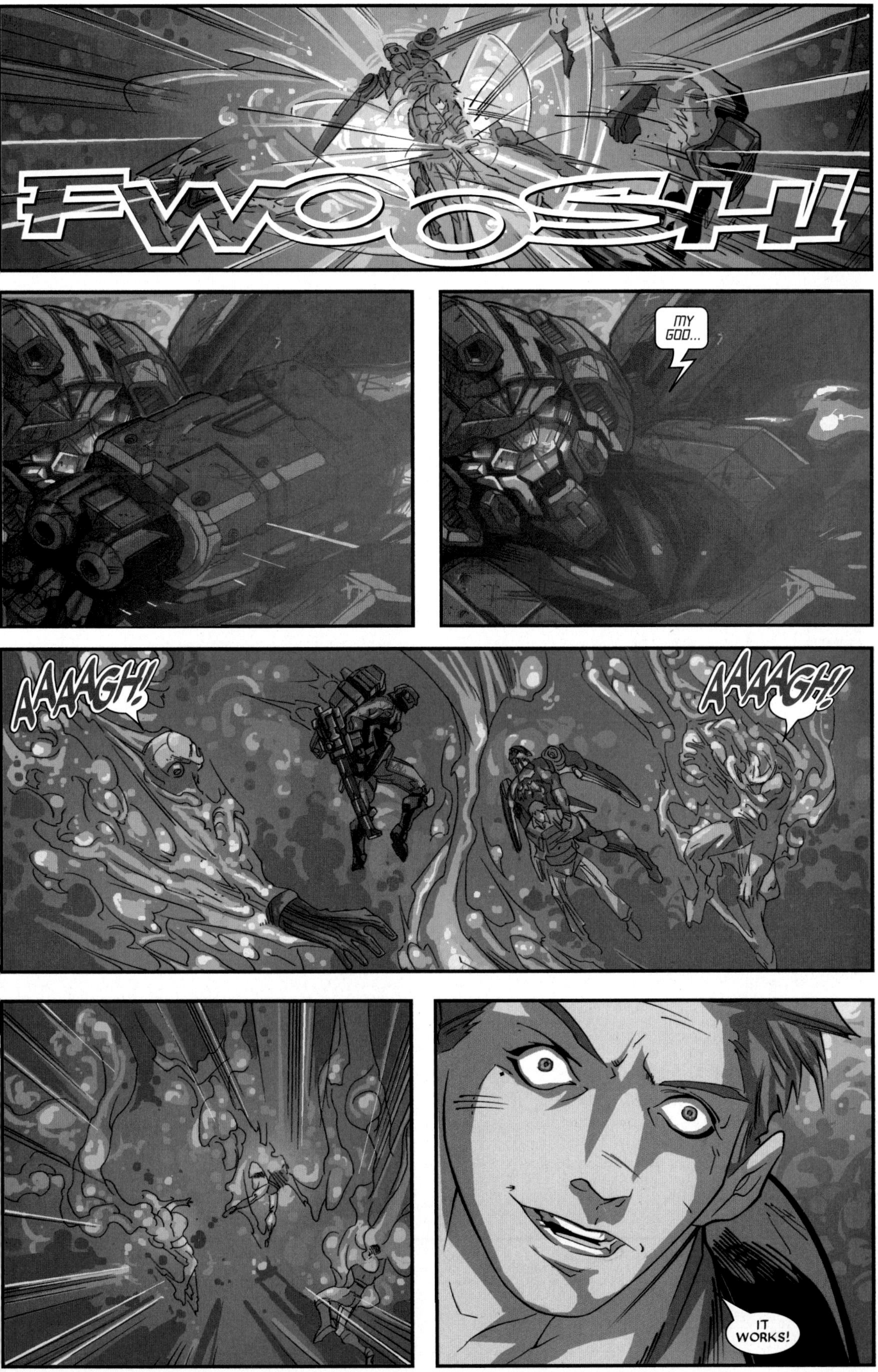
FWOOSH!
MY GOD...
AAAAGH!
AAAAGH!
IT WORKS!

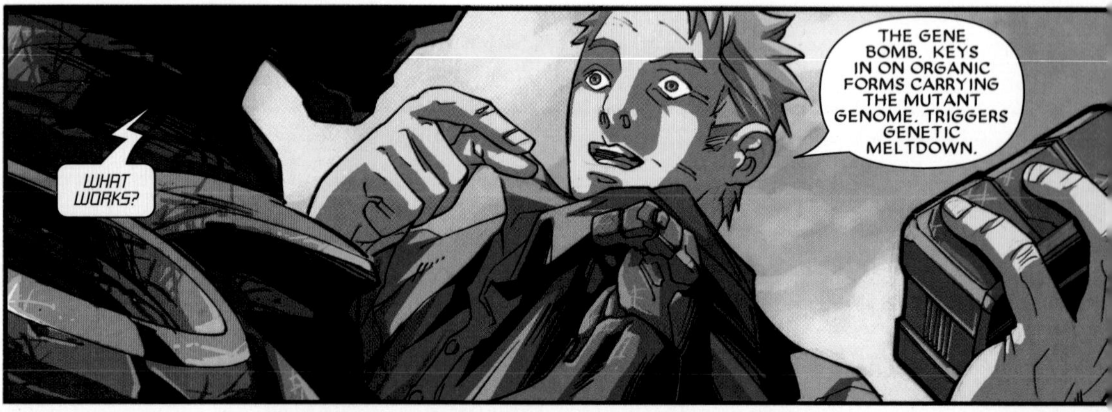

WHAT WORKS?
THE GENE BOMB. KEYS IN ON ORGANIC FORMS CARRYING THE MUTANT GENOME. TRIGGERS GENETIC MELTDOWN.

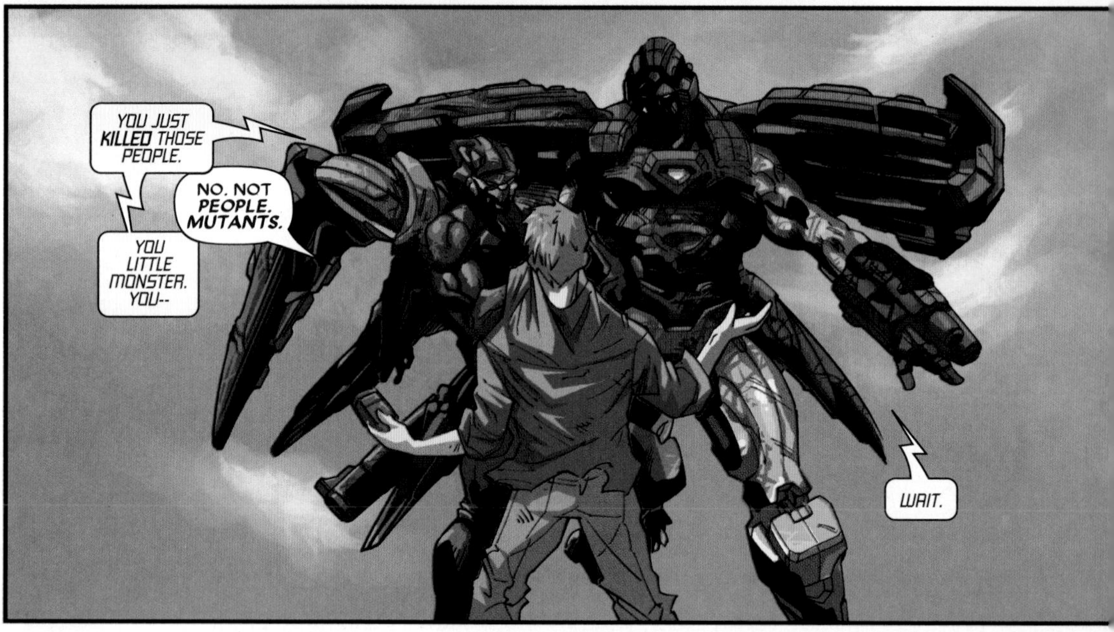

YOU JUST KILLED THOSE PEOPLE.
NO. NOT PEOPLE. MUTANTS.
YOU LITTLE MONSTER. YOU--
WAIT.

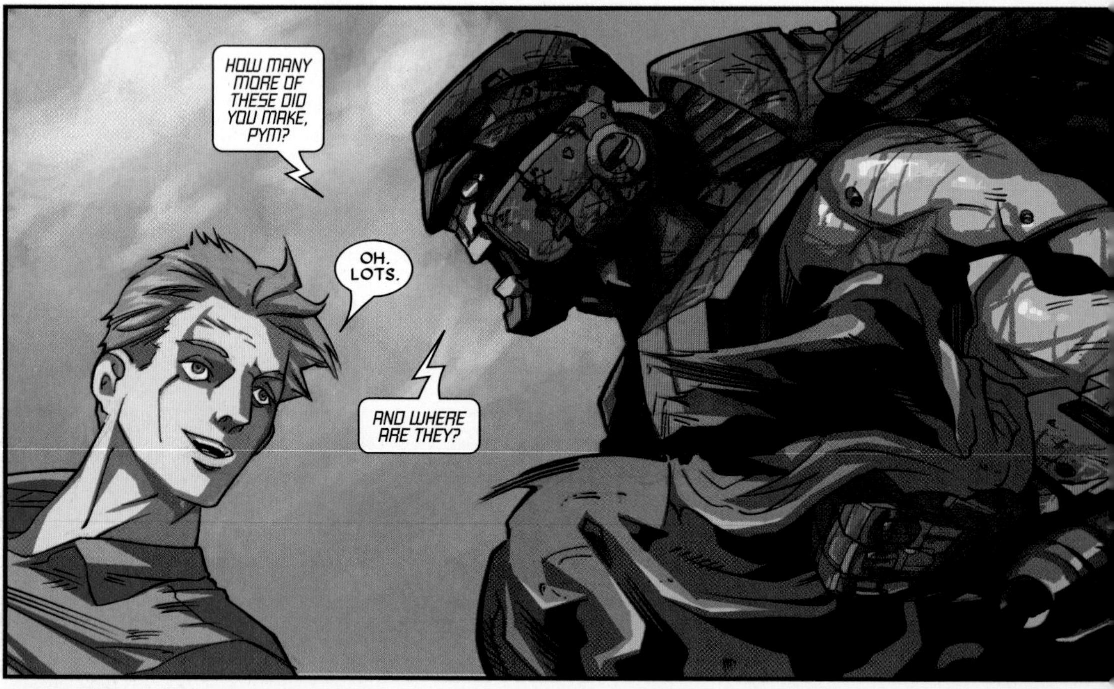

HOW MANY MORE OF THESE DID YOU MAKE, PYM?
OH. LOTS.
AND WHERE ARE THEY?

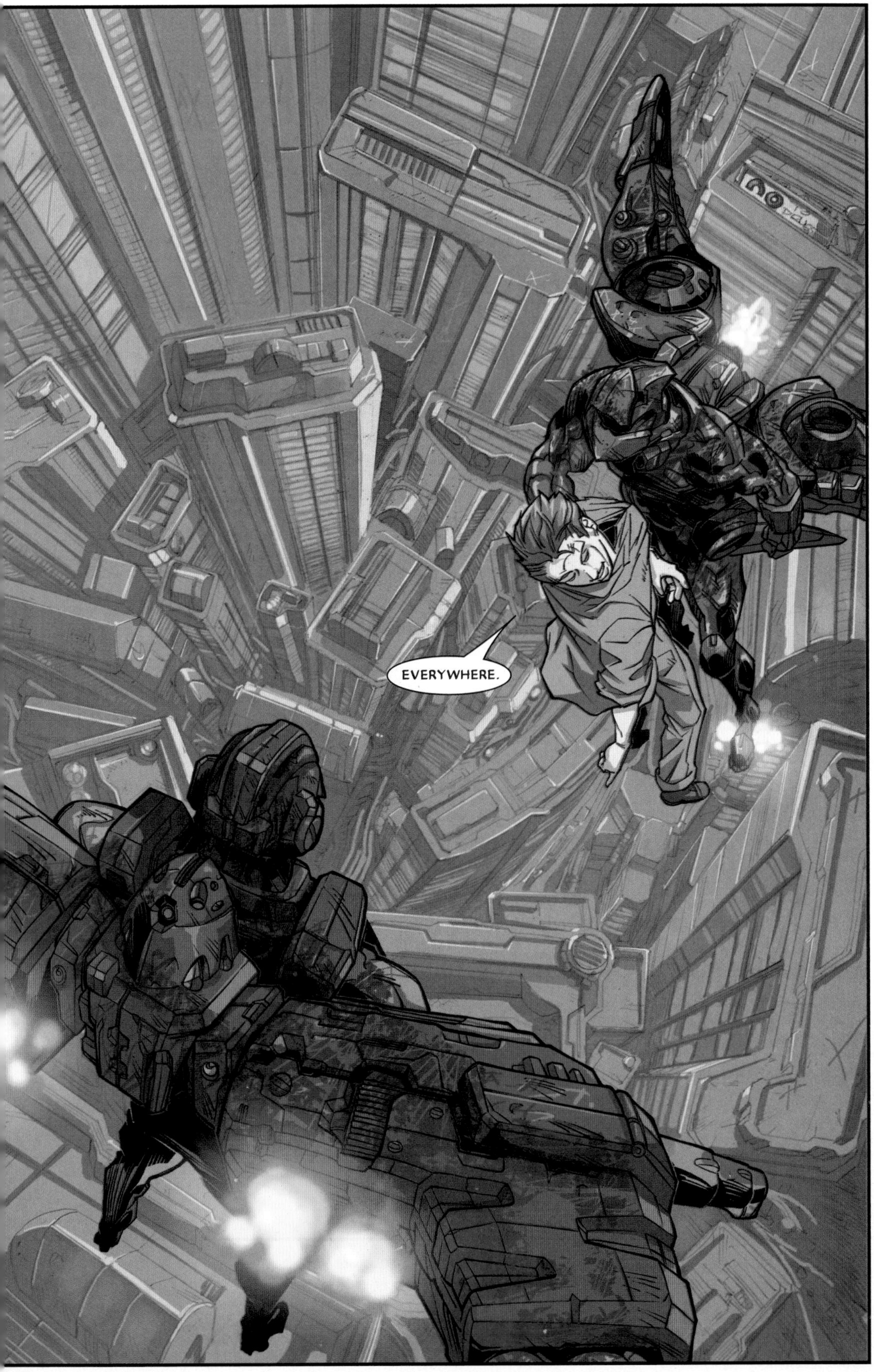
EVERYWHERE.

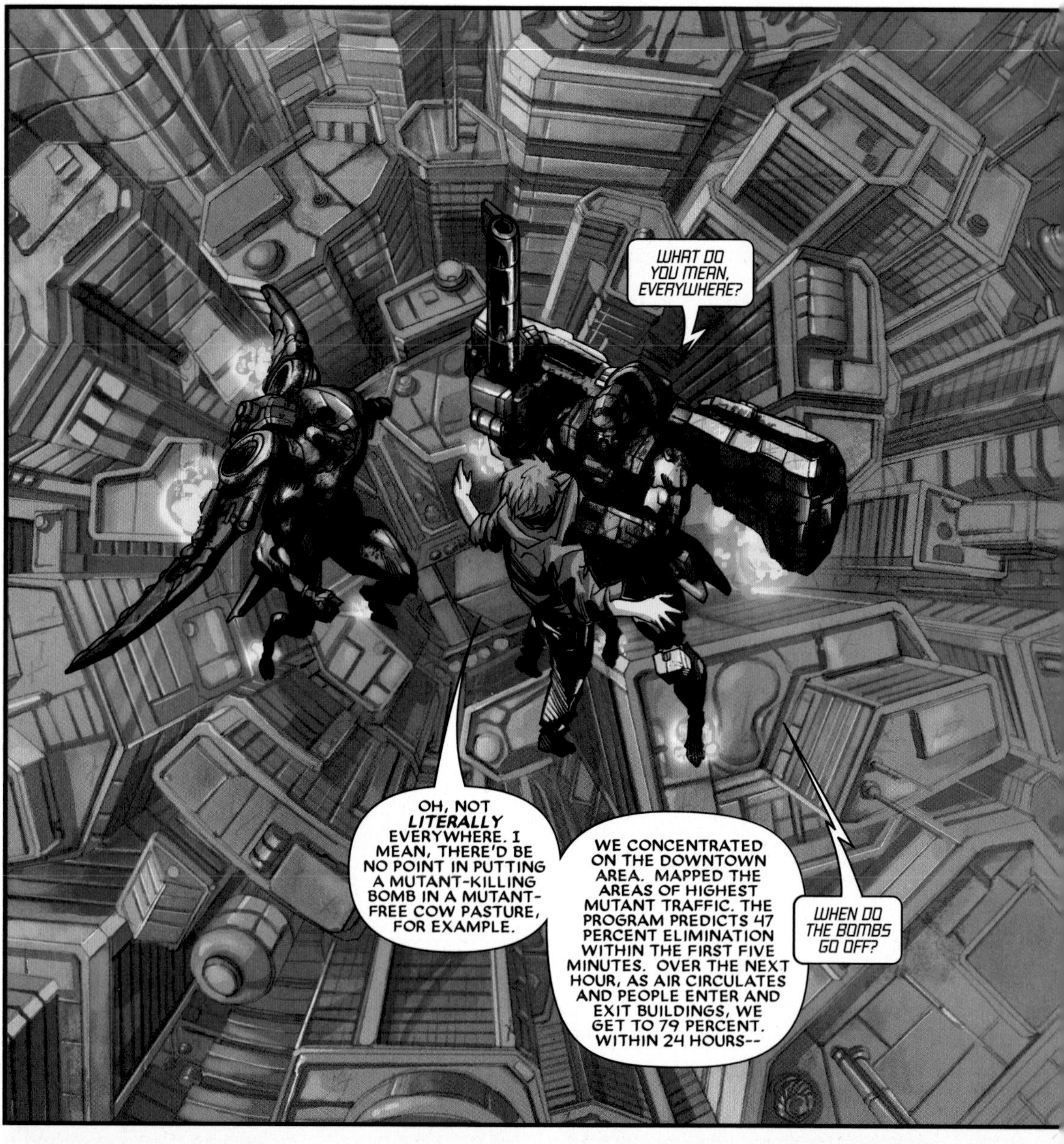
WHAT DO YOU MEAN, EVERYWHERE?
OH, NOT *LITERALLY* EVERYWHERE. I MEAN, THERE'D BE NO POINT IN PUTTING A MUTANT-KILLING BOMB IN A MUTANT-FREE COW PASTURE, FOR EXAMPLE.
WE CONCENTRATED ON THE DOWNTOWN AREA. MAPPED THE AREAS OF HIGHEST MUTANT TRAFFIC. THE PROGRAM PREDICTS 47 PERCENT ELIMINATION WITHIN THE FIRST FIVE MINUTES. OVER THE NEXT HOUR, AS AIR CIRCULATES AND PEOPLE ENTER AND EXIT BUILDINGS, WE GET TO 79 PERCENT. WITHIN 24 HOURS--
WHEN DO THE BOMBS GO OFF?

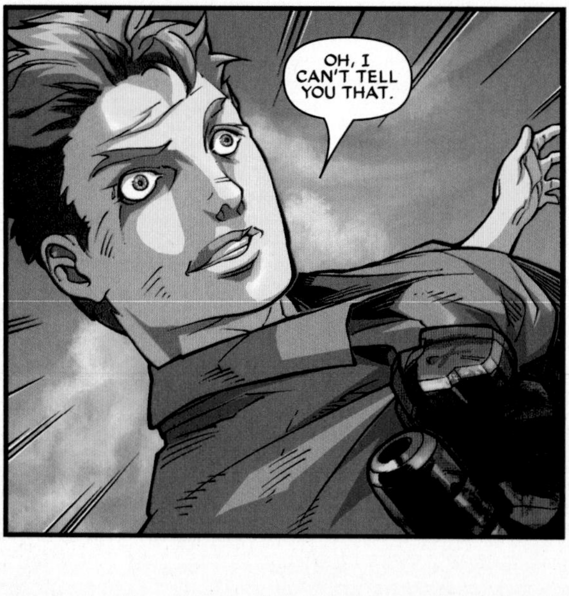
OH, I CAN'T TELL YOU THAT.

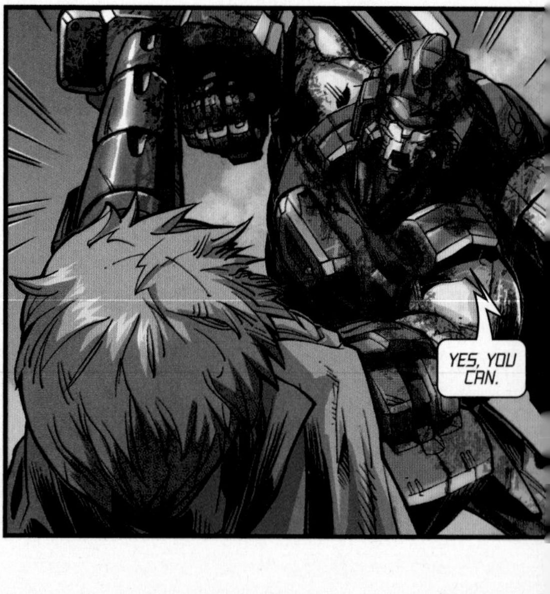
YES, YOU CAN.

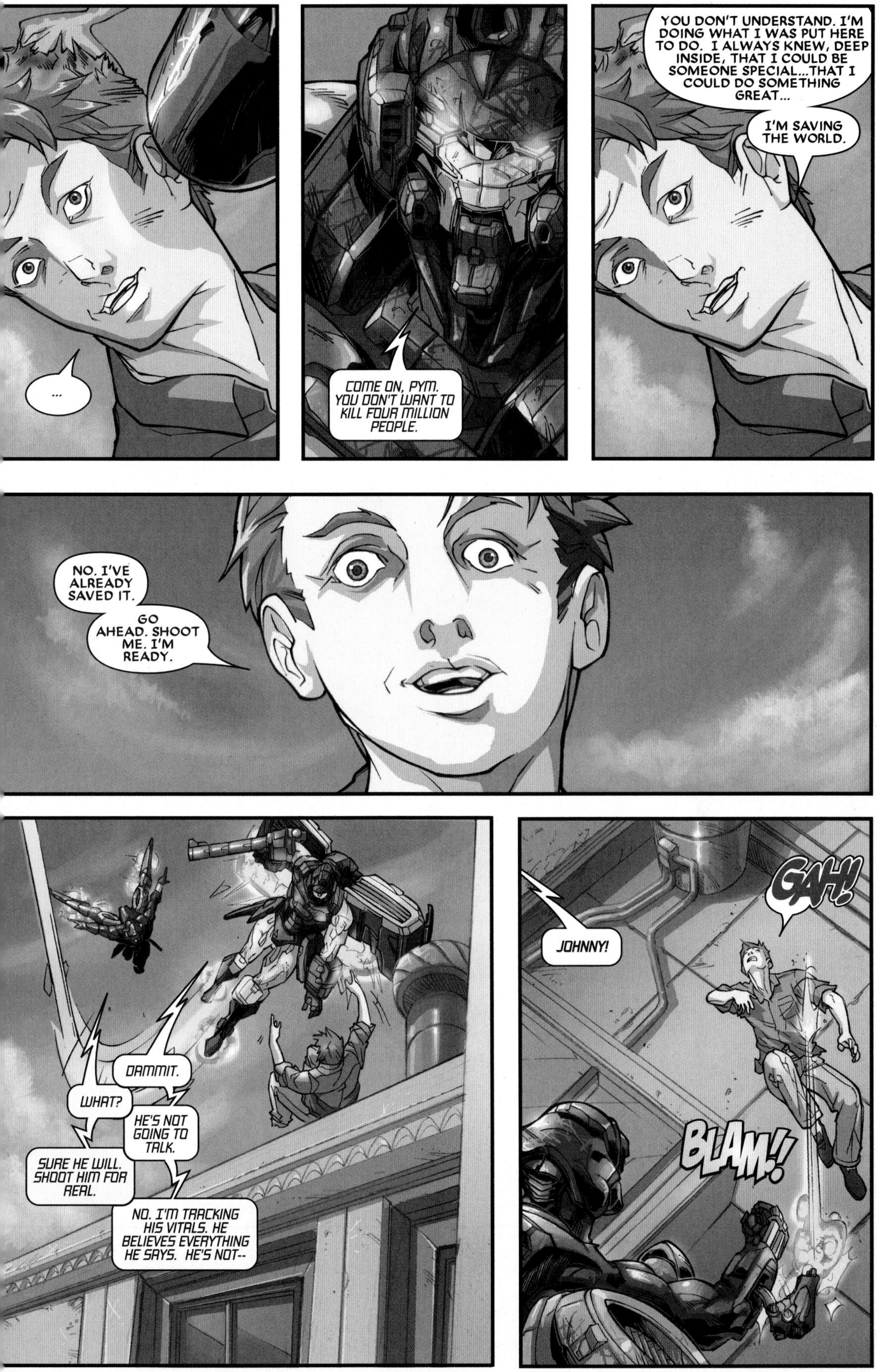

...
COME ON, PYM. YOU DON'T WANT TO KILL FOUR MILLION PEOPLE.
YOU DON'T UNDERSTAND. I'M DOING WHAT I WAS PUT HERE TO DO. I ALWAYS KNEW, DEEP INSIDE, THAT I COULD BE SOMEONE SPECIAL...THAT I COULD DO SOMETHING GREAT...
I'M SAVING THE WORLD.
NO. I'VE ALREADY SAVED IT.
GO AHEAD. SHOOT ME. I'M READY.
DAMMIT.
WHAT?
HE'S NOT GOING TO TALK.
SURE HE WILL. SHOOT HIM FOR REAL.
NO. I'M TRACKING HIS VITALS. HE BELIEVES EVERYTHING HE SAYS. HE'S NOT--
JOHNNY!
GAH!
BLAM!!

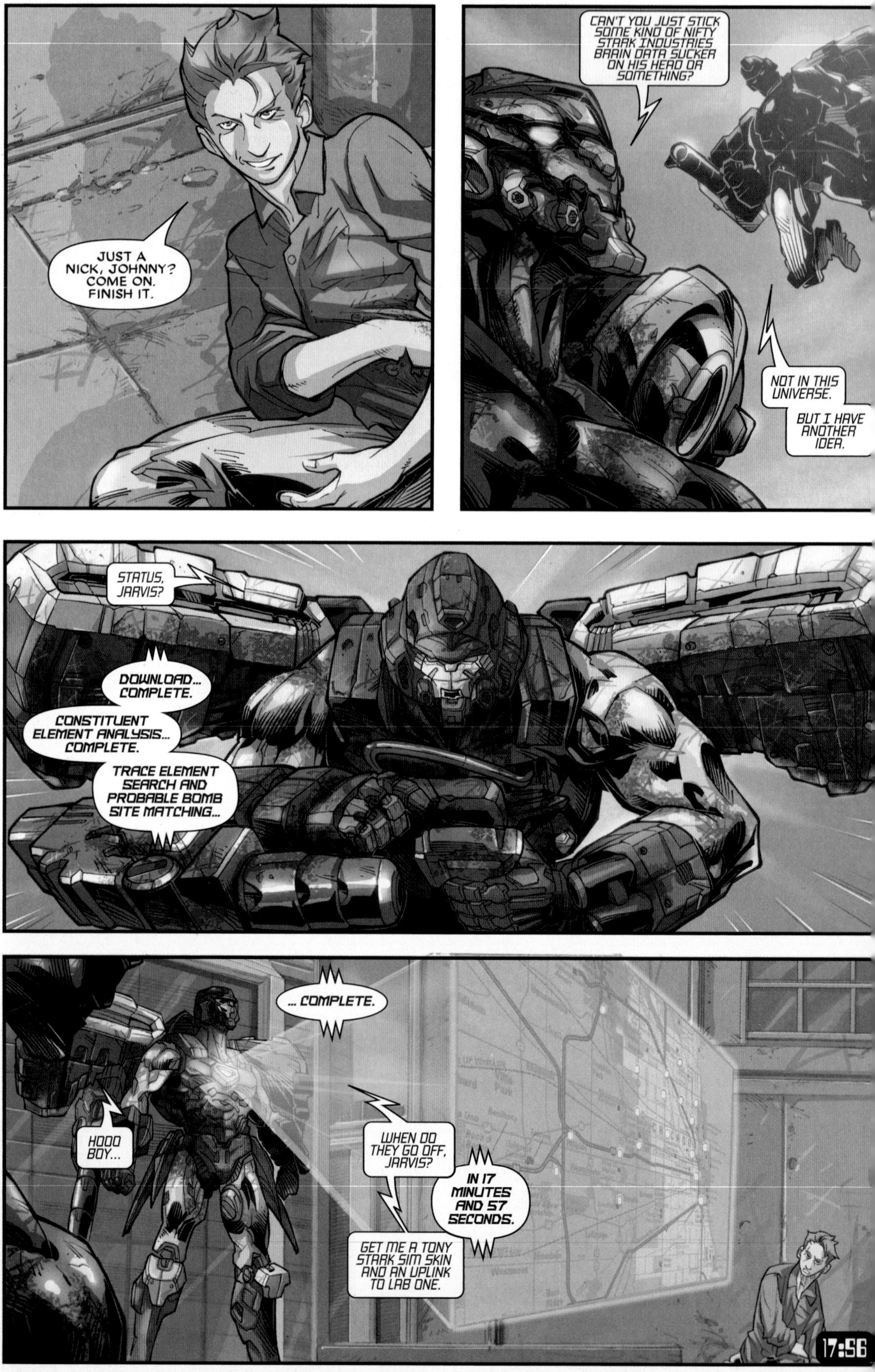
JUST A NICK, JOHNNY? COME ON. FINISH IT.
CAN'T YOU JUST STICK SOME KIND OF NIFTY STARK INDUSTRIES BRAIN DATA SUCKER ON HIS HEAD OR SOMETHING?
NOT IN THIS UNIVERSE.
BUT I HAVE ANOTHER IDEA.
STATUS, JARVIS?
DOWNLOAD... COMPLETE.
CONSTITUENT ELEMENT ANALYSIS... COMPLETE.
TRACE ELEMENT SEARCH AND PROBABLE BOMB SITE MATCHING...
... COMPLETE.
HOOO BOY...
WHEN DO THEY GO OFF, JARVIS?
IN 17 MINUTES AND 57 SECONDS.
GET ME A TONY STARK SIM SKIN AND AN UPLINK TO LAB ONE.
17:56

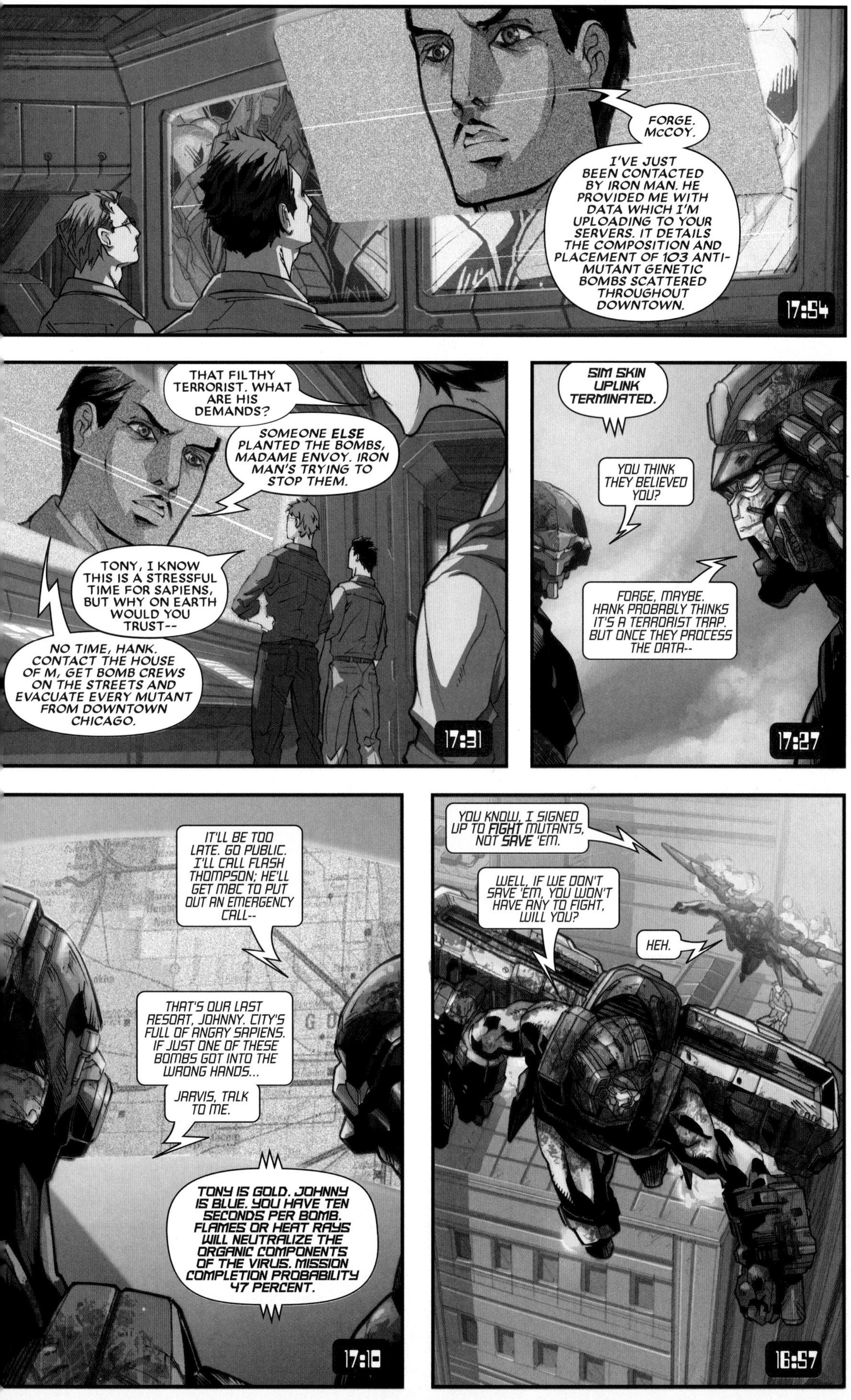
FORGE. McCOY.
I'VE JUST BEEN CONTACTED BY IRON MAN. HE PROVIDED ME WITH DATA WHICH I'M UPLOADING TO YOUR SERVERS. IT DETAILS THE COMPOSITION AND PLACEMENT OF 103 ANTI-MUTANT GENETIC BOMBS SCATTERED THROUGHOUT DOWNTOWN.
17:54
THAT FILTHY TERRORIST. WHAT ARE HIS DEMANDS?
SOMEONE ELSE PLANTED THE BOMBS, MADAME ENVOY. IRON MAN'S TRYING TO STOP THEM.
TONY, I KNOW THIS IS A STRESSFUL TIME FOR SAPIENS, BUT WHY ON EARTH WOULD YOU TRUST--
NO TIME, HANK. CONTACT THE HOUSE OF M, GET BOMB CREWS ON THE STREETS AND EVACUATE EVERY MUTANT FROM DOWNTOWN CHICAGO.
17:31
SIM SKIN UPLINK TERMINATED.
YOU THINK THEY BELIEVED YOU?
FORGE, MAYBE. HANK PROBABLY THINKS IT'S A TERRORIST TRAP. BUT ONCE THEY PROCESS THE DATA--
17:27
IT'LL BE TOO LATE. GO PUBLIC. I'LL CALL FLASH THOMPSON; HE'LL GET MBC TO PUT OUT AN EMERGENCY CALL--
THAT'S OUR LAST RESORT, JOHNNY. CITY'S FULL OF ANGRY SAPIENS. IF JUST ONE OF THESE BOMBS GOT INTO THE WRONG HANDS...
JARVIS, TALK TO ME.
TONY IS GOLD. JOHNNY IS BLUE. YOU HAVE TEN SECONDS PER BOMB. FLAMES OR HEAT RAYS WILL NEUTRALIZE THE ORGANIC COMPONENTS OF THE VIRUS. MISSION COMPLETION PROBABILITY 47 PERCENT.
17:10
YOU KNOW, I SIGNED UP TO FIGHT MUTANTS, NOT SAVE 'EM.
WELL, IF WE DON'T SAVE 'EM, YOU WON'T HAVE ANY TO FIGHT, WILL YOU?
HEH.
16:57

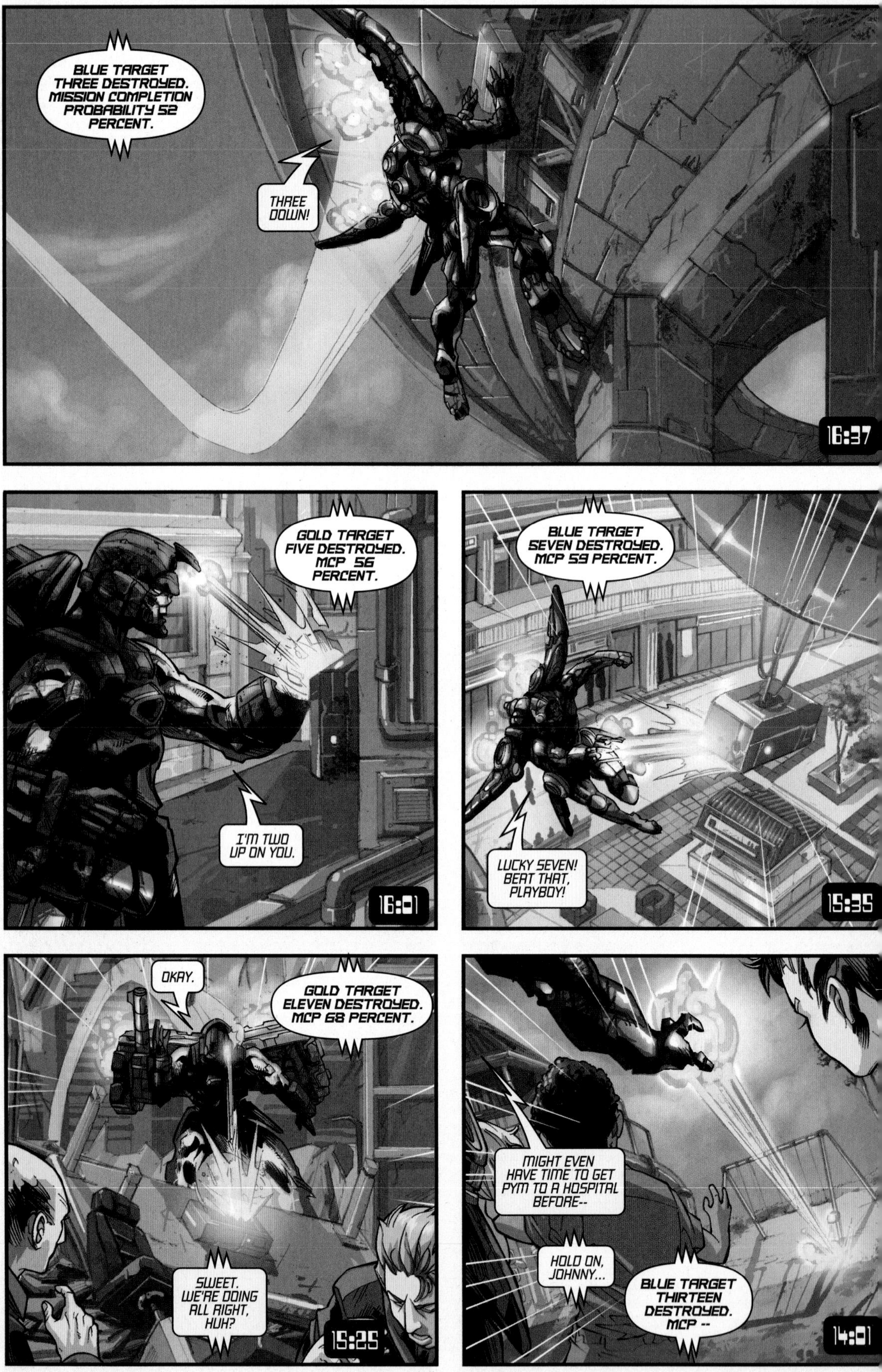
BLUE TARGET THREE DESTROYED. MISSION COMPLETION PROBABILITY 52 PERCENT.
THREE DOWN!
16:37
GOLD TARGET FIVE DESTROYED. MCP 56 PERCENT.
I'M TWO UP ON YOU.
16:01
BLUE TARGET SEVEN DESTROYED. MCP 59 PERCENT.
LUCKY SEVEN! BEAT THAT, PLAYBOY!
15:35
OKAY.
GOLD TARGET ELEVEN DESTROYED. MCP 68 PERCENT.
SWEET. WE'RE DOING ALL RIGHT, HUH?
15:25
MIGHT EVEN HAVE TIME TO GET PYM TO A HOSPITAL BEFORE--
HOLD ON, JOHNNY...
BLUE TARGET THIRTEEN DESTROYED. MCP --
14:01

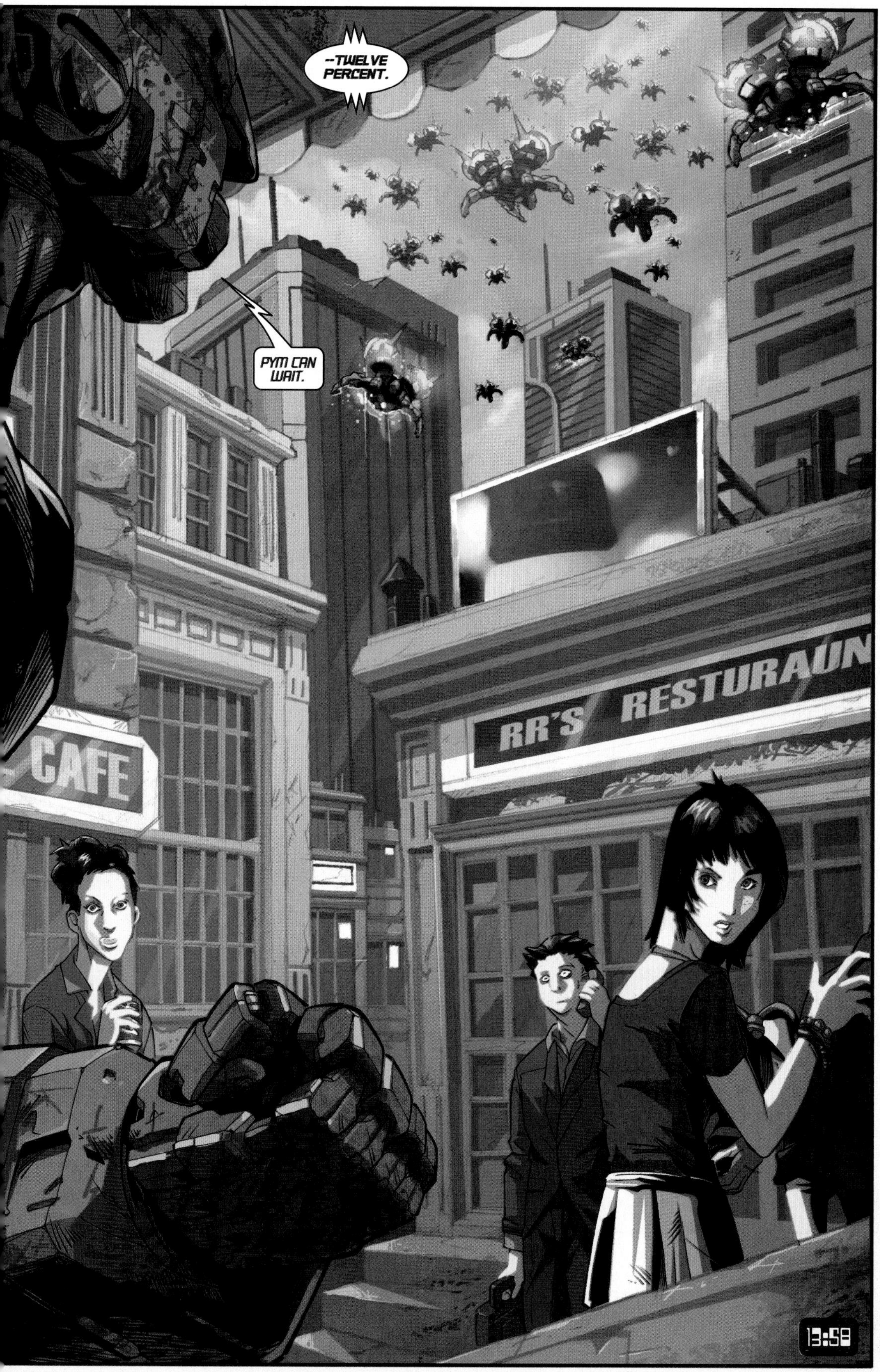
--TWELVE PERCENT.
PYM CAN WAIT.
CAFE
RR'S RESTURAUN
13:58

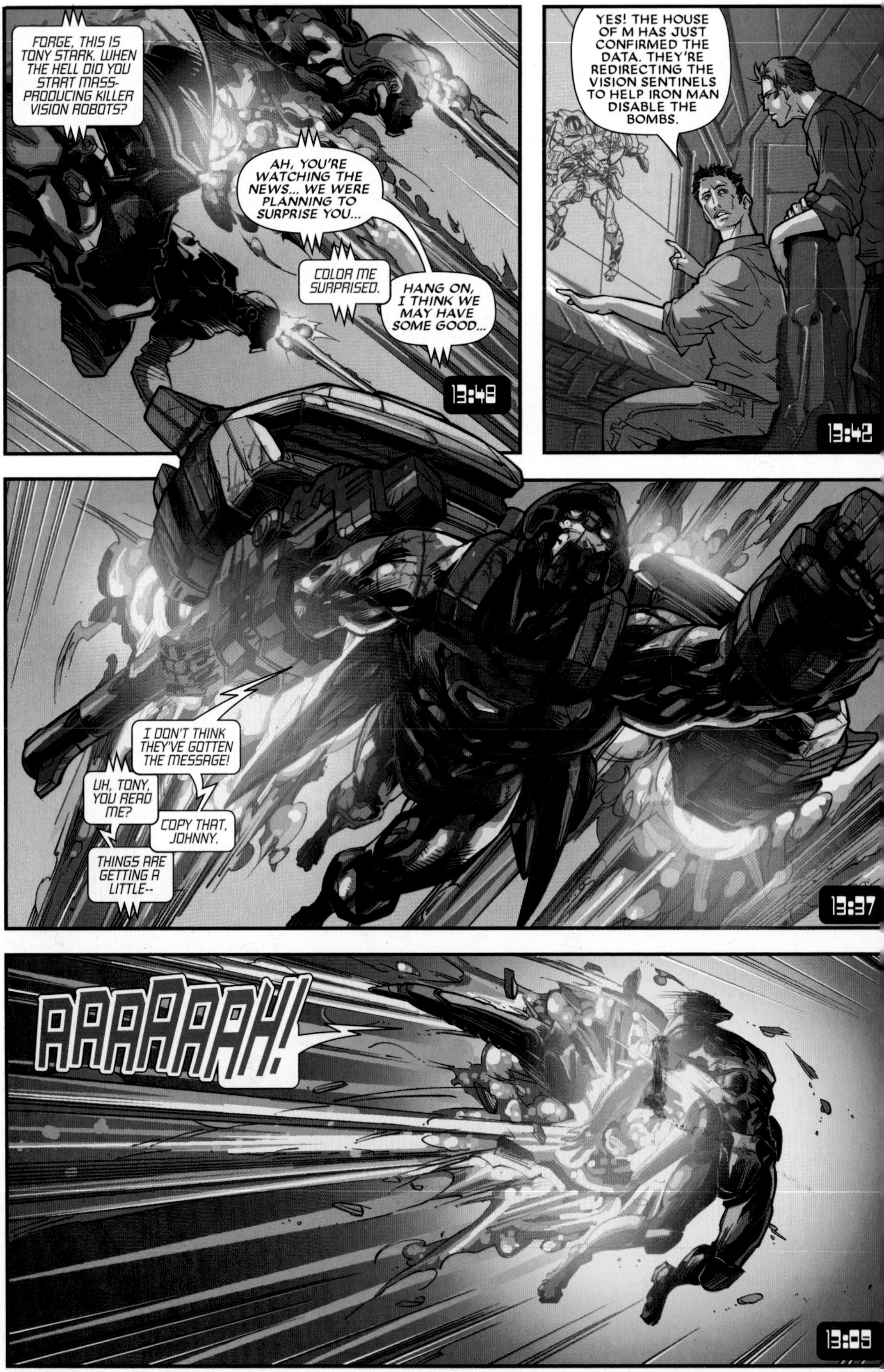
FORGE, THIS IS TONY STARK. WHEN THE HELL DID YOU START MASS-PRODUCING KILLER VISION ROBOTS?
AH, YOU'RE WATCHING THE NEWS... WE WERE PLANNING TO SURPRISE YOU...
COLOR ME SURPRISED.
HANG ON, I THINK WE MAY HAVE SOME GOOD...
13:48
YES! THE HOUSE OF M HAS JUST CONFIRMED THE DATA. THEY'RE REDIRECTING THE VISION SENTINELS TO HELP IRON MAN DISABLE THE BOMBS.
13:42
I DON'T THINK THEY'VE GOTTEN THE MESSAGE!
UH, TONY, YOU READ ME?
COPY THAT, JOHNNY.
THINGS ARE GETTING A LITTLE--
13:37
AAAAAAAH!
13:09

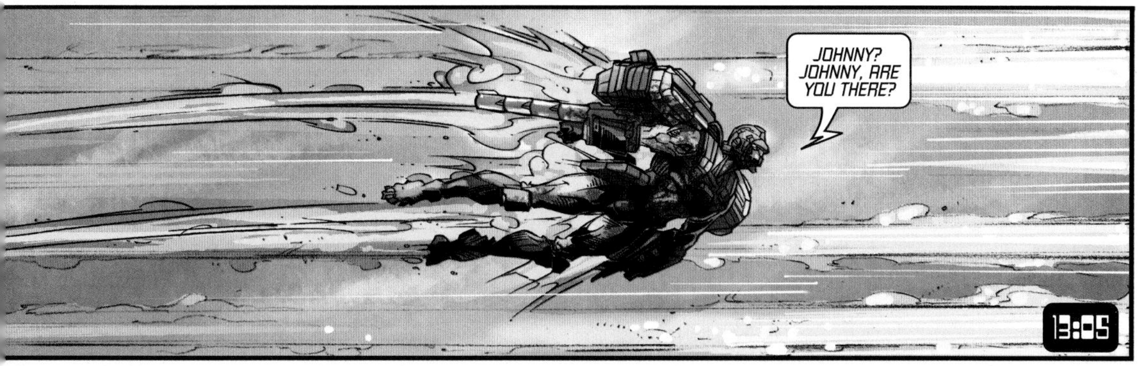
JOHNNY? JOHNNY, ARE YOU THERE?
13:05

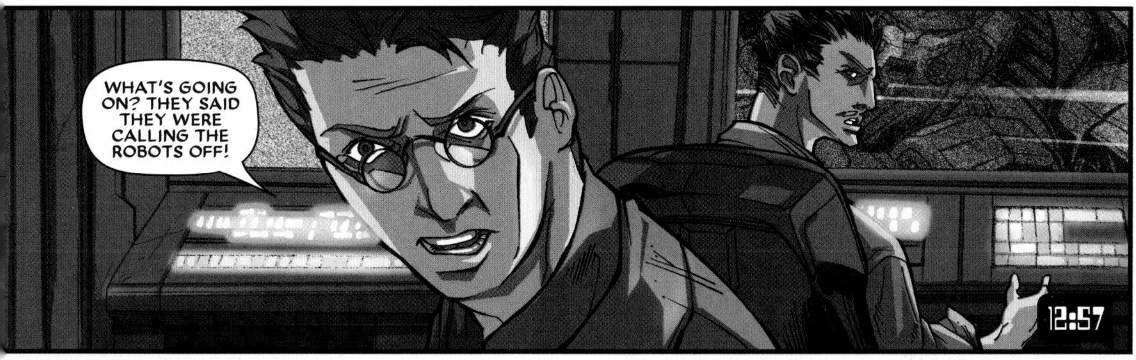
WHAT'S GOING ON? THEY SAID THEY WERE CALLING THE ROBOTS OFF!
12:57

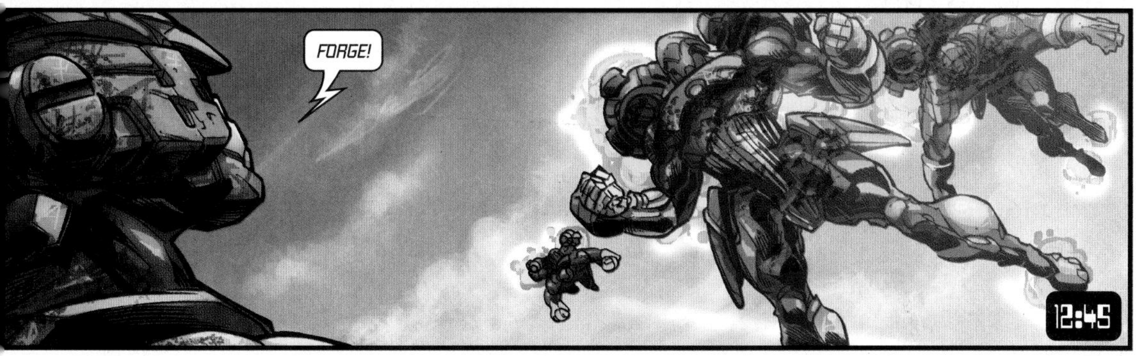
FORGE!
12:45

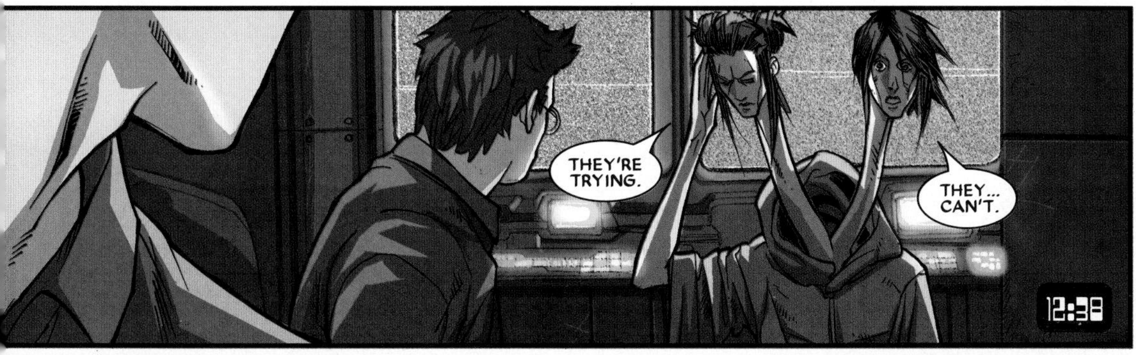
THEY'RE TRYING.
THEY... CAN'T.
12:38

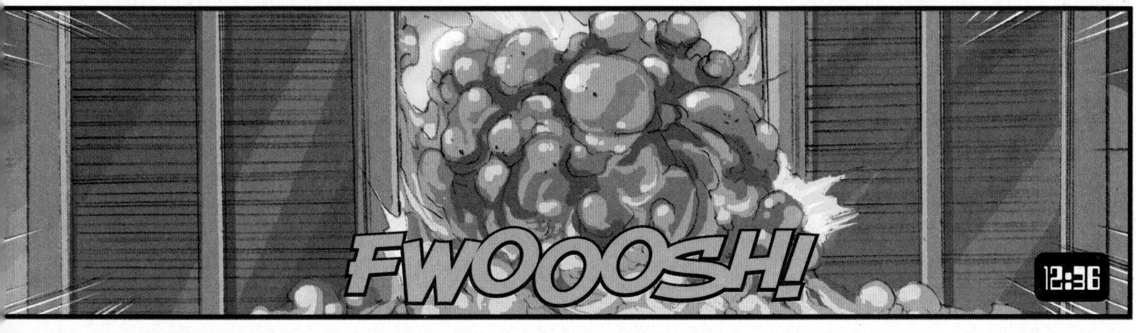
FWOOOSH!
12:36

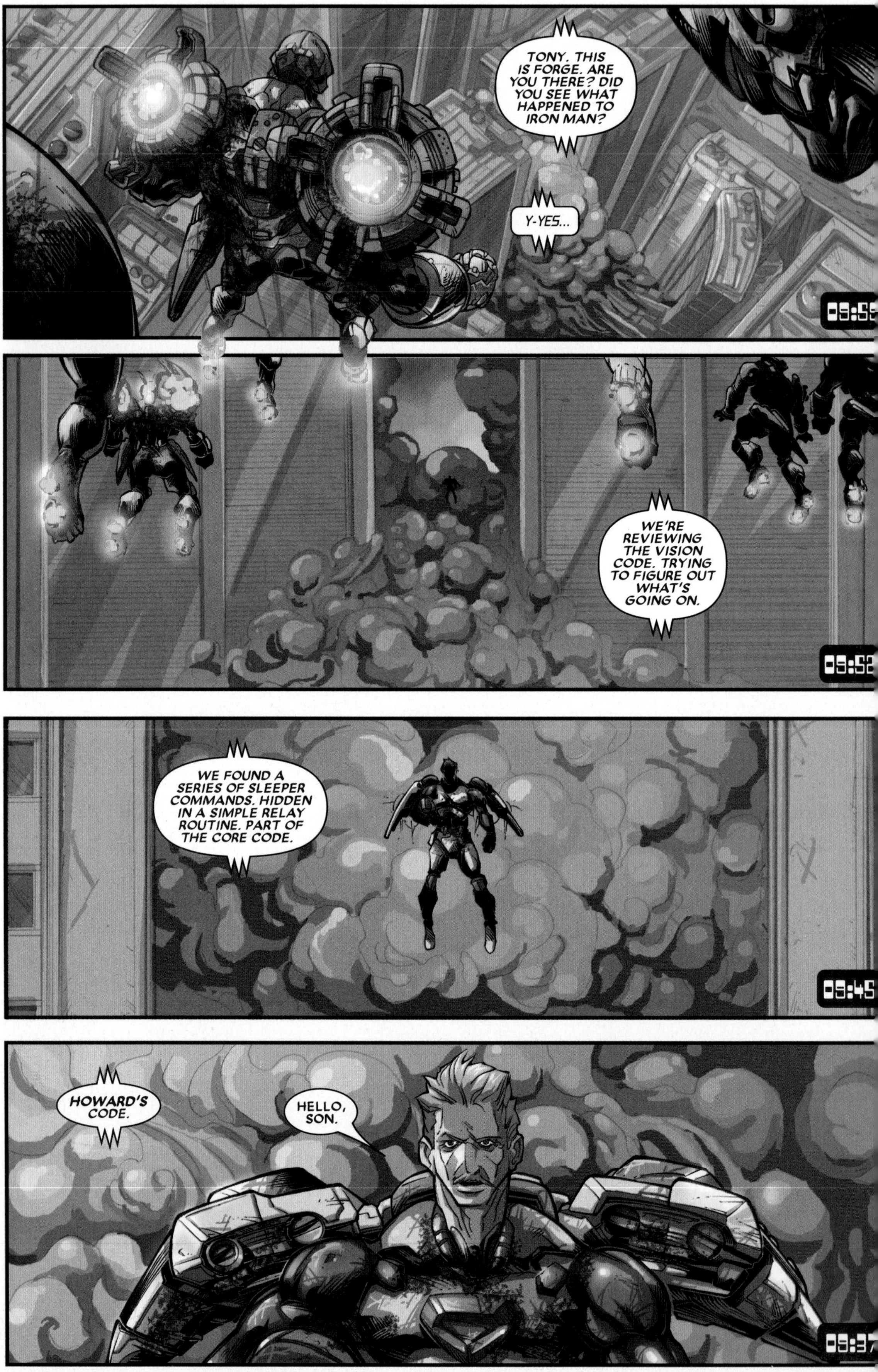

TONY. THIS IS FORGE. ARE YOU THERE? DID YOU SEE WHAT HAPPENED TO IRON MAN?
Y-YES...
WE'RE REVIEWING THE VISION CODE. TRYING TO FIGURE OUT WHAT'S GOING ON.
WE FOUND A SERIES OF SLEEPER COMMANDS. HIDDEN IN A SIMPLE RELAY ROUTINE. PART OF THE CORE CODE.
05:45
HOWARD'S CODE.
HELLO, SON.

NO, DAD. YOU DON'T UNDERSTAND.
NO WHINING, TONY. NOBODY LIKES A WHINER.
WE...HAVE TO STOP THESE BOMBS...
NOT WE, TONY. YOU. IF YOU CAN.
05:31
REMEMBER THIS, TONY: I GAVE YOU AN OUT. YOU COULD HAVE DESTROYED THE ARMOR. BUT NO. YOU WANTED TO BE A HERO.
YOU CHOSE THIS PATH.
05:17
YOU SET THIS WHOLE THING UP. THE BOMBS... YOU AND PYM...
AND YOU, TONY. COULDN'T HAVE DONE IT WITHOUT YOU. YOU PLAYED IT SO BEAUTIFULLY. SO CALLOW, SO EAGER TO PLEASE. DANCING FOR YOUR MUTANT MASTERS, KEEPING THEM DISTRACTED.
YOU REALLY ARE A MONSTER, AREN'T YOU?
NO. JUST A DIFFERENT BREED.
05:08
ALL RIGHT, THEN. GOODBYE.
DON'T OVERDRAMATIZE, SON. I'M NOT GOING TO KILL YOU. YOU HAVE AN IMPORTANT--
05:02
I'M NOT YOUR SON.
05:00

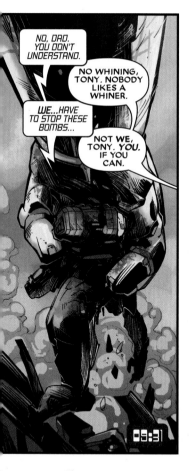

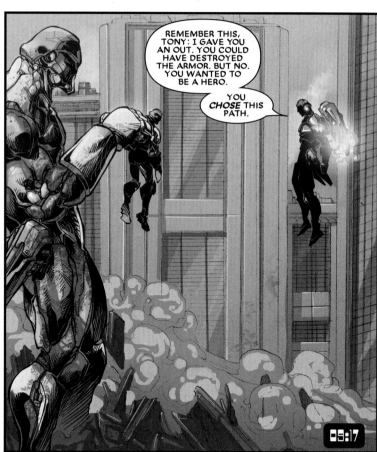

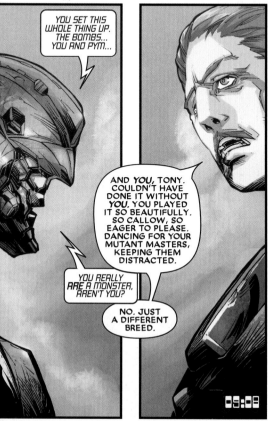

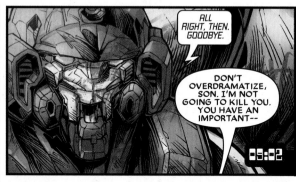

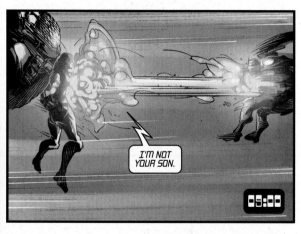

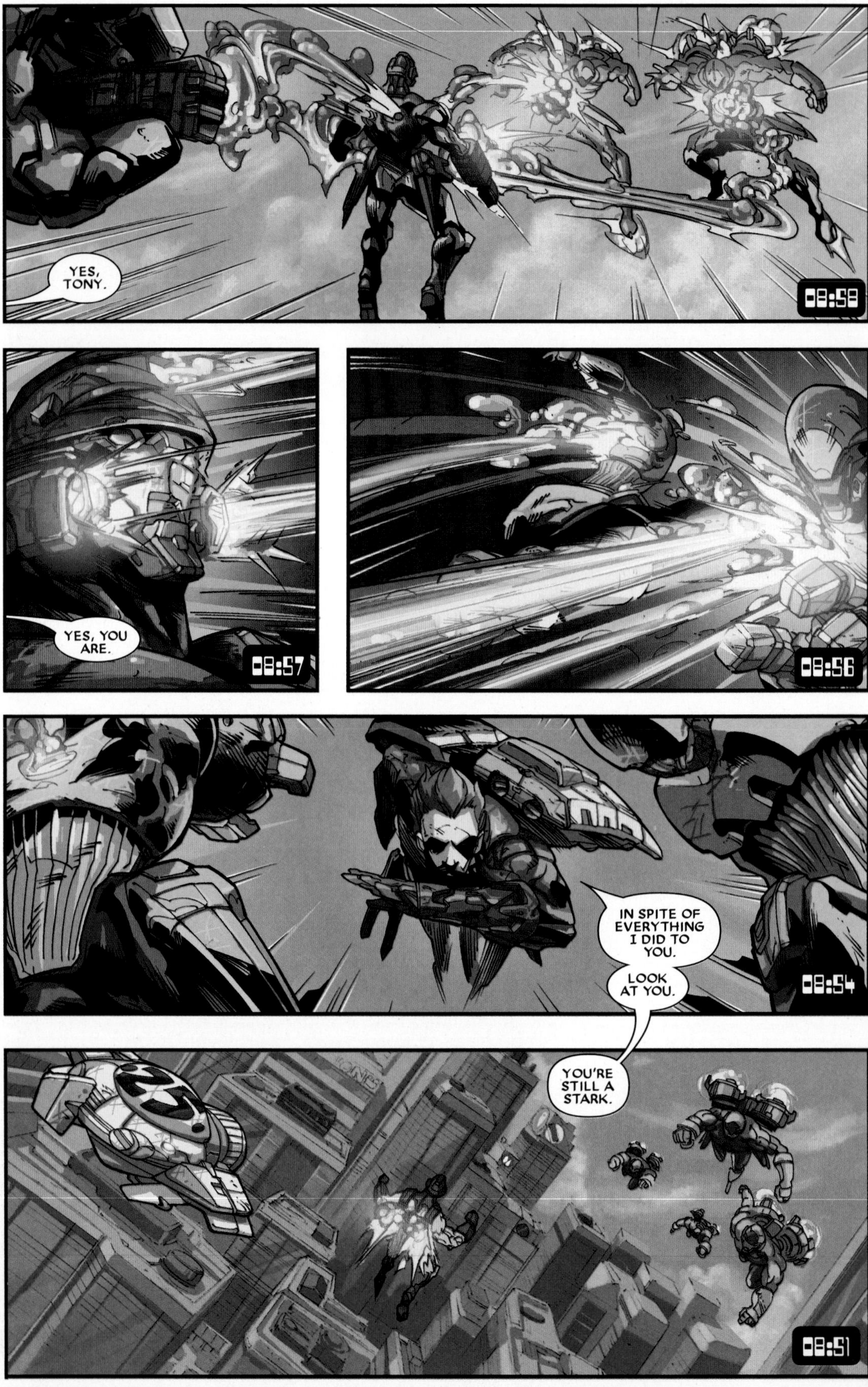
YES, TONY.
08:58
YES, YOU ARE.
08:57
08:56
IN SPITE OF EVERYTHING I DID TO YOU.
LOOK AT YOU.
08:54
YOU'RE STILL A STARK.
08:51

BEEP
BEEP
BEE--

FLASH THOMPSON HERE.

07:37

I'M ON IT.

07:35

SOUNDS LIKE FUN.

07:21

ALREADY ON OUR WAY.

SWEET.

07:12

COOL. CAN I BRING MY COUSIN?

06:56

TONY, IT'S FLASH. LISTEN, NO TIME TO EXPLAIN--IRON MAN NEEDS HELP. ARE YOU IN?

I'M A LITTLE TIED UP RIGHT--

TONY?

05:11

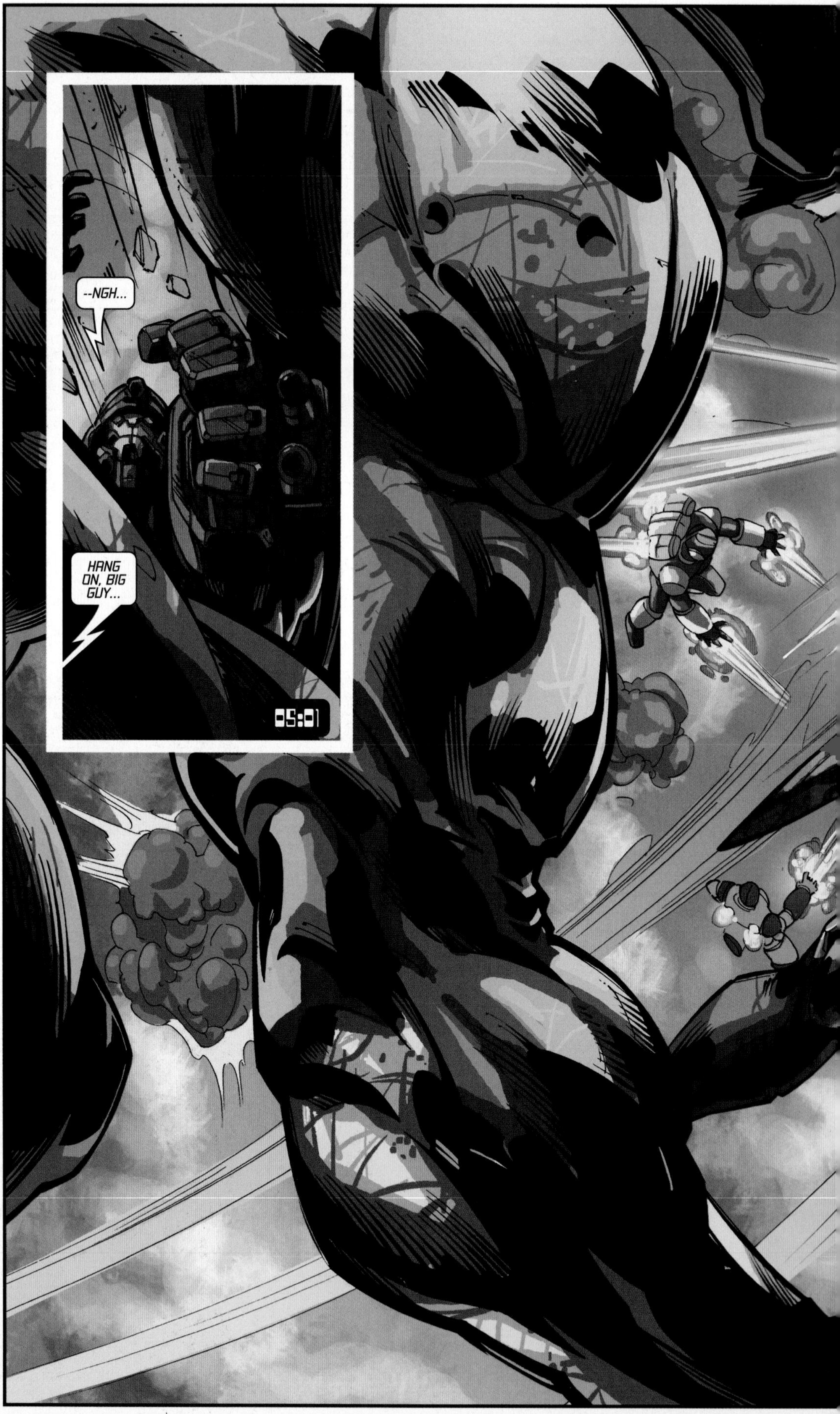
--NGH...
HANG ON, BIG GUY...
05:01

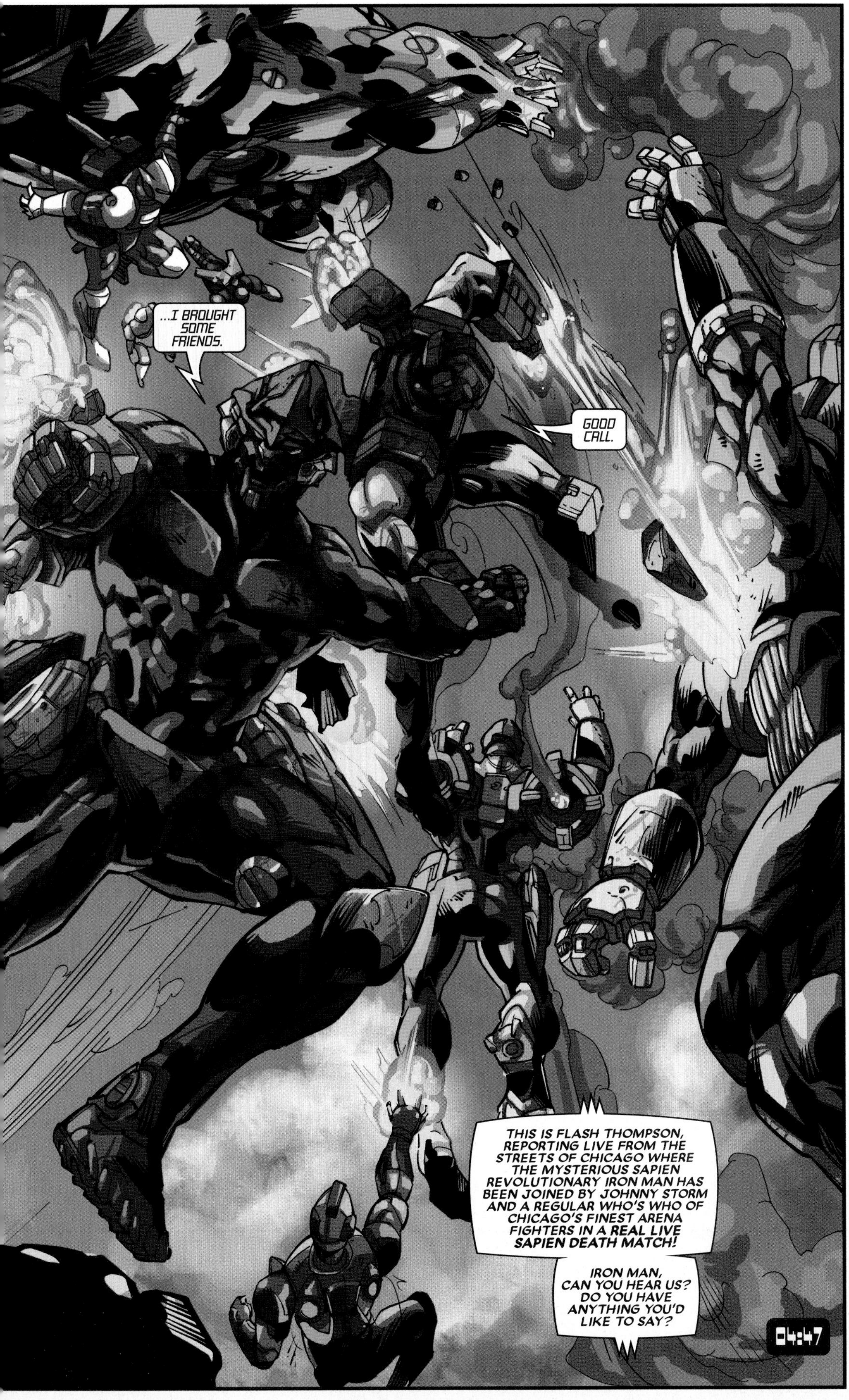
...I BROUGHT SOME FRIENDS.
GOOD CALL.
THIS IS FLASH THOMPSON, REPORTING LIVE FROM THE STREETS OF CHICAGO WHERE THE MYSTERIOUS SAPIEN REVOLUTIONARY IRON MAN HAS BEEN JOINED BY JOHNNY STORM AND A REGULAR WHO'S WHO OF CHICAGO'S FINEST ARENA FIGHTERS IN A REAL LIVE SAPIEN DEATH MATCH!
IRON MAN, CAN YOU HEAR US? DO YOU HAVE ANYTHING YOU'D LIKE TO SAY?
04:47

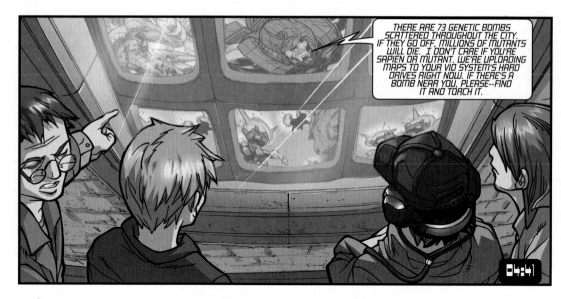

THERE ARE 73 GENETIC BOMBS SCATTERED THROUGHOUT THE CITY. IF THEY GO OFF, MILLIONS OF MUTANTS WILL DIE. I DON'T CARE IF YOU'RE SAPIEN OR MUTANT. WE'RE UPLOADING MAPS TO YOUR VID SYSTEM'S HARD DRIVES RIGHT NOW. IF THERE'S A BOMB NEAR YOU, PLEASE--FIND IT AND TORCH IT.

04:41

WE'VE GOT ONE!

RIGHT HERE, CHIEF!

03:55

THERE IT IS!

GOOD EYE!

03:16

THANKS, IRON MAN!

02:37

WHAT DO WE HAVE, JARVIS?

THIRTEEN LEFT. IN A CLUSTER.

WHERE?

01:57

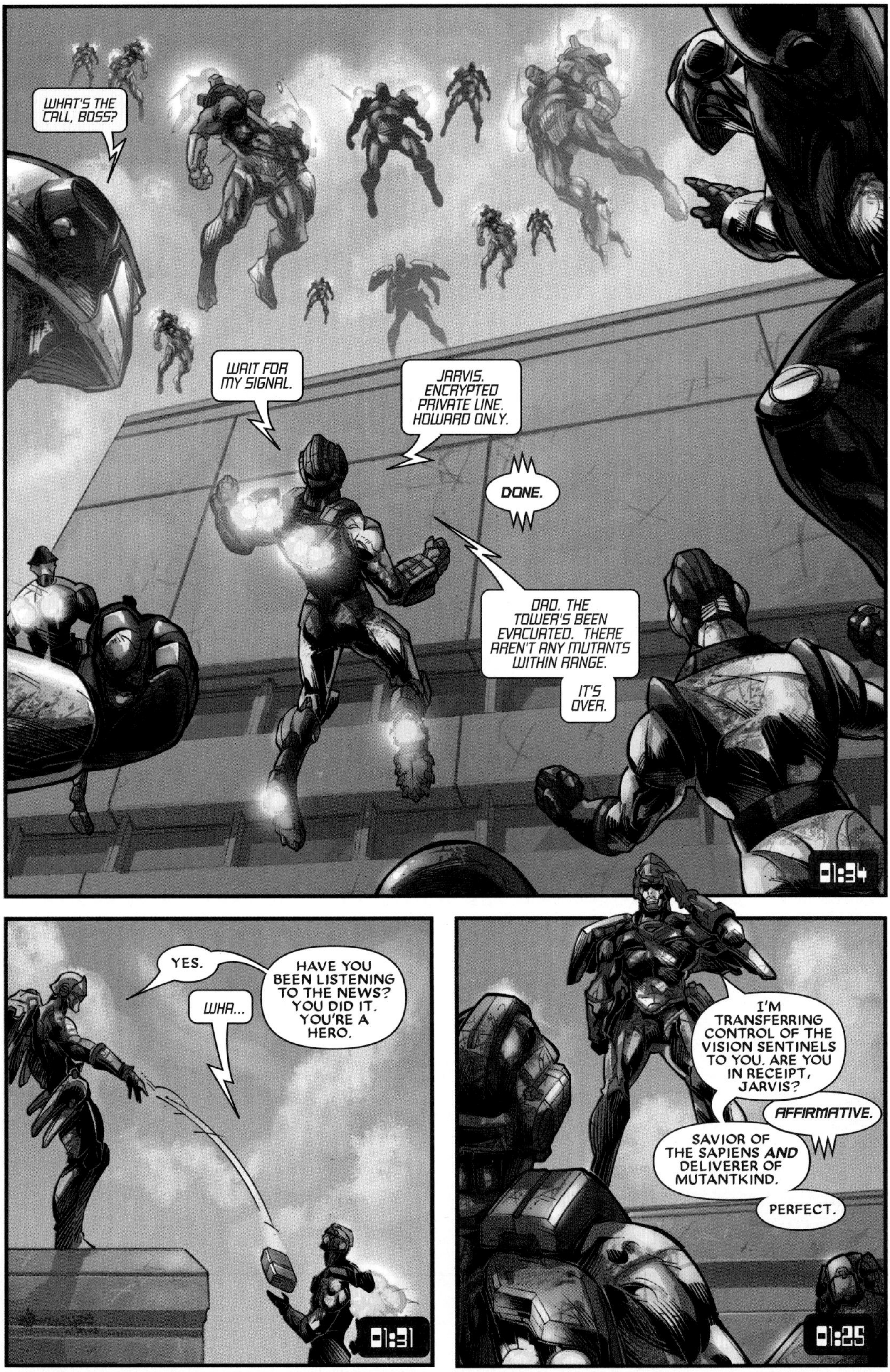

WHAT'S THE CALL, BOSS?
WAIT FOR MY SIGNAL.
JARVIS. ENCRYPTED PRIVATE LINE. HOWARD ONLY.
DONE.
DAD. THE TOWER'S BEEN EVACUATED. THERE AREN'T ANY MUTANTS WITHIN RANGE.
IT'S OVER.
01:34
YES.
HAVE YOU BEEN LISTENING TO THE NEWS? YOU DID IT. YOU'RE A HERO.
WHA...
01:31
I'M TRANSFERRING CONTROL OF THE VISION SENTINELS TO YOU. ARE YOU IN RECEIPT, JARVIS?
AFFIRMATIVE.
SAVIOR OF THE SAPIENS AND DELIVERER OF MUTANTKIND.
PERFECT.
01:25

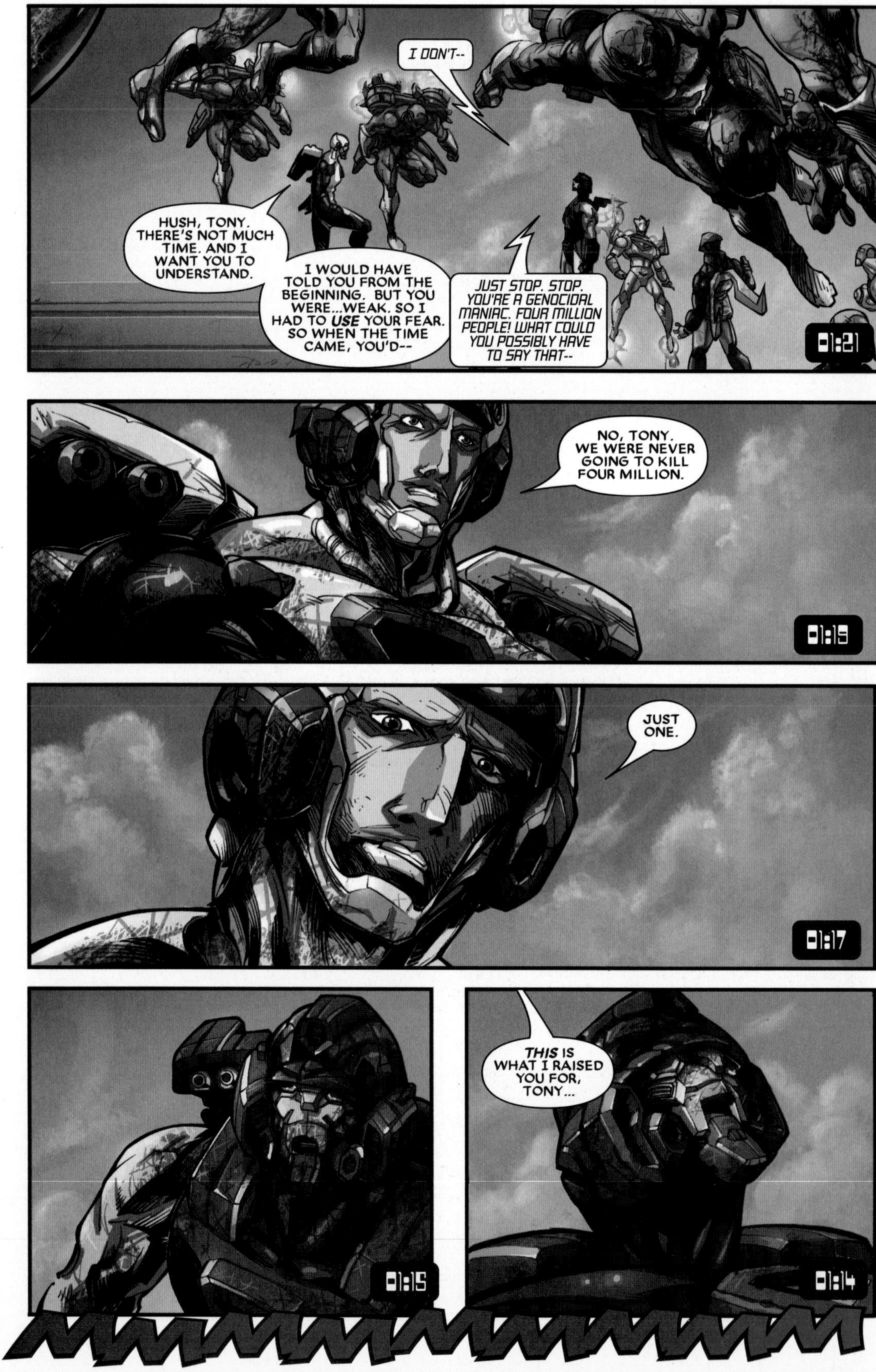
I DON'T--
HUSH, TONY. THERE'S NOT MUCH TIME. AND I WANT YOU TO UNDERSTAND.
I WOULD HAVE TOLD YOU FROM THE BEGINNING. BUT YOU WERE...WEAK. SO I HAD TO USE YOUR FEAR. SO WHEN THE TIME CAME, YOU'D--
JUST STOP. STOP. YOU'RE A GENOCIDAL MANIAC. FOUR MILLION PEOPLE! WHAT COULD YOU POSSIBLY HAVE TO SAY THAT--
01:21
NO, TONY. WE WERE NEVER GOING TO KILL FOUR MILLION.
01:19
JUST ONE.
01:17
01:15
THIS IS WHAT I RAISED YOU FOR, TONY...
01:14

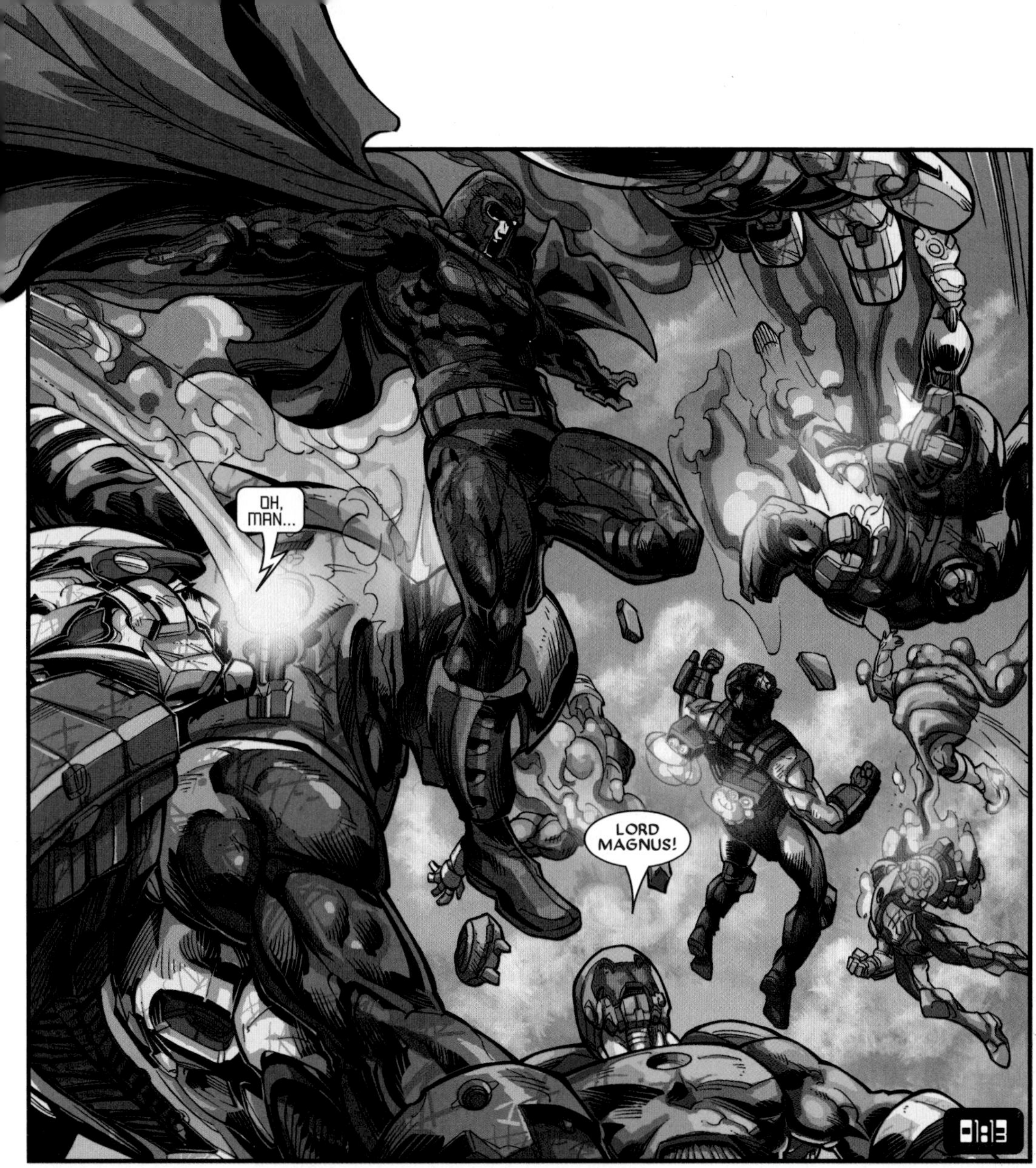
OH, MAN...
LORD MAGNUS!
01:13

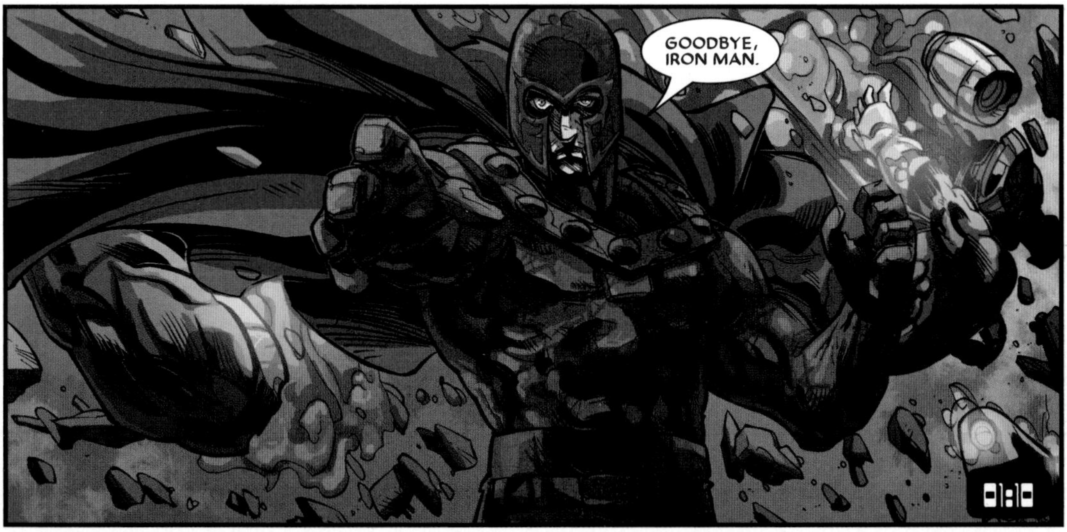
GOODBYE, IRON MAN.
01:10

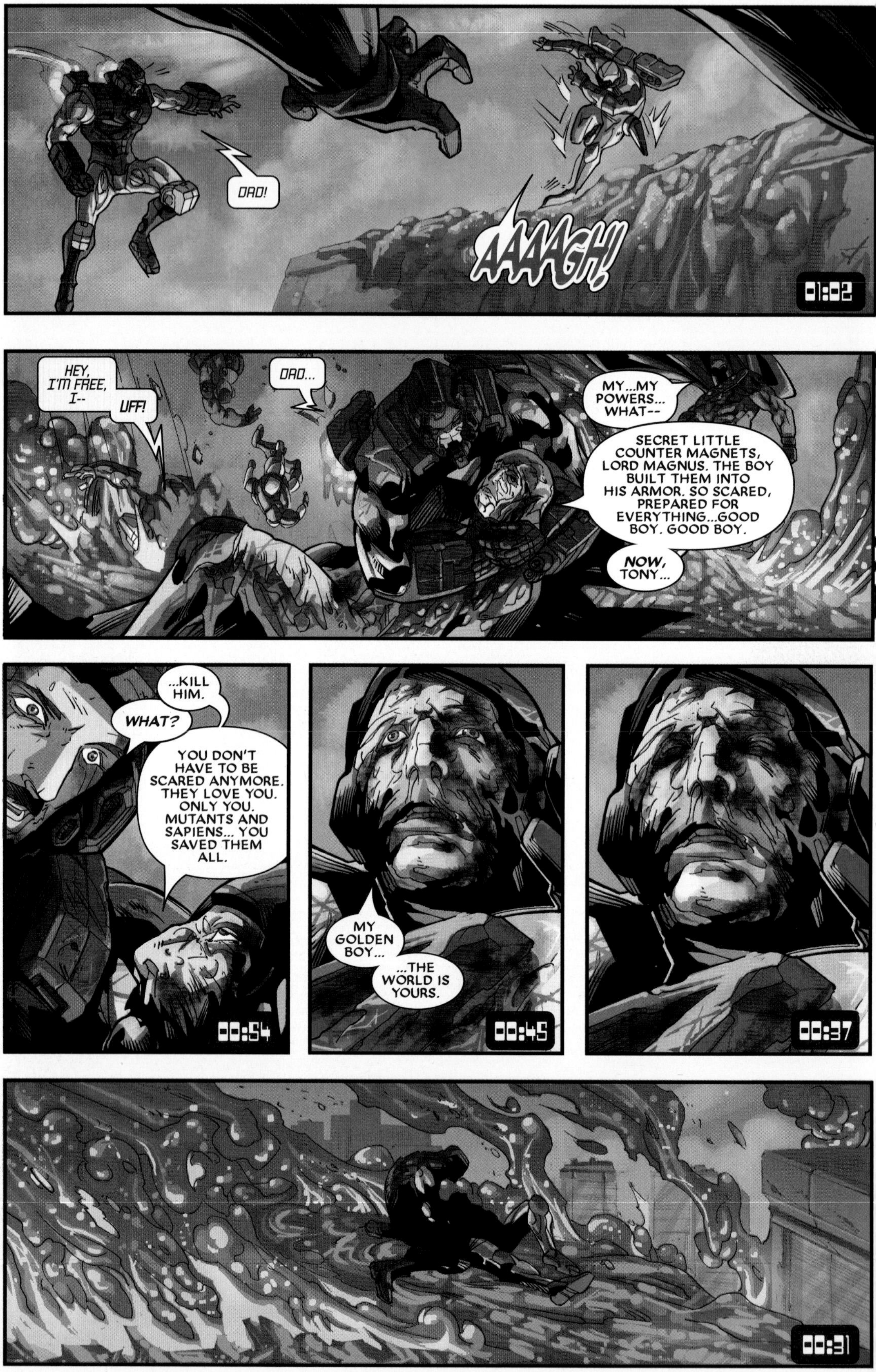
DAD!
AAAAGH!
01:02
HEY, I'M FREE, I--
UFF!
DAD...
MY...MY POWERS... WHAT--
SECRET LITTLE COUNTER MAGNETS, LORD MAGNUS. THE BOY BUILT THEM INTO HIS ARMOR. SO SCARED, PREPARED FOR EVERYTHING...GOOD BOY. GOOD BOY.
NOW, TONY...
...KILL HIM.
WHAT?
YOU DON'T HAVE TO BE SCARED ANYMORE. THEY LOVE YOU. ONLY YOU. MUTANTS AND SAPIENS... YOU SAVED THEM ALL.
00:54
MY GOLDEN BOY...
...THE WORLD IS YOURS.
00:45
00:37
00:31

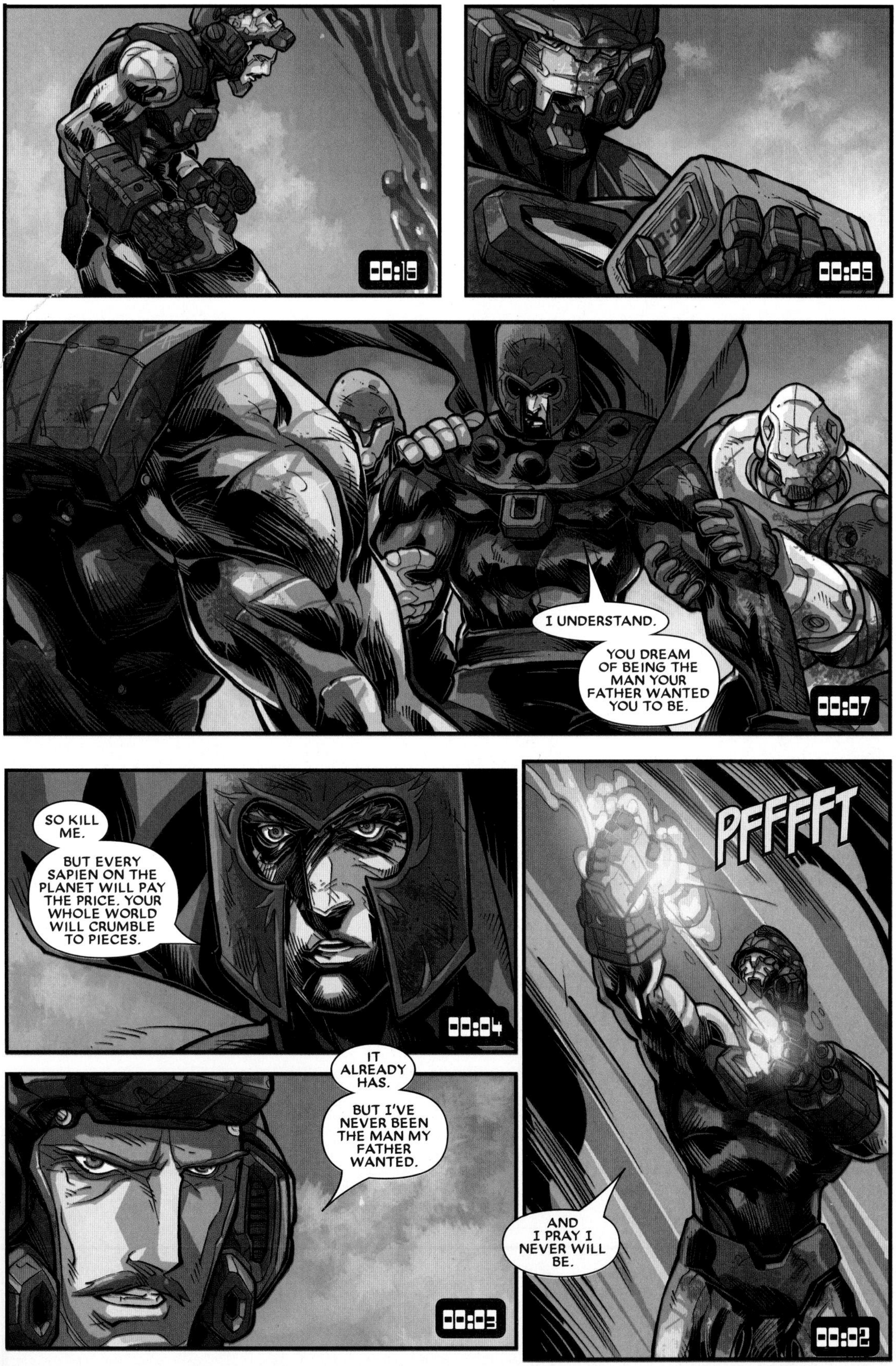
00:15
00:05
I UNDERSTAND.
YOU DREAM OF BEING THE MAN YOUR FATHER WANTED YOU TO BE.
00:07
SO KILL ME.
BUT EVERY SAPIEN ON THE PLANET WILL PAY THE PRICE. YOUR WHOLE WORLD WILL CRUMBLE TO PIECES.
00:04
IT ALREADY HAS.
BUT I'VE NEVER BEEN THE MAN MY FATHER WANTED.
00:03
PFFFFT
AND I PRAY I NEVER WILL BE.
00:02

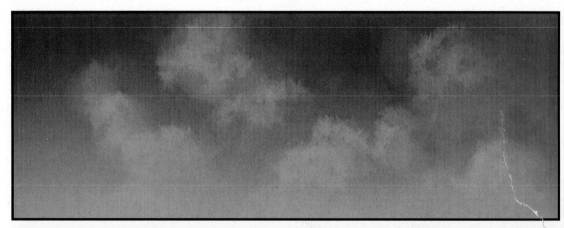

THIS IS TONY STARK.

MR. STARK! OH, THANK GOD THANK GOD THANK GOD. WHERE ARE YOU? NO, DON'T TELL ME. WAIT A MINUTE, LET ME GET LEGAL ON THE LINE, AND THE BOARD--

NO, NO TIME. I'M LOCKED OUT OF THE SYSTEM. CALLING FROM AN UNENCRYPTED LINE. THEY'LL TRACE IT IN A FEW SECONDS. JUST TELL ME WHAT'S GOING ON.

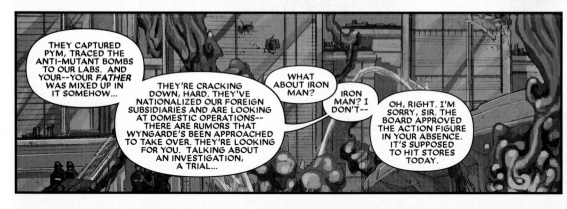

THEY CAPTURED PYM, TRACED THE ANTI-MUTANT BOMBS TO OUR LABS. AND YOUR--YOUR *FATHER* WAS MIXED UP IN IT SOMEHOW...

THEY'RE CRACKING DOWN, HARD. THEY'VE NATIONALIZED OUR FOREIGN SUBSIDIARIES AND ARE LOOKING AT DOMESTIC OPERATIONS-- THERE ARE RUMORS THAT WYNGARDE'S BEEN APPROACHED TO TAKE OVER. THEY'RE LOOKING FOR YOU. TALKING ABOUT AN INVESTIGATION, A TRIAL...

WHAT ABOUT IRON MAN?

IRON MAN? I DON'T--

OH, RIGHT. I'M SORRY, SIR. THE BOARD APPROVED THE ACTION FIGURE IN YOUR ABSENCE. IT'S SUPPOSED TO HIT STORES TODAY.

THEY KNEW YOU DISAPPROVED BEFORE, BUT NOW THAT HE'S A HERO... HE SAVED THE CITY. HE SAVED LORD *MAGNUS*. IT SEEMED LIKE A GOOD--

DON'T WORRY. IT'S FINE.

BUT--BUT WHAT ABOUT *YOU*, SIR? ARE YOU ALL RIGHT? LEGAL IS DESPERATE TO TALK--

LEGAL CAN WAIT.

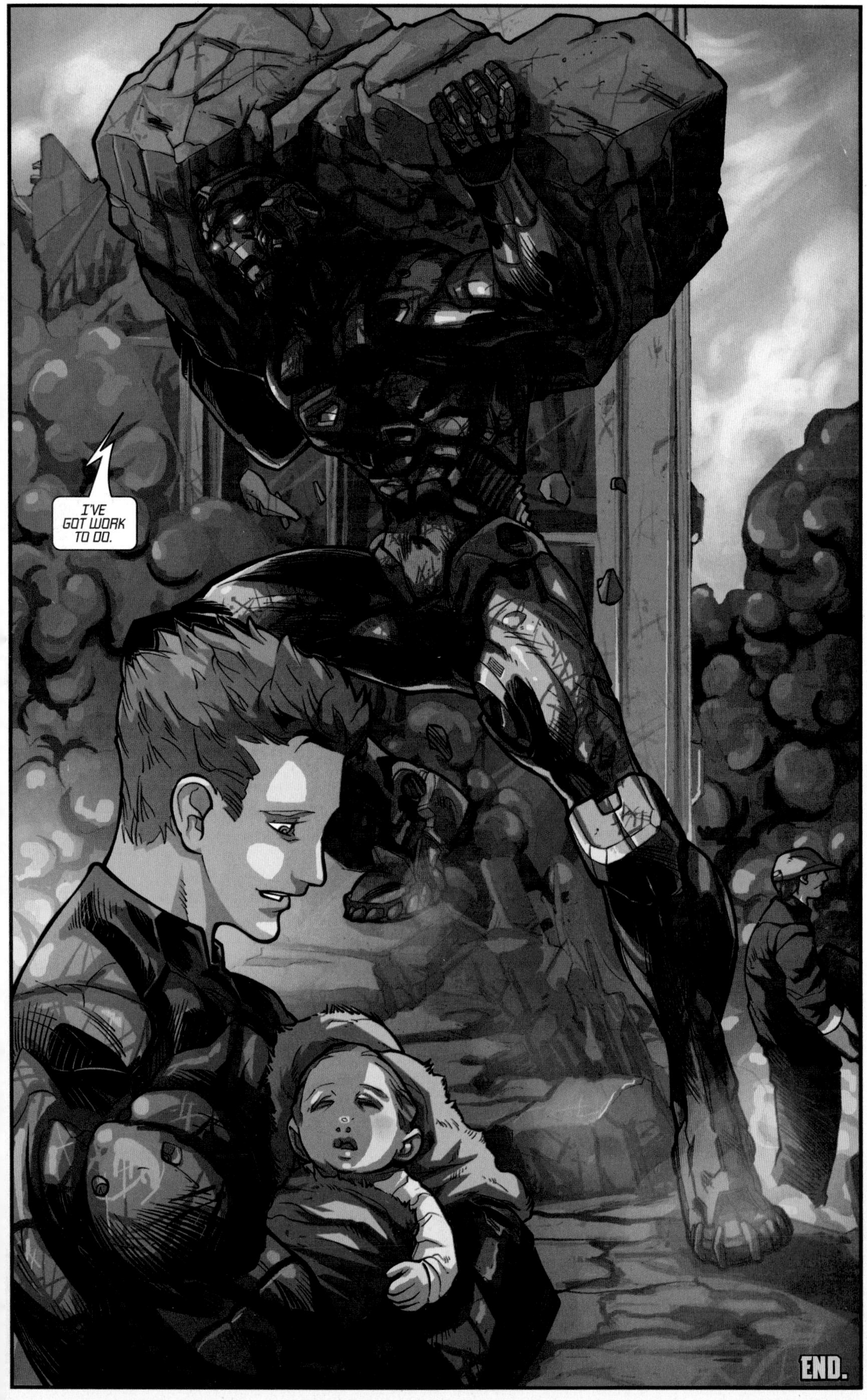

I'VE GOT WORK TO DO.
END.

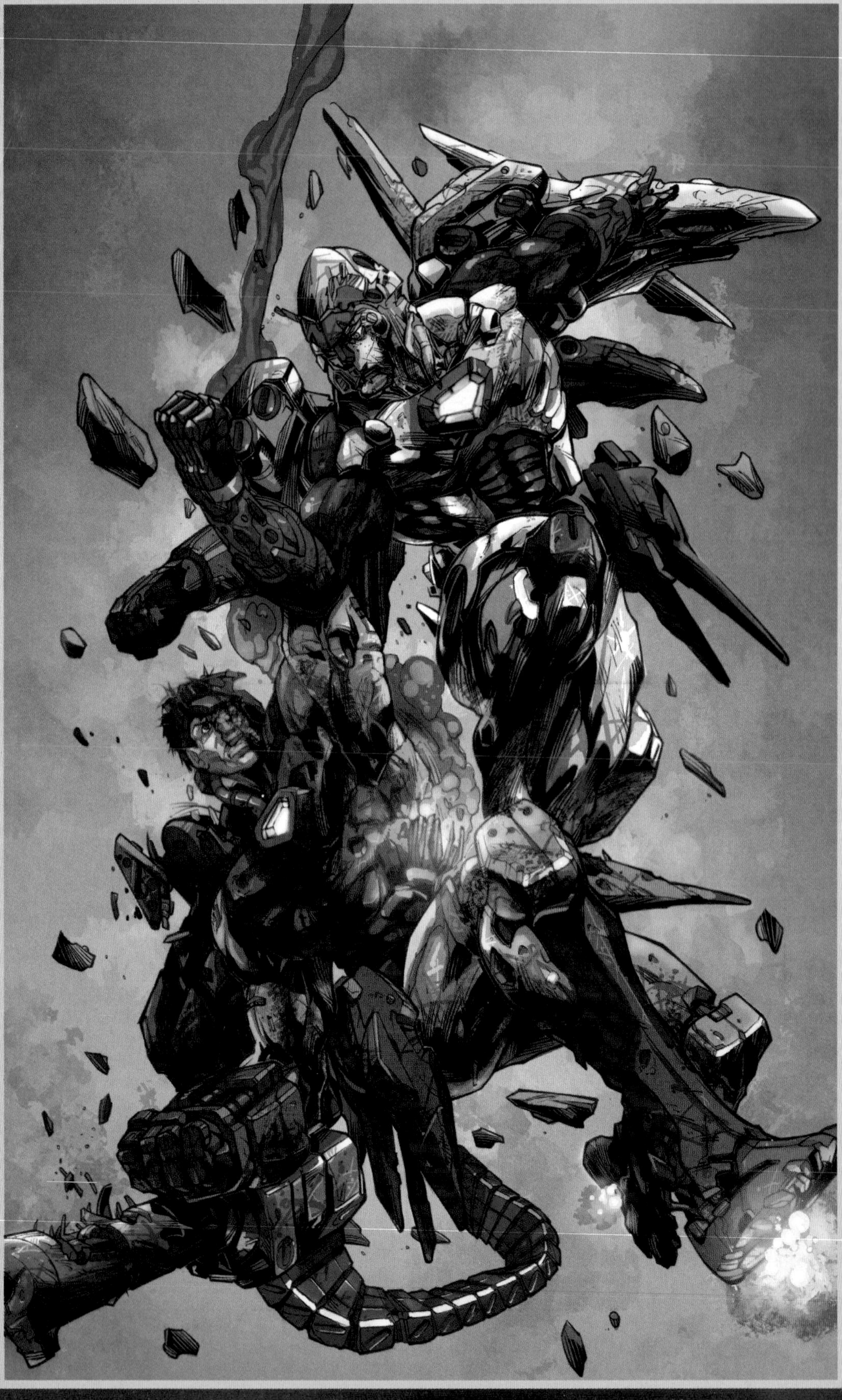

IRON MAN: HOUSE OF M #3